Shapeshifting

FOR CORRECTIONAL FACILITY CNT/HNT

Ellis Amdur, M.A., N.C.C., C.M.H.S.
Ret. Sgt. Lisbeth Eddy

Effective Scenario Training for
Crisis / Hostage Negotiation Teams

An Edgework Book
www.edgework.info

Notes and Notices

SHAPESHIFTING FOR CORRECTIONAL FACILITY CNT/HNT: Effective Scenario Training for Crisis/Hostage Negotiation Teams

By Ellis Amdur, M.A., N.C.C., C.M.H.S. and Lisbeth Eddy © 2018

ISBN: 978-0-9985224-7-0

A Message to Our Readers

Edgework is committed to offering the best of what our years of experience and study have taught us. We ask that you express your respect for these intentions and honor our work by adhering strictly to the copyright protection notice you will find below. Please know that by choosing NOT to reproduce these materials, you are supporting our work and making it possible for us to continue to develop materials that will enhance both officer and public safety. We thank you sincerely for your vigilance in respecting our rights!

Credits
Design: Soundview Design Studio
Cover photograph by: Jukka from Helsinki, Finland (Storm clouds) [CC BY 2.0 (http://creativecommons.org/licenses/by/2.0)], via Wikimedia Commons

Contents

Published Works by Ellis Amdur (and Co-Authors)

On Crisis Intervention, De-escalation of Aggression, and Psychology

BODY AND SOUL: Toward a Radical Intersubjectivity in Psychotherapy – Ellis Amdur

COOLING THE FLAMES: Communication, Control, and De-escalation of Mentally Ill & Aggressive Patients – *A Comprehensive Guidebook for Emergency Medical Services* – Ellis Amdur & John K. Murphy

EVERYTHING ON THE LINE: Calming and De-escalation of Aggressive & Mentally Ill Individuals on the Phone – *A Comprehensive Guidebook for Emergency Dispatch (9-1-1) Centers* – Ellis Amdur

FROM CHAOS TO COMPLIANCE: Communication, Control, and De-escalation of Mentally Ill, Emotionally Disturbed & Aggressive Offenders – *A Comprehensive Guidebook for Parole and Probation Officers* – Ellis Amdur & Alan Pelton

GUARDING THE GATES: Calming, Control and De-escalation of Mentally Ill, Emotionally Disturbed & Aggressive Individuals – *A Comprehensive Guidebook for Security Guards* – Ellis Amdur & William Cooper

GRACE UNDER FIRE: Skills to Calm and De-escalate Aggressive & Mentally Ill Individuals in Outpatient Settings: 2nd Edition – *A Comprehensive Guidebook for Those in Social Services or Helping Professions* – Ellis Amdur

IN THE EYE OF THE HURRICANE: Skills to Calm and De-escalate Aggressive & Mentally Ill Family Members: 2nd Edition – Ellis Amdur

SAFE BEHIND BARS: Communication, Control, and De-escalation of Mentally Ill & Aggressive Inmates – *A Comprehensive Guidebook for Correctional Officers in Jail Settings* – Ellis Amdur, Michael Blake & Chris De Villeneuve

SAFE HAVEN: Skills to Calm and De-escalate Aggressive & Mentally Ill Individuals: 2nd Edition – *A Comprehensive Guidebook for Personnel Working in Hospital and Residential Settings* – Ellis Amdur

SAFETY AT WORK: Skills to Calm and De-escalate Aggressive & Mentally Ill Individuals *A Comprehensive Guidebook for Corporate Security Managers, Human Resources Staff, Loss Prevention Specialists, Executive Protection, and Others Involved in Threat Management Professions* – Ellis Amdur & William Cooper

SHAPESHIFTING FOR LAW ENFORCEMENT CNT/HNT: Effective Scenario Training for Crisis/Hostage Negotiation Teams – Ellis Amdur & Ret. Sgt. Lisbeth Eddy

SHAPESHIFTING FOR CORRECTIONAL FACILITY CNT/HNT: Effective Scenario Training for Crisis/Hostage Negotiation Teams – Ellis Amdur & Ret. Sgt. Lisbeth Eddy

THE COORDINATOR: Managing High-Risk High-Consequence Social Interactions in an Unfamiliar Environment – Ellis Amdur & Robert Hubal

THE THIN BLUE LIFELINE: Verbal De-escalation of Mentally Ill & Emotionally Disturbed People – *A Comprehensive Guidebook for Law Enforcement Officers* – Ellis Amdur & John Hutchings

THREAT DE-ESCALATION: HOW TO EFFECTIVELY ASSESS AND DIFFUSE DANGEROUS SITUATIONS (Book & DVD) *A Publication of the United States Concealed Carry Association* – Ellis Amdur

Published by Freelance Academy Press www.freelanceacademypress.com

DUELING WITH O-SENSEI: Grappling with the Myth of the Warrior Sage – Revised & Expanded Edition – Ellis Amdur

HIDDEN IN PLAIN SIGHT: Tracing the Roots of Ueshiba Morihei's Power – Revised & Expanded Edition – Revised & Expanded Edition – Ellis Amdur

OLD SCHOOL: Essays on Japanese Martial Traditions – 2nd Expanded Edition – Ellis Amdur

Fiction

Published by Jet City Comics

THE CIMARRONIN: A SAMURAI IN NEW SPAIN: *A Graphic Novel* Neal Stephenson, Charles Mann, Ellis Amdur & Mark Teppo

Published by Edgework Books

THE GIRL WITH THE FACE OF THE MOON – Ellis Amdur

Published Works by Lisbeth Eddy

CRIMINAL PSYCHOLOGY, Jacqueline B. Helfgott, PhD, Editor. **Volume Three: Implications for Forensic Assessment, Policing and the Courts—Chapter 7**, Eddy, Lis, "The Elements of Hostage (Crisis) Negotiation" Praeger Press, Santa Barbara, California, 2013

In Gratitude for Expert Critique

First of all, the writers wish to express their gratitude to the Hostage Negotiation Team of the Monroe Correctional Complex. First of all, it was due to their push that we wrote this follow-up to our first book, **SHAPESHIFTING FOR LAW ENFORCEMENT CNT/HNT: Effective Scenario Training for Crisis/Hostage Negotiation**. Beyond that, they undertook a rigorous, comprehensive review of this manuscript so that the scenarios conform to the actual environment within a prison setting. Their assistance has been invaluable.

The following professionals have also closely reviewed this book. With each draft, we corrected errors of fact, added new information, and fine-tuned the manuscript. One of the qualities of good law enforcement and correctional officers is the understanding that the task supersedes protecting someone's feelings: therefore, we have appreciated all the direct criticism.

All responsibility for this book, however, must lie in our hands. Any errors, in particular, are ours alone. Given lives are on the line in work such as this, please do not hesitate to contact us if you believe any part of this book is inaccurate or needs additional material. We will revise the book, as needed, in future editions.

The authors also wish to thank the following reviewers:

Retired Sergeant James Detrick is a retired sergeant of the Auburn Police Department, Auburn, Washington. He has thirty-five years of law enforcement training experience, is a trained hostage/crisis negotiator, mental health first aid instructor, and assists with the Crisis Intervention Training program in King County, Washington.

Assistant Commander Ian Edwards began his career in Corrections in 2007 as a Corrections Deputy at the Snohomish County Jail. He stepped away from his position as the Training Sergeant ten years later to accept the position of Assistant Commander for the Basic Training Division of the Washington State Criminal Justice Training Commission, overseeing the Corrections Officers Academies. He has worked as a corrections trainer for a number of years. Also a Blue Courage instructor, he assisted with the development of the Blue Courage Corrections curriculum. Certified through the HeartMath Institute, Ian's passion is delivering resiliency training to public safety professionals.

Deputy Sheriff Ben Hecht has worked for the DuPage County Sheriff's Office for eighteen years. He spent the first seven months as a Correctional Officer/Deputy before beginning his career in the Patrol

Division. He has been a Crisis Negotiator since 2006, and is currently a Team Leader (Dupage County maintains two complete teams). Officer Hecht notes that I his negotiation background has been effective not only in hostage/barricaded subject incidents, but also in dealing with anyone who is having any type of mental health episode.

I

Foreword

This book concerns crisis/hostage negotiation within correctional facilities. It is not only for 'in-house' CNT/HNT teams within prisons. Most jails and other community level correctional facilities do not have their own negotiation team and when incidents occur, a local law enforcement team is called in to negotiate working in tandem with the facility's Emergency Response Team. So this book can be used for inter-agency practice when the team will, by necessity, come from outside the correctional facility.

Crisis negotiation—of which hostage negotiation is a subset—is one of the most remarkable areas of law enforcement and corrections. Through a combination of tactical communication, empathic connection and, at times, subterfuge, negotiators persuade desperate, suicidal or homicidal inmates, often intoxicated or mentally ill, to relinquish their position of power and submit to correctional authority. Not all barricaded or static situations, however, are truly negotiable. A perpetrator of an act of mayhem may merely desire an audience to his or her crime, or someone to keep him or her company before executing a suicidal act.[1] In other cases, their actions are attempts to draw responders into a position of vulnerability so that they can enact either a 'suicide by cop' or an ambush. In all such cases, the negotiator serves a vital function: by focusing the subject's attention upon his or her voice, this gives emergency responders time and position to directly intervene to stop the crime in process.

To achieve a successful crisis negotiation, two things must be present: 1) containment of the subject; and 2) the subject must be willing to live. In the correctional setting, containment is almost always far easier to achieve than out in the everyday world. At the same time, there is always the risk that reducing the space the subject has to move around will make them feel even more confined, and less in control. Willingness to live is innate in most individuals—in the correctional setting, however, because of a long sentence, depression, loss of family connections, etc, this might be a very large hurdle to overcome. These factors make the skills of the negotiator extremely important in a stand-off in any correctional setting.

Even in cases where the situation is either a 'victim taking,' or some form of 'suicide by cop,' the role of the negotiation is absolutely essential—the negotiator can distract or delay the subject, or gather Intel so that tactical forces can achieve a rescue or a neutralization of the threat.[2] Even in some dire situations, negotiators can achieve small concessions, or release of some hostages (ill, wounded, or inconvenient to the hostage taker) that make the situation safer for some. This also reduces the complexity of the tactical problems that emergency responders must overcome.

Tactical Responders – Who is called (and how will we refer to them)?

There are thousands of prisons in the United States, encompassing state and federal prisons, military prisons, civil commitment facilities, immigration detention facilities, not to mention local jails, Indian Country jails, and juvenile correctional facilities. Emergency response systems vary widely within these institutions. It would be impossible to construct scenarios that correspond in detail to all particular emergency response systems. First of all, let us consider negotiators—The authors will refer to negotiators either as crisis negotiators (CNT) or hostage negotiators (HNT).

As for tactical responders, here is one example of any emergency response system from a correctional institution within whom the authors consulted. It is possibly quite different from yours:

In our facility, initial response is usually some variation of the Quick Response Strike Team (QRST), which is comprised of people who are filling specific jobs for that shift. For example, our strike team consists of the Shift Sergeant, Response and Movement Officers, and nursing staff. No matter whether the person has response experience or not, if they are filling one of those spots for that day, they are a required responder. This is different from the secondary specialty teams that are called in later, based on the severity and nature of the situation. Those teams are all made of people who applied and interviewed for that team and receive specialized monthly training based on the team's mission. In general, the initial response is QRST, and one or more of the following will be activated or deployed for more serious situations:

- Special ERT (SERT) – Lethal force options (i.e. Sharpshooters). Very small team who go through the SWAT Academy as part of their initial training.
- ERT (ERT) – Less-Lethal force options such as specialty impact munitions. This team's focus is riot control, and as a result is a larger team (we have 30), trained through a specialized Department of Corrections academy.
- Crisis Negotiation Team (CNT) – Hostage negotiators with initial training through basic FBI negotiator course.

All of these specialized response teams are made of people who have regular posts in the facility—being on the team is something they do in addition to their regular job. As a result, we might use members of one of those teams who are already working on the hill and leave it at that, or we might do a full activation and activate people from home to respond. That increases response time obviously, but it shows that tactical response changes based on the scale of the emergency.

The focus of this book is on the development of true-to-life scenarios that require crisis negotiation, not all the ins-and-outs of tactical response. ***Within each scenario, therefore, we will write something to the effect of "Emergency Tactical Responders are called." We will usually abbreviate this as ERT. It is the responsibility of the training director of the scenario to integrate the various component*** teams of your emergency responders, as appropriate to that specific scenario, given the resources at your facility. In many scenarios, only one of your teams will be required (if you have more than one). In a complex or long scenario several teams may be involved.

The Role Player

Crisis negotiation requires a high level of skill. This can only be developed through practice. Such practice also gives a team leader the opportunity to assess his or her negotiators, to assure their abilities remain at peak levels, and also pick out weak points in their repertoire. First-rate training, however, is not easy. Consider the maxim: "As you practice, so you will do." In this light, training must conform closely to real crises. This requires realistic role-play, something easier said than done. Such training has a number of requirements:

- The role-play must be true to life. This means it must conform to the way people truly act in such crises. A role player must, therefore, either have an understanding of crisis negotiation, or be coached *during* the scenario by a 'shadow' who is in the room with the role-player. Hostage takers as well as victim takers, tend to follow—and negotiators definitely *must* follow—certain patterns of behavior that differ from what the uninitiated might assume from watching movies or reading novels;
- The role-play should be true to the behaviors of a person in that particular crisis;
- Additionally, the role-play must be true to the behaviors a person suffering from a mental disorder would genuinely display in such a situation;
- As the role-play is set up for the purpose of improving skills, the training exercise should, in almost all cases, end in success. 'Table-top' or other informal training exercises can be repeated over and over until it is done perfectly, but it would certainly be counter-productive were the department invest in the expense to set up a full training exercise, only to have it aborted or terminated in the first half hour when the hostage-taker 'kills' the hostage. The role player, therefore, in cooperation with the team leader, must monitor the exchange he or she is having with the lead negotiator, and at times, give *in-character* cues when the negotiator is off-target. For example, if the negotiator is talking too much, or trying to tell the subject what to do (instead than practicing tactical paraphrasing), the subject should yell, "You are not listening!" followed, perhaps, by hanging up the phone;
- Sometimes, when necessary, the subject will demand a new negotiator. This is for the purpose of keeping the exercise going when the initial negotiator has lost his or her way. It can also be deliberately programmed into the scenario so more than one negotiator can use the opportunity to practice. However, another aspect that should be built into practice is a manipulative subject,

or one who is so unorganized they cannot focus on either progress or a positive outcome. When *they* demand a change of negotiators, this is a good opportunity for the team to practice refusing their demands in a way that doesn't flame them up

- The only exception to 'building in success' would be if the negotiating team is so incompetent or lackadaisical that they need a hard wake-up call. In such a case, the hostages should be killed or the subject kills himself or herself to underscore the deadly seriousness of the training. At this point, there should be an immediate after-action review, and the exercise can be restarted or closed down, whichever would make the team stronger.

All in all, this is a tall order. You will need someone who is not only familiar with the behaviors of desperate, drug affected, and/or mentally unstable individuals. They also need to be someone who is familiar with crisis negotiation *and* is a good actor. Finally, you need someone who is familiar with the prison or jail environment, and what an inmate can expect from staff in a given situation. Given a negotiation team is usually a small entity within a correctional institution with a variety of competing demands on limited funds, most agencies cannot hire such a professional on a regular basis. Furthermore, once used, could the professional actor be used again? His or her voice would be familiar, and he or she will have participated in the debriefing, thereby establishing a personal relationship with the team. Familiarity may hopefully not breed contempt, but it also takes away the edge that makes the training exercise feel real. Because training should be a regular rather than one-time occurrence, professional trainers should be a rarity rather than the norm.

Who, then, should be a role player? One option is to use acting students, or amateur actors from a local theater company. A second can be staff from a local mental health agency, if they have been properly vetted. One can also use people known to the negotiation team who are both teachable and have acting talent. In all cases, you must have people who have a positive (neutral is not enough!) attitude towards the role that correctional facilities have in helping maintain public safety. In any event, they must be educated in several things:

- The purpose of scenario training
- The requirement to follow the direction of the 'shadow coach'
- They should be assessed in a short audition to ascertain if they can simultaneously think on their feet, follow directions and not go 'off message,' because they imagine they know what a hostage taker would do.

Another option is to use correctional or law enforcement officers. The authors believe correctional officers who are part of the same team are rarely suitable as role-players. Team members recognize their voice and style of interaction on both sides of the role-play, and with such familiarity, it is very hard to make things realistic. Even the use of officers from another agency can be problematic. There is a tendency among all too many officers to become overly competitive with the team and break character or lose sight of the exercise. Another flaw can be that the officer second-guesses the team's strategies, based on his or her beliefs on how s/he personally would interact with an inmate who was acting as the role-play demands. To be sure, the use of officers from another agency, unfamiliar to the team, can be successful, but the aforementioned factors must be taken into account by both the organizers of the training exercise and the role-player.

The Scenario

The reader will find in the following pages thirty-two different training scenarios. They are colorful, unpredictable, and multi-layered. Just as a real situation can change radically when new information is brought in, most of the scenarios will have unexpected twists requiring the negotiators to think on their feet and sometimes diametrically change directions.

Many of the scenarios can be programmed in two ways: for a successful negotiated scenario or an impasse. In the latter case, failure is deliberately architected, so negotiators can learn to recognize a situation gone bad and ERT is given a chance to practice their skills for which they have mustered.

Using this book, a team should be able to orient role-players on how the team wants the training to go. You will have scenario training that you can make as realistic as possible. Each scenario has instructions on best-practice communication strategies for someone displaying the particular type of disturbed behavior highlighted in the scenario. The role-player and coach, if used, are both informed of these strategies. The role-player responds positively when the team uses them, and negatively when they do not. There are three ways to use these strategic communication tactics:

- The team is instructed in the strategies. The exercise is agenda-driven so specific skills are honed and practiced to pattern them as part of one's repertoire. Think of this as a 'tabletop' exercise;
- They are used by a psychological consultant, or members of the team act as 'runners' who hypothetically received information from a consultant, mid-exercise, to drive the exercise forward towards a successful conclusion;
- The team is NOT informed of such strategies. It's sink or swim. At the end of the exercise, be it successful or not, these strategies are brought up in an after-action review, as a comparison with what the team actually tried.

We have tried to give role-play scenarios covering the gamut of mental illness and personality disorders, as well as common crises that lead otherwise ordinary people (inmates or employees) into desperate violent acts.

- It is quite easy to rework a scenario based on your own specific training needs and resources. <u>You can, of course, change gender, age, race, etc. of the role players: just write out a script with the changes.</u> In such a case, our scenario can serve as a guide to the type of personality the role-player must assume, even though specific details are changed. If you decide to change ethnic or cultural details, consult with a subject matter expert in the culture you are concerned with, showing them the scenario. You may find something that is a dilemma in one culture may not be a major problem in another. For example, consider Scenario 12, where you have an inmate from a Middle Eastern Islamic culture, suicidal because her family believes her honor has been inescapably destroyed. Should you change this to a young American, she is more likely, in modern times, to be suicidal because she believes she disappointed and shamed her parents or she is experiencing bullying and harassment. In essence, you can use the same scenario as a core template to make alternative scenarios for a number of training exercises, each time focusing on cultural and religious issues that may drive a crisis situation. They can look very different, while following the same essential plotline.

- <u>The team-leader can also 'pare' down the complexity of the situation, particularly when working with a new team, or when time is limited, feeding the team the information in increments, making the 'role-play' to be an 'educational exercise,' rather than a true-to-life scenario.</u>

Recycling Scenarios

Once familiar with the procedures in this manual, teams can productively recycle scenarios building a new character from traits found elsewhere: based on a character elsewhere in this book, or based on an inmate in your institution. Let us take Scenario 2 as an example. Here we have a hostage incident in a Special Offender's Unit, where one of the inmates takes a therapist hostage. He is a 'jumped-up' pseudo-Intellectual: pretentious and narcissistic. You could take the same plot line, and superimpose the character of the sociopathic characters you find in several of the other scenarios, the paranoid 'control freak,' a developmentally disabled inmate or someone psychotic, also surely part of the prisoner population of such a unit.

Training Procedure

The team leader gives the initial information—who, what, where—to the team, once everything is staged (Of course, the organizer of the exercise will not reveal the title of the scenario, which would give the team members too much of a 'lead' in the negotiation).

Further information is acquired in the same way Intel is gathered in real situations. Preferably, the team leader should recruit persons to act as 'interviewees' for the Intel-gathering members of the team to work with. Depending on the way the scenario is set up (and how many actors/participants the team leader has available), additional role players (family, friends, professionals) pass on the information through secondary interviews, exactly as would happen in real life. In this way, the secondary members of the team get a chance to practice their interview skills. The secondary interviewees can be coached on how to make the interview challenging in a realistic way. If the secondary interviewers are ineffective, they will NOT receive necessary information from the interviewees. In cases where secondary interviewees are not available:

- The team leader (or coordinator of the training i.e. the 'director'), can pass out envelopes containing the appropriate background material, etc. This information should only be given out if the team member asks the right questions of the coordinator of the training exercise, and explains to him or her who they would interview and what information they are looking for.
- If there is an assistant team leader, he or she becomes the 'information person' and takes on the role of each person the Intel gatherers would wish to interview. They don't have to act the part,

but would merely provide information when the proper questions and requests are posed. For example, a team member states they would try to interview other inmates or family members. The information person would state whether that individual is or is not available. If available, they would provide information to appropriate inquiries. If the Intel states they understand the subject has a sister who lives in San Francisco, and would like to interview her, the information person would ask how they intend to locate her. Once the Intel officer describes a reasonable way to find and contact that person, the information person 'becomes' that sister and answers questions accordingly, thus providing the necessary information. This removes the need for an additional role-player, and reduces the need for the preparation of all the written Intel to be done ahead of time. It also allows for some flexibility in problem solving for the Intel officers when figuring out how to go about finding and retrieving information.

The scenario, as written out in the book, is NOT passed to the team as a cheat sheet. We have had critical readers object that the scenarios are 'too complex.' That complexity is for the role player, so that he or she can actually build a character. Furthermore, it gives the 'director', usually the team leader, suitable opportunities to introduce other characters who can be debriefed by the team.

ERTs' Role Within The Training Scenario

If ERT (which may encompass several different teams) is part of the exercise, the exercise should be deliberately crafted and role-player instructed for eventual 'failure' so ERT does not simply stage for hours without anything to do. That said, boredom and stasis are realistically part of the tactical team's job description, and teams that have not honed the ability to tolerate boredom may sometimes act in ways that are not tactically sound.

If possible, various 'exercises' for ERT should be developed for them to actually practice, such as food deliveries, release of an injured hostage, delivery of the throw phone, or documents the subject has demanded. They can plant listening devices, or attempt to get a visual on the scene. As said earlier, team leaders can program the negotiation exercise for failure, something that ERT will not be informed. When it is suddenly time to go, they must be ready to go. Right now.

Effective Coordination between HNT and ERTs

One of the biggest problems that occurs in 'barricade subject' situations of any type, much less hostage situations, is poor coordination and communication between ERTs and HNT. These two divisions must practice together so that flaws in communication as well as development of a clear chain of command are highlighted and addressed. The writers are aware of far too many situations where HNT and ERTs inadvertently function in opposition to each other or when Emergency Responders are not aware of what progress (or lack thereof) HNT has made with the barricaded subject.

HNT and Emergency Response must function together as a 'meta-team.' Problems of coordination, communication and command should be ironed out during training, not on the ground while an incident is in progress.

And, keep in mind, as the Emergency Responder Team(s) develop ideas, it's certainly useful for them to practice them, even if those ideas are never put to use in the particular scenario. For example, as unique and special needs come up in a given situation, there might be a requirement for responders to practice and become familiar with equipment they have never used before. Quite possibly, a situation could resolve itself in many different ways before tactical teams have the need to actually execute the plan as developed. (In 1997, Seattle Police had a stand off with a man armed with a samurai sword in downtown Seattle. The situation took 11 hours to resolve. Ultimately, it was resolved using fire hoses and a ladder. The ERT team had to practice for many hours with equipment they borrowed from Seattle Fire, before executing the plan that took this man safely into custody).

The trainer may be creative, enacting a scenario with tactical intervention, and then, later, 'picking up' at that point, essentially having a second round as a 'do-over.' However, done this way, the exercise does lose an element of adrenaline. It is our sense that the 'do-over' should follow a *successful* negotiation. The negotiation team and role-player should 'rewind' approximately ½ hour to one hour (time for a second negotiator to practice), but this time the role-player should escalate into a negative situation, enabling Emergency Responders to fully practice their skills.

Some of these scenarios may seem rather outlandish. However, life is truly more bizarre and savage than fiction. Each scenario is based on real incidents and real people, the majority of whom the authors have actually encountered.

Essential Information on Communication with Emotionally Disturbed Individuals

This book assumes that the reader has already acquired basic knowledge of emotionally and disturbed individuals as their behaviors pertain to law enforcement or corrections. Whatever the reader's level of knowledge in this area, comprehensive basic information can be acquired through

- **SAFE BEHIND BARS:** Communication, Control, and De-escalation of Mentally Ill and Aggressive Inmates – *A Comprehensive Guidebook for Correctional Officers in Jail Settings* by Ellis Amdur, Michael Blake & Chris De Villeneuve
- **THE COORDINATOR:** Managing High-Risk High-Consequence Social Interactions in an Unfamiliar Environment by Ellis Amdur
- Both of these books, as well as a future companion volume, **SAFE WITHIN THE WALLS:** Communication, Control, and De-escalation of Mentally Ill and Aggressive Inmates – *A Comprehensive Guidebook for Correctional Officers in Prison Settings* can be acquired at www.edgeworkbooks.com

SCENE COMMANDER

HNT Team Leader

- Sergeant or senior team member
- Liaison with scene commander and ERT
- Coordinates written sit-rep
- Monitors stress level of HNT members
- Plans for relief, if necessary
- Determines selection of positions and changes, if necessary

ERT

- Tactical response

Primary

- Communicates with subject
- Not anyone of rank
- Distraction free (should be isolated except secondary and team leader
- No promises made
- No agreements without consult

Secondary (coach)

- Controls access to primary
- Monitors negotiation and provides feedback and ideas
- Is a second ear
- Watches primary's stress level

Intel (likely more than one officer)

- Gathers ALL info on subject
- Interviews family, friends, doctors, mental health providers, etc.
- Runs records checks and computer searches
- Provides relief for other positions

Scribe (recorder)

- Keeps written time line
- Documents everything
- Provides notes for primary and secondary
- Hangs posters, etc.

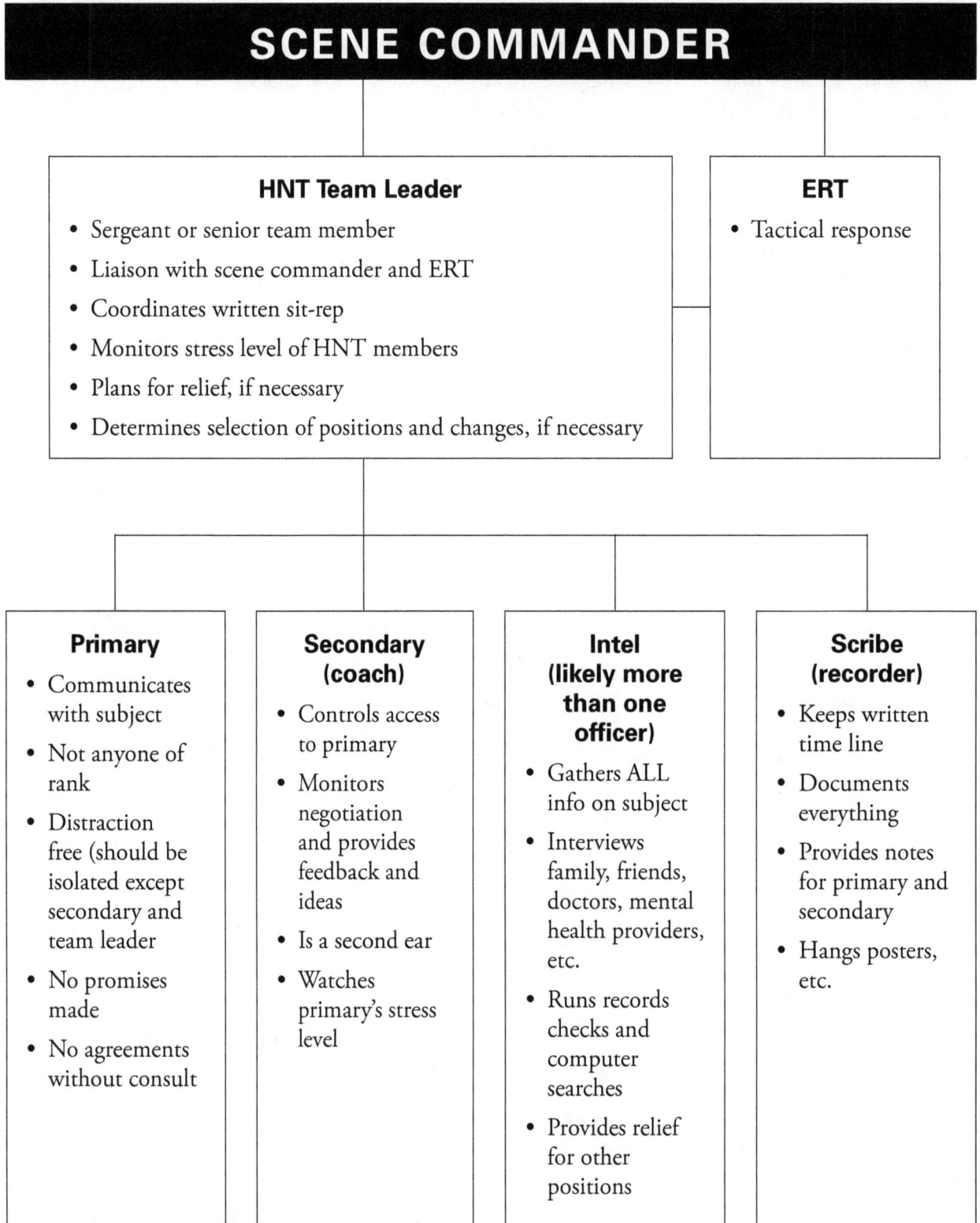

NOTE: This should be regarded as a general model.
Details will vary depending such factors as your organizational structure, available resources and the size of your team.

II

A Note On
Psychological Consultation

Best practice demands a negotiation team has a psychological consultant. Mental health professionals (psychiatrist, psychologist, and counselor) almost never participate in direct negotiation. A correctional crisis negotiator must be prepared, in certain situations, to abet in the killing of the hostage taker. Few mental health professionals, by training, experience, or disposition, are suited for this. A psychologist-negotiator may find himself/herself in an ethical dilemma, known as a 'dual relationship,' where his/her professional responsibility to offer therapeutic interventions may conflict with the negotiator role, which may require misdirection, manipulation, distraction, even lying to the hostage taker in order to ensure the safety of the victims.

This principle is not ironclad. There are teams who use mental health professional/non-corrections personnel in direct negotiations, but this is justifiably rare. Generally speaking, the mental health professional functions as a consultant, either by having a situation sketched out to them at a distance, or listening in on negotiations as they occur and offering their insights to aid the negotiation team. The best consultant, of course, should be a psychological expert already working in the correctional environment. In any event, all negotiators and consultants to the team *must* go through standard negotiation training, and furthermore, we strongly recommend all non-law enforcement personnel associated with a crisis negotiation team should go through defensive tactics training and also engage in 'job shadowing' within the correctional environment to gain some understanding of actual corrections work and culture. In particular, they should experience some simulated training in 'shoot/no-shoot' decision-making, less-lethal and lethal options, as might occur within your facility. There are strict protocols concerning force response that have been learned through bitter experience. You should never have a non-law enforcement negotiator or consultant trying to learn protocols in the middle of a negotiation, particularly corrections procedures, which are far different, in many respects, than the civil rights we enjoy in the free world.

As stated above, the more usual role for the mental health professional is as a consultant: listening in on the conversation, and trying to get a handle on the psychological organization or disorganization of the hostage taker or barricaded subject, or responding to a phone call off-site, and offering informed suggestions on how best to carry out the negotiations.

Hopefully, the team leader, typically a sergeant, has already developed credibility with the command staff, and, if fortunate, with ERT. Having a solid mental health professional on scene to back up the negotiations team can add even more 'weight,' causing command staff consider the negotiators' requests, recommendations and assessment with more gravity. Of course, this requires a mental health professional who is not only able, but also confident enough in his/her abilities that he or she make clear recommendations.

In terms of training scenarios, the mental health professional can provide a vital role in setting up a role play, and in particular, teaching the role player how to understand the subject he or she is playing from the 'inside out.' Based on extensive experience with that 'type' of person, the consultant can give cues on how to talk, and literally how to move (physical organization—body language that mirrors the behaviors of people suffering from a particular illness or mindset—is the best avenue to effective role playing, just as it is in acting). In some scenarios, the mental health professional works as part of the team doing the negotiation. In other trainings, he or she can be in the room with the role-player, coaching them so they stay true to the character and scenario.

The mental health professional must have some humility here. If he or she does not have *direct* experience with the type of individual in a particular role-play, he or she should assist the department in securing a consultant with that knowledge. This can often be done without incurring costs—for example, let us imagine a role play with a head injured hostage taker, where the negotiation team avails itself of a specialist from the local mental health agency, thereby ensuring the actor stays true to character. Joint training exercises are the perfect opportunity for CNT members to meet and 'train' mental health agencies in their community. This is a good time for the Team leader, or training coordinator to reach out to agencies that might be working with this population upon their release. Or, perhaps the agencies that send their representatives into the facility to meet with the population on a regular basis. Connect with them. Talk to them. They would more than likely be excited about assisting in a joint exercise. Both sides have much to learn from each other.

How to Effectively Use Psychological Consultation in the Training Exercises

Some teams start with a psychological consultant on scene and others bring on the consultant only in more complicated cases. You should, of course, follow your standard operating procedures.

- If you start with a consultant, he or she should go into the scenario 'cold,' just like the officers, and offer consultation as he or she usually does. After an hour or two, the consultant should look at the 'consultation' in the book, and use it to augment his or her own advice.

- If you only use a consultant when cases get complicated, or you call 'outside' for help when needed, treat the 'consultation' in the text as if it were a simulated call to a consultant midway through the crisis.

- You could conceivably use this book to assess a potential or actual consultant. If their assessment of the subject in the scenario radically diverges from the psych assessment in the book—particularly if this happens several times—you very likely have someone who is not suitable as a consultant, because they have demonstrated themselves as really misreading the situation (of course, this is not necessarily so if your role player arbitrarily goes off script and is no longer true to the character).

In general, you can either have your psych consultant use the material, adding their own suggestions, or you can read it, as if it was sent by email from consultants far away. If you wish to challenge a member of the team, have someone read it to the team member on the phone, as if from a consultant. The team member must take good notes and report what s/he learned to the rest of the team. Any data not accurately reported will not be available to the team. This will be discussed during the after-action review.

III

How To Set Up
The Role-play

1. The scenario can be set up from simple to elaborate, depending on personnel and resources. The authors have participated in some excellent scenarios that involved no more than two rooms, and a phone in the same building. Other, more complicated training scenarios have entailed taking over a fire station while armed with a sword, holding three hostages in sub-freezing weather in an abandoned building on the grounds of a correctional institution (trading two hostages for hot soup!); providing consultation in the middle of a forest while sitting in an armored personnel carrier; and holding hostages in a building booby-trapped by the ERT team leader so his team could meticulously practice safely going through a huge, dark, unknown environment without getting blown up.

2. Decide if this will be a 'negotiating team alone' exercise, or will include Emergency Response. If it is going to include ERT participation, it is important to have a representative from the designated tactical teams participate in development and implementation of the training exercise, so that their team's time is well spent.

3. Decide on the goals for both teams: Will they be programmed in beforehand to hone specific training objectives, or will it be open-ended?

4. Pick the scenario you want your team to work on. Either the team leader (or if he or she wants to participate in the exercise, another team member) is the director.

5. Role-play (fictitious) information can be inserted into inmate records so that support staff, when asked, can 'pull up' criminal history and other records which thereby make Intel gathering more realistic (remember to pull these fictitious records at the end of the exercise!)

6. Provide the role-player with the scenario. Have them go over the character with the psych consultant or director (if the latter is familiar enough with the personality type), and rehearse with him or her, including having them move like such a person might move. They need to get into character.

7. The information in the psych consult in each chapter can be used to help coach the role player how to play the part. <u>However, do not simply give it to him or her to read, as they will, unavoidably, start tracking the strategies used for de-escalation.</u> Rather, instruct them on the relevant aspects of the subject's behavior, motive and psychological make-up, much like a film director would to an actor, and help them, thereby, get in character.

8. The director should clearly explain the objectives of the exercise. Teach the role player what are effective strategies that will be used by the hostage negotiator, such as active listening. Particularly with a role-player new to negotiation, either the director or an assistant (someone who is

very familiar with hostage negotiations) will be present in the barricaded inmate's location to coach the person so they do not do or say something unrealistic to disrupt the training exercise. You may have to coach (whisper) responses congruent with how barricaded inmates respond to maintain realism. This 'shadow coach' needs to be somehow identified as not being 'in play,' usually by wearing a traffic vest or something of that nature. Whatever 'identifier' is chosen, it must be consistent with all personnel who need to be moving about in the scenario who are NOT in play. It is important to keep these numbers of personnel to an ABSOLUTE minimum. They are 'invisible' to the negotiation team and/or the ERT, if they are listening:

9. If space is limited, because of the location/venue of the 'incident', such as in a vehicle, a two-way radio can be used to communicate and direct the role player. There are some limitations to this, as whoever is doing the directing needs to be able to follow both sides of the conversation, and really stay on top of things:

10. How to respond when the negotiator is 'off track':

   • If the negotiator is talking at the subject and neither listening nor 'lining up' with them, the subject will go into a tirade, yelling, "You are not listening!" They may hang up the phone;

   • If the negotiator says something stupid, which the actor might not realize, the coach will tell the role-player how to react;

   • When the role-player needs a break they can cut off the call in a variety of ways. They can use statements like, "I'm sick of you" to "I'm hungry. I'm going to eat something. Call me later;"

   • If the team is not taking the exercise seriously, (this happens, on occasion), the role-player should be instructed to kill himself/herself or the hostage. Then the team gets the privilege of the sharp edge of the team-leader's tongue.[3]

   • The coach will help the role-player bargain for things—anything from something that is do-able, food for example, to a police escort to the airport—so that the negotiators can practice gaining concessions, taking control incrementally, tiring the subject out, etc;

   • If this is not a hostage situation, but rather a 'victim taking,' the negotiator should practice communicating with the subject, engendering enough interest/connection so that they stay on the line, enabling the ERT to get into a tactical position to neutralize them.

   • If the role player starts to go off message, either 'creatively' or ignorantly, the coach of the exercise should cut them short, using a signal to them that indicates that they slam the phone down saying, for example, "Call me in ten minutes." The director must, as strongly as is required, require the role player to play the character according to script.

11. If the exercise is time-limited, the coach will be essential in assisting the role-player to realistically, pace concessions, the development of rapport, etc.

IV

Core Principles—
Make It Personal

One hallmark of crisis situations is we forget the obvious. The crisis negotiator is striving to establish a connection with the hostage/victim taker or barricaded subject. In different ways, a hostage taker and a victim taker are in an apocalyptic situation. The hostage taker cannot conceive of any better way out of his or her crisis than taking someone prisoner. The victim taker wants to create his or her own personal apocalypse, but they: want a witness (you) while they do it; they are still trying to amp themselves up further; unconsciously, they are looking for a way out. The barricaded inmate sees contact with the officers as a threat. In all cases, the connection you are striving to establish is human. Such a connection immediately establishes that the individual in crisis is no longer isolated. S/he has someone working *with* him or her. When an individual no longer feels alone, new ideas, including hope, arise and they are, at best, willing to surrender power to the correctional officers, or at minimum, divided in their intentions (part of them wanting to surrender and part of them still wanting to cause harm). Even in the latter case, an individual with divided intentions loses situational awareness and may, therefore, be easier to neutralize if that is required.

You cannot establish a connection with an individual unless they perceive you as human. Therefore, as expeditiously as possible, introduce yourself. (There are several viewpoints on this: some negotiators introduce themselves with their first name; others with their title and the department for whom they work). Outline, in the most general sense, what you are trying to do in talking with them. In crisis negotiation, human connection is the ultimate tactic. Without it, no other tactic will have any power at all.

V

Core Principles:
Tactical Paraphrasing—A Reminder

"I don't need good talkers. I need good listeners"
– Ret. Sgt Don Gulla, King County Crisis Negotiation Team

Paraphrasing is perhaps the most important technique in crisis negotiation, particularly in the early stages. As many times as we have worked with negotiation teams, and as often we have seen this emphasized, all too many negotiators neglect to use this strategy effectively.

Tactical paraphrasing is NOT repeating what the other person has said, or even summarizing, in your own words, what they said. Rather, using a phrase or a sentence, you inform the subject your <u>UNDER-STANDING</u> of what they said. If you paraphrase effectively, you have established that you have 'gotten it' that far, so they don't have to repeat themselves, or try to say it in other words. <u>It is like peeling off a single layer of an onion so you can be shown the next one.</u> If you don't show you 'get it,' the hostage taker or barricaded inmate will get frustrated, and feel forced to repeat and/or elaborate that layer of the problem with more and more intensity. As the situation gets more intense, they usually get more irrational, and their ability to communicate breaks down even further. The wonderful thing about paraphrasing is you don't have to be 'smart' and interpret anything. You simply have to listen carefully.

Returning to our image of an onion, as you peel off each layer, the hostage taker/barricaded subject reveals the next layer of whatever is driving them. The inmate might start out complaining about so many officers outside the building. You paraphrase by saying, "You don't want those guys around." Then, they begin to tell you their wife sent the children to live with her aunt, while she took up with a new boyfriend, and you paraphrase, "That's terrible, man. You had no idea your wife would pull that kind of thing. Now things are so bad, there you are with your cellmate, holding a shank in your hand – who you say you DON'T want to cut—with officers right outside your cell," and then the inmate starts talking about suicide.

Paraphrasing establishes you're truly listening and have understood what they have said. An additional component of tactical paraphrasing is where we also take a slightly activist approach. We <u>select</u> what we will paraphrase, subtly steering them in the direction of safety.

This method is 'self-correcting,' whereas passive reflection can make things worse. If you sum up an angry person's worst impulses, they may find themselves in full agreement with you. Here is an example of an incorrect response. "Seeing Tactical Officers outside your cell makes you want to cut off his head." You have lined up with the part of them that desires destruction! However, if you sum up an aspect of what they have said in the direction of conflict resolution, you will draw out of them that which desires a favorable outcome. On the other hand, if they're, in fact, bent on mayhem, they will correct you by escalating what they're saying, believing you aren't getting the message. <u>Remember, they're trying to communicate, or they wouldn't be talking to you.</u>

Example of self-correction:

HNT – "You didn't want it to come to this. You've been hoping you could simply talk this through peacefully."

Subject – "No, you don't get it. I don't want to 'talk this through.' I wanted him right where I got him, sitting here, unable to move, while I tell him how much I hate his guts. When I'm finished with that, we'll see what happens next."

Why not simply ask the hostage taker/barricaded subject what's going on? If they want to tell you, won't they just answer your questions? Sometimes, of course, that's the simplest approach, and it can work. However, asking too many questions is usually not a good idea with really angry people. They already believe you don't understand what they're saying, and a question proves that you don't. (That's why you hear such angry demands as "Don't you get it?" or "How many times do I have to say the same thing?" or "Suppose I spell this out for you slow enough for even you to comprehend." Or even, "If I cut off one of his ears, will you get it now?") Furthermore, they may perceive your questions as an interrogation, of you trying to take control. The subject, particularly if angry, can easily view your questions as a 'power grab,' and will often escalate to take back control.

Of course, there are some basic questions one asks right at the beginning, such as "Are you alright?" or "Is anybody hurt?" Beyond that, and particularly if they are not forthcoming with answers, tactical paraphrasing helps get communication going, focuses the hostage taker on you rather than the victim(s), often fixes their position, and gives them a sense that someone is hearing them out.

How to Use Paraphrasing Successfully

- It is very important that your voice is calm and strong. You speak to the individual as someone who has the power within to take care of both himself and his problem, not as someone who is fragile or volatile . . .even if he is.
- Contact the strong aspect of the individual, the 'future-looking' side, which is striving for a resolution to the situation rather than an apocalypse. If you 'support' the weak or the insecure aspects of the person, you may foster regression to a less mature level of action. Childish action is often impulsive or violent.

- Sometimes, you can use a dramatic summation, "You're really ticked off!" Here, you sum up the individual's mood with your voice, in addition to what is being said.

Using Paraphrasing to Communicate with Individuals with Severe Mental Illness

Paraphrasing can be remarkably effective for communication with severely mentally ill inmates. Given the internal chaos people experience when psychotic, manic, drug intoxicated (a time-limited, externally-induced mental illness), or disorganized, it is essential we don't add to their sense of confusion by barraging them with questions or attempting to solve their problems by taking over and telling them what they should feel or do. When the mentally ill inmate gets confused, losing track of what he was saying, or drifts off into a tangent, just paraphrase the last thing they said. This will help them reorient to the subject of concern.

Core Level within Paraphrasing

We know we have reached the core level when there is no more 'progress.' The person spins his wheels. They may use different words, but they say essentially the same thing over and over again. Some express relief at being finally understood. Some exhibit an intensification of emotion, because you have reached that which is most distressing. When you reach the core, and it is clear you have truly established rapport, you can begin problem-solving. This can be:

- Further paraphrasing, where you show greater and greater understanding about what they're upset about;
- A summation of the core problem, followed by a puzzled question. For example, "You are due to get out in six months. You trusted him, and let him work with you on your business. He stole from you. I can understand why you'd be so mad at him. What I'm confused about is this: if you kill him, he wins. He's hurt or dead, sure, but you stack up more charges, and there will be no one home to protect your family for years – or ever. We have to figure out a way you can win so you keep your respect here, but still are able to get home to your family."
- With some individuals, you have, by paraphrasing them every step of the way, established that you're a person of trust. In some cases, you can now be quite directive, because people are often willing to accept advice or even instruction from those they trust;
- With others, we're ready to engage in a collaborative process of problem-solving, trying to figure out a way to solve the situation in the best interest of everyone involved.

How to Efficiently Develop Skills in Paraphrasing

Outside of realistic scenario training, many find it hard to practice paraphrasing in a manner that does not seem utterly contrived. <u>Taking five minutes at every 'shift change' to practice paraphrasing in pairs while sitting back-to-back is simply not going to happen, and won't be effective anyway.</u> Furthermore, if you view paraphrasing as a 'specialized,' pseudo-counseling technique, you probably won't want to do it—and you won't be good at it anyway. When you are hit by adrenaline, dealing with an angry, perhaps mentally deranged individual, you will stumble over your words if you try to speak 'psychologese,' saying things like:

- "So what you are sharing with me is . . ."
- "What I hear you saying is . . ."

Don't do this! Many subjects will find you irritating, and you will be trying to speak in a way that you never talk like in daily life. You must be absolutely present to what is going on right now, not 'stuck in your head,' trying to say things in the 'right' way.

You are, in fact, a master of paraphrasing. You do it all the time simply keeping a conversation going, saying things like:
- "Your kid flunked out, huh?"
- "You're not getting a raise."
- "You hate that guy."
- "She's the one."

In short, the natural statements you intersperse in any conversation are perfect paraphrasing. However, because you do this unconsciously, it's hard to tap into as an **emergency technique**. You need to make this a conscious skill, something that's easy to perfect. Consider this—how many conversations do you have a day? Twenty? Thirty? Forty? In each and every conversation, at an arbitrary moment of your choosing, decide to paraphrase the next thing they say. <u>Only one statement</u>. For example, your friend says: "I'm thinking of going hunting this weekend." You, instead of asking a question, say, "You got your license already," or "You want to get an elk again this year, huh?" Or another example: your friend says, "My daughter got on the honor role. Finally." You reply, "Her grades really went up this quarter, didn't they," or "You've been waiting a long time." Then, whatever the response, you go back to your conversation in your usual manner.

Your conversational partner won't even notice. <u>But because you made a conscious decision to do this, your brain notices</u>. That means you have practiced that skill twenty to forty times a day. Consider how good your shooting skills would be if you do twenty, thirty, forty perfect shots a day—it would become automatic! Similarly, if you do this every day, you will be able to step into crisis-oriented paraphrasing without hesitation. It will be so natural to you that you do not even have to think about it.

VI

Don't Forget The Value Of Scenario Training To Hone The Skills Of Potential 'Coaches' Or 'Secondary Negotiators.'

When debriefing true hostage negotiation/barricaded subject incidents, most all eyes are on the primary negotiator. The primary is the position most (if not all) HNT members aspire to become. All HNT members are waiting for their turn in the 'hot seat.' This is where the action is, and most consider it the most important position on the team. Nonetheless, all members will concede that crisis negotiation is a team effort. Successful outcomes would not be as common without the efforts of the Intel officers, and the other team members helping out in the background, not to mention the presence and security that ERT(s) provide.

In all actuality, the most important member of the team is probably the 'secondary' or 'coach' negotiator. This position is usually occupied by one of the most skilled team members. This member is in a position where the adrenaline is running a little lower than for the primary. This enables the secondary to see things with a broader view, thereby processing the information through a different filter. This coach is not only involved in the processing of the information and development of the negotiation strategies, but is also tasked with keeping an eye on the primary negotiator. There have been incidents where the primary has become too emotionally involved with the subject, and has inadvertently tipped them off as to developing tactical actions. In other cases, primaries have become so close to the subject, that they lose their objectivity when discussing possible outcomes. Finally, the primary can get his or her buttons pushed and lose that objective distance that an effective negotiator must maintain. The coach has the responsibility to ensure the primary does not go astray with regard to their feelings for the subject (either positive or negative). If the coach sees this issue developing, it is their responsibility to bring it to the attention of the team leader, who can discuss it with the primary, and secondary, and a decision can be made as to whether or not to switch negotiators.

The coach truly is a critical role. Scenario-based training provides the team leader/director with an opportunity to watch to see how different members can perform in this role. This is not a role that comes naturally to most negotiators, and just because one is very experienced in the field does not necessarily mean they will perform well as a coach.

Some of the very best negotiators are very poor coaches. When placed into the role of coach, they cannot help but take over. Instead of 'coaching' the primary by listening and providing suggestions as needed, they begin to feed the primary lines, one at a time, as if the primary had no idea what to say. This can be very annoying, and also does not let the team leader assess the skills of the person who is acting as primary for the training.

On the other hand, some 'coaches' may not participate at all. Instead, they sit with a set of headphones on, neither engaging in strategy sessions nor paying attention to what they need to.

The role of the secondary is a difficult role to fill. As stated before, most negotiators would rather be 'doing it themselves' than observe and help. It takes a very disciplined negotiator to fulfill this role. Scenario-based training is a good time to find who can do so when needed. The best coach is one who can listen, guide and direct an inexperienced or new negotiator through an exercise. That way, the new negotiator gains some skill and confidence by learning from one of the veterans. The coach can also provide a different kind of guidance when a negotiator, even a veteran, begins to lose focus and the situation goes sideways.

Built-In Secondary Negotiator Training

The team leader can deliberately create a stealth training scenario, in collaboration with the primary, where the latter develops too strong of rapport with the subject, interfering with the process. This challenges the secondary to step up and do something about it, and enables the team leader to observe how the rest of the team reacts. Having to make decisions about changing negotiators is something the team needs to be comfortable with; furthermore, all must understand that there can be no arguments when/if the time comes. If good reasons are provided, the changes need to be made, so the process can continue.

VII

Texting

The authors recently heard about an excellent training exercise by the Snohomish County Sheriff's Office of Washington State that was carried out entirely through texting. A bright young teenager was recruited and oriented towards a suicidal situation. She was simply asked to reflect on some of her friends that have had trouble with parents, bullying or the like and to construct the character as the training went along. She was also coached by the director on how hostage negotiation works, and how it should be resolved. Because of the technological challenge, the director decided to do a straightforward negotiation, rather than a complex one. Texting was more than enough of a challenge!

There are two circumstances where texting/communication is likely to occur:
- A hostage is surreptitiously communicating with officers (or texting a friend, who communicates in turn with law enforcement). In this case, the communication will likely be in brief, short bursts
- A subject communicates directly. The negotiators were really challenged! They didn't understand the various emoticons and slang, and they were too slow with their thumbs. The young person was often confused by the negotiator's response, because he was six or seven texts behind what the kid was saying.

Because texting is becoming almost ubiquitous, it is an essential skill that at least several team members should be expert. Like touch-typing, the expert 'texter' thumbs words at an amazing rate of speed. Your texting specialist should familiarize himself/herself with various emoticons and abbreviations. They must go on line frequently to find out what the new slang is.

While the "text-negotiation" is taking place, a secondary should be ready, logged into Google or Bing, so they can instantly type various incomprehensible-to-the-negotiator abbreviations, so they can signal the negotiator what each of them means.

The authors are well-aware that cell phones are interdicted in correctional settings. To state the obvious, so are drugs, yet both get inside. So as unlikely as it might be, prepare for the possibility of a texting situation. If it ever does happen, and no one is prepared, someone may die.

On Texting Scenarios

We have not set up a specific scenario drill here for text negotiations or hostage communication, but as described above, it should be easy to integrate into a training exercise.

VIII

On Social Media

It would be naïve to assume that social media does not impact hostage situations in prison or jails. Inmates, particularly those in minimum security, may have access to social media of one kind or another, and may use it to communicate to the outside world. A riot or other incident may be impacted on such communication, from both sides. Not only will the inmates receive information, they may also get encouragement, incitement and Intelligence. On the other hand, social media can become a conduit for false (or managed) information that spreads like wildfire ('goes viral').

In addition, family and associates may have been communicating with the inmate through a variety of media, including visitation, smuggled cell phones or through trustees, etc., who have access to computers. In the event of a hostage taking, check the social media accounts of their friends, family and known associates. Vital information may be acquired through this medium.

Do not confine your search to Facebook. There are a number of other social media sites more popular with many these days. Other popular sites include Twitter, LinkedIn, Pinterest, Google+, Tumblr, Instagram, VK, Flickr and Vine, to name a few. Even MySpace, considered to be out of fashion, is still used, particularly by many with 'alternative' lifestyles – most who post on the latter site are harmless people with unusual intimate recreational activities, but MySpace has also been a venue for more predatory and aggressive sexual predators.

A general project for your team should be to assemble data on all these conduits of information.

IX

On The Names Used
In The Scenarios

The writers have chosen many names that are hard-to-pronounce or associated with a particular ethnic group. One reason is that this should be a clue to at least think about if a cultural consult is necessary. There are times when it is not necessary—for example, a 2nd or 3rd generation American may have received the name of his or her ancestors, but culturally, that person is mainstream American. Sometimes, however, the cultural factors are very relevant, and the name can be a clue.

A second reason is that many people are very defensive and easily upset about their name being mispronounced. Some people, grievance collectors, look for a reason to get upset, and one's name being misspelled or mispronounced is an excuse to 'pop off.' So when you get a report of the name, look it up online to: a) determine the ethnic background, and b) find out the proper pronunciation, if you don't know it. Imagine you have an inmate who has had his or her name mispronounced by correctional officers and inmates on a repeated basis. If you can't correctly determine the proper pronunciation through quick research, the negotiator could say something like "I want to be respectful. Would you tell me the proper pronunciation of your name?" Given that pronouncing it wrong can flame them up, saying their name correctly can be the first step toward rapport building.

X

"That's Not The Way We Do It Here"
—Rewrite As Necessary!

The authors have tried to provide a scenario that tells a story that is realistic enough that the role player can properly prepare for it. However, to tell a story requires details. It is very likely that we may describe a scenario that is, in some detail, large or small, impossible at your facility: the floors have drains so one can't flood anything; there are no tiers to jump off; staff are not provided with stab vests or conducted electrical weapons (CEW), etc. It is the responsibility of the director to rewrite the scenario so that it fits your institution. The character of the subject does not need to change when you rewrite the circumstances or environment that he or she acts out.

XI

On Scenario Training

**This chapter—and only this chapter—is copied and given as a handout
to the team before the training exercise.**

Important

This training is for educational purposes. This includes not only the negotiating team, but also all the observers. The role player will be presenting an inmate encompassing specific behaviors associated with mental disorder/personality disorder/substance abuse, etc. Within the designated time period, our intention will be to allow both observers and participants to experience what interacting with someone of this style might be like. This includes recognizing some of the signs and symptoms, trying out various interventions, and experiencing some of your reactions, the negative ones in particular, that someone of this style might engender.

Be Aware

At various times, the inmate may hang up the phone or otherwise stop communicating:
- Because it's what the person would do in the situation;
- To indicate, clearly, that the negotiator is off-course;
- So the supervisor of the exercise is able to use the time to pass new info to the team or to bring in new role players, such as family members or escaped hostages for collateral interview practice. The collateral subjects may need to be de-escalated themselves: escaped hostages and other inmates, from whom you are attempting to gather Intel, are often very agitated, showing everything from hysterical fear to anger at the negotiating team.

Possible Outcomes & Situations

- An interaction will take place throughout the time period, with no resolution. Progress will be made, and we will debrief what worked well, or what might have worked better, etc.
- A resolution truly occurs and the hostage taker surrenders.
- The situation is going somewhat badly, and will likely get worse. Ensuring the exercise continues, rather than it ending in disaster, the role player may get very belligerent, and demand another negotiator. The role player will probably cut off communication. If such a situation occurs, the team should discuss if the situation is really going poorly. If so, both in the interests of continuing the exercise, and also increasing the learning process, we sometimes recommend changing negotiators. Otherwise, the hostages might be killed. On the other hand, the demand for another negotiator may be just a power play. Thus, you have to be aware of the connection/control you

have or do not have with the hostage taker, because the latter situation requires you continue and do not change. The former, however, allows the role player and supervising observers to signal a potentially fatal situation without completely aborting the exercise.

- The situation goes badly, for whatever reason, and the hostage is in danger. Tactical forces are called in and the hostage taker is neutralized.

Guarantees

- The role player will make this an educational exercise.
- No attempt will be made to 'cheat', to make the scenario a no-win situation, or to shame the team. This does not include the difficult, perhaps obnoxious behaviors typical of the type of inmate we are training to deal with.
- Whoever the role player is, they will have the humility to be directed in how to play the role by the team leader, and when included, a psychological consultant. They will be 100% willing to accept direction throughout, so the training exercise makes the team and individual members stronger. Everyone is training for life-and-death events, so scenario training will be treated that way.

SCENARIO 1

Bipolar Disorder

1 – Incident

Inmate Joseph Cooper has tied his cellmate to his bunk, and is holding a shank to his throat. ERT is outside his cell. He shouts that if they enter or use gas, he will cut his cellmate's throat to the bone before they can get to him. HNT and ERT are called.

1 – Interview with Staff from Mental Health Unit

Joseph Cooper is a 32-year-old male, who has been in-and-out of the mental health unit. He's been diagnosed with bipolar disorder (AKA manic-depression). Typically—there've been three such incidents in the past—he stops taking his medications. He gets energetic and loud, and increasingly sleep deprived. In the past, his typical pattern was to get verbally aggressive and defiant of orders. At the same time, he would get boisterous, singing loudly, and making obscene statements and jokes. Medical staff has always been unable to convince him to start taking his medications again. Eventually, he gets hypersexual, stripping off clothing and masturbating, and getting into conflicts with other inmates. He has previously been moved to the mental health unit due to self-harm: in those three previous incidents, he has, in order: slashed his face with a razor blade, repeatedly bashed his head against the wall and swallowed a number of objects. However, there is no previous record of him being aggressive to others while in custody.

1 – Criminal History

Cooper is eight years into a twelve-year sentence for first-degree assault, his first incarceration. He got in a physical fight with his brother during a family party, and gouged out one of his eyes, only failing with the second when his uncle knocked him out. There had been no signs of mental illness noticed at that time, although mental health professionals now suspect that this violent incident was probably a manifestation of the emergence of his illness. Overt symptoms of his bipolar disorder emerged in the second year of his incarceration.

1 – Interview with an Inmate

One of the other inmates states that Joseph is not acting the same as he has in previous incidents. "He's different now. He has a bad attitude. Always arguing. I mean, he's like he always is when he goes off his meds, but he aint happy this time. He's usually kind of funny when he goes dingy, a least before the jerking off starts, but he aint funny this time."

Information from collateral contacts

Essential information will only be revealed if the interviewer asks the right questions. The fellow inmate role player is free to adopt any kind of role (belligerent, scared, cautious), and the interviewer must effectively work with whatever they present. The role player, however, must give the information IF the interviewer is effective. If the interviewer is 'phoning it in,' is rude or rushed, terminate the contact

---

1 – First Contact with Negotiator

Joseph, upon first contact, sounds buoyant and happy, but on the edge of being out of control. He talks really fast, seeming hardly to breathe between sentences. The negotiator will find it very hard to get a word in edgewise. He says his cellmate never shuts up, talks at him all the time, and he has twenty-two hours and seventeen minutes of things to say to him, but he kept interrupting, so he tied him up and gagged him so he could be sure he stayed still to listen. He tells the officer to wait because he's got to be in top shape 'to handle the coming storm,' and he jumps up and starts stabbing the air in sewing machine fashion, well away from his tied up roommate, nonstop for three minutes. He starts talking again. Then he starts doing burpees, dropping to the floor, knife in hand, does a push-up, jumps up and repeats. This kind of action happens repeatedly (the role player, if they can't do the exercises, should breathe as if they are doing some kind of fast, active, chaotic movement.

He is volatile, and talks very rapidly. He will be easily irritated, will misunderstand what the negotiator says, and will go off on a lot of tangents. He is also provocative, saying things to get a rise out of the officer.

Joseph will keep changing the subject. It'll be really hard to get him to focus on your agenda – just when you think you've made progress, he'll talk about something completely different. There will be a lot of sexualized references, inquiries about the negotiator's sex life, provocative statements bringing up celebrities and politicians who sexually harass women and men, then he'll ignore you and start talking about anything that comes into his head, first to the captive cellmate, then back to you

1 – Interview with Another Inmate

Joseph has been obsessing about his son. He heard from his wife that the boy has been diagnosed with ADHD and was put on medication. He says the pills "are called Adival or Addital or Amital or something like that, and Joe says that he needs to know what his son is taking to figure out if they are good for him. He said he heard that the pills are like some kind of speed, so he copped some meth on the yard. Nah, I aint saying any more about it, but he's a good guy, so I don't want to see him get messed up with you guys."

1 – Further Interviewing with Joseph, After Getting Info Regarding His Son

Joseph, when asked, tells the officer the school told him his son has ADHD, which " . . . is a lie. He's just smart and bored. But my wife made him go to the doctor and take the meds. I love my son. I don't want him to take something that's bad for him. So I've been taking them too, both to see what effect they have and out of solidarity. But I have to take some more and anyway, I have to make this asshole listen for once, instead of talking all the time." He wonders if crystal meth is really the same as Adderal and demands that he be supplied with the latter – "or Ritalin, that'll work too, won't it?" – so he can adequately assess his son's medications.

1 – Psych Consult Regarding Bipolar Subjects

If you haven't picked it up already, the consultant will suggest the strong possibility Joseph is manic, either because he has bipolar disorder, and/or due to his taking meth. You will recognize the manic person because they will display super high energy. They will often be talking very fast and their ideas will 'zigzag' from one to another. They often act like comedians, with a rapid-fire delivery. Their behavior may also be either sexualized or hair-trigger aggressive. In either case, they will very likely be provocative. Here are some things you should do:

- Remain calm and centered;
- Be conscious of their 'brittle' state of mind, in spite of how confidently they behave. Grandiose doesn't mean strong! So, if you question their competence, or make them feel vulnerable or stupid, they may explode with rage;
- Don't bluntly criticize their actions;
- Don't laugh at them, either deliberately, or involuntarily;
- If you use any humor, it is for the purpose of slowing them down, not joking around. If you joke around, you will 'wind them up.' They may start to fool around like they are a character in a cartoon, where no one *really* gets hurt—they just 'see stars.' Or, they may be caught off-guard by your humor and they will think you are laughing at them (because they will interpret the 'surprise' of a good joke as a 'surprise attack');
- They may try to provoke you (think of the Road Runner and Coyote);
- They can be very volatile, exploding into rage with the slightest provocation. Be relaxed but ready for the worst.

Mania PLUS Psychosis

At its extreme, mania (either from bipolar disorder or stimulant drug intoxication) can develop into full-blown psychosis – it is NOT so in this scenario. IF the manic person is also psychotic, the psychosis, particularly the delusions, will probably take precedence in terms of your tactics, but it will be very hard to get the person to track you because of their mania. In these situations, you essentially have a hallucinating or delusional person who also happens to be moving and talking very fast. See other sections of this book, as well as other source books, cited in the Text Box in the Forward: **"Essential Information on Communication with Emotionally Disturbed Individuals"**

1 – Conclusion of the Exercise

This exercise can go on for some time. Ideally, using the principles above, the negotiator should try to get Joseph focused on his son's well-being rather than on the tied-up inmate.

Things that a negotiator might offer would be a conversation with a mental health professional to talk about ADHD and what good or bad the meds might do. On the other hand, Joseph may simply get hungry or tired and surrender – you extend the negotiation in order that he 'runs down,' particularly if, in the process, he is detoxing from the methamphetamine he took.

This scenario could also be primed for cell-extraction/rescue of the hostage. It would be a valuable exercise to calculate just when Joseph is far enough away from the hostage – on the floor doing exercises or moving towards the cell-door to yell at the negotiator – to move in and cut him off from the hostage.

SCENARIO 1 – Checklist for After Action Review

The after action assessment/critique will depend on what was expressed and expected of the team going into the exercise. In other words, what was the desired training goal or outcome? Not just the outcome of the scenario, but what are the skills the director (team leader) is hoping to see exercised by the team, as these scenario/situations develop?

Team recognized what was going on with subject?
- ❏ Did not meet goal
- ❏ Partially met goal
- ❏ Fully met goal

Negotiator dealt appropriately with subject?
- ❏ Did not meet goal
- ❏ Partially met goal
- ❏ Fully met goal

Negotiator demonstrated good listening skills?
- ❏ Did not meet goal
- ❏ Partially met goal
- ❏ Fully met goal

Negotiator did not challenge or criticize subject?
- ❏ Did not meet goal
- ❏ Partially met goal
- ❏ Fully met goal

Negotiator did not get sidetracked by all the subject's tangential communication?
- ❏ Did not meet goal
- ❏ Partially met goal
- ❏ Fully met goal

Negotiator did not misinterpret subject 'sounding funny' with 'being funny' and use humor that aggravated the subject or took him off guard?
- ❏ Did not meet goal
- ❏ Partially met goal
- ❏ Fully met goal

SCENARIO 2

Brittle Narcissism

2 – Call to Main Control and Redirection to HNT

The prison receives a call through main control from the spouse of one of the therapists, Alicia Thompson, in the Special Offender Unit (NOTE: Twenty states currently have civil commitment laws for violent sexual predators. If your facility does not have such a unit, or your state does not have civil commitment laws, rework the plotline to involve an inmate in the Mental Health Unit).

The spouse received a text from the therapist that s/he is being held captive by one of the inmates. The first level of communication will be through main control. The caller will be provided with relevant information through the text. It is up to the calltaker to get this initial information.

On Communication 'Outside'

The writers are aware that cell phones are forbidden for most job classes to bring inside correctional facilities. This can be built into the scenario in two ways:
1. The therapist smuggled in the phone because her spouse was so worried about her, and demands texts.
2. An alternative method of communication outside is used – the therapist has a direct phone and was on the phone with her spouse when the inmate went into her office. She dropped the phone and the spouse heard the incident as it occurred before the inmate hangs up the phone.
3. That the therapist has the phone can also be a combination of an oversight by the therapist coupled with inattention on the part of corrections staff.

The gender of therapist and spouse can, of course, be adapted as the director of the role play chooses. This can add another layer to the communication, as decided by the director of the scenario. For example:
- Therapist and spouse can be same-sex and the spouse is hyper-sensitive and argumentative to any delay in the calltaker realizing that they are, in fact, married.
- The spouse can be an argumentative, aggressive male, who never liked his wife working with "those perverts," and he gets focused on "holding you people responsible if anything happens to my wife."
- The spouse, of either gender, is panicky and tearful and it is hard to get information from them.

Working with Main Control Call-takers

The call-taker will be responsible for passing the information on to the negotiation team. The training goal is for the call-taker to get practice in getting through the noise and emotion, and conveying all the accurate information to the negotiation team. If the call-taker is not able to get past the spouse's heightened emotions, the latter should hang up. You then figure out if the call-taker should call back, another call-taker should do so, or HNT should call back.

2 – Subjects Located – Background Information

Through the initial call, the hostage taker and hostage are located. The subject is Henry Forsythe. A record check will reveal that he received a six year sentence for rape of a child, an eleven year old niece, whom he abused for over a year before she disclosed and he was arrested. He claimed that the sex was consensual, even though the young woman has subsequently personally contacted his parole board, so that he served his full sentence. Forsythe claims that her mind was poisoned by 'the feminists.'

After he served his sentence, he was placed in the Special Offender Unit under the state's civil commitment statute governing dangerous sexual offenders. Forsythe has maintained his innocence based on his claim that young women in Biblical times were married upon reaching puberty. He has been at odds with staff because he refuses to participate in mandated treatment.

Additional Plot Line

Forsythe has been informed by the therapist (a Sex Offender Treatment Specialist) that because of his non-compliance with treatment, she will not be recommending him for release to the Indeterminate Sentence Review Board.

An alternative plotline justifying the therapist regarding him as non-compliant could be that another member of the offender's family alleges that she, too, was one of his victims. A condition of the offender's release is successful completion of the Sex Offender Treatment and Assessment Program, which requires that he fully disclose all crimes he committed, whether adjudicated or not. The new victim matches a vague story the offender told during treatment, however the offender changed numerous details to lessen the significance of the crime.

The most likely for the offender would be that he has taken her as a 'victim' – he's not trying to bargain for anything. He simply wants revenge.

You could change the scenario, however, making him less Intelligent and manipulative, and in that case, create a storyline where he actually thinks that taking his therapist hostage will help him.

2 – Interview with Therapist's Colleague

Jason Allred is part of the therapy team. He states that Forsythe has been particularly hostile to Dr. Thompson, because he claims she is anti-man, anti-sex and has singled him out. Forsythe says that he doesn't belong in this unit, that he is not a pedophile. He claims that he's never had any sexual desire towards a child, that the girl he molested (and others, staff suspects) were past the age of puberty, and as they could be impregnated, they were young women. He also states that rape requires force and he didn't use any violence at all.

Allred is off site and reception is poor, but he states that Forsythe is a flaming narcissist.

2 – For the Role Player

Contact is made with Forsythe. He is a pretentious guy. He intersperses his conversation with a lot of "you know what I mean" phrases, and alludes to travel to Europe, visits to fine museums, beautiful vistas. He sprinkles his sentences with phrases in French. It's unclear if he's ever been to Europe, or if he can speak French, really knows ballet, etc. The role player will try to keep the conversation about these matters – not the hostage taking or his demands. He has a 'captive audience' in HNT and he intends to draw things out as long as he can.

This is an example. The role player should have several hobbies, travel experience or other interests that they can use to build the role. If they speak another language, they are free to use that.

Henry will have a prissy manner—but NOT someone's stereotype of a 'queen.' More like an arrogant prep school graduate. Henry will be disdainful and contemptuous:

- If the officer is female and attempts to be friendly or jocular, or if she softens his voice offering to help, Henry should be flirtatious, trying to push the officer's buttons. If the officer, male or female, is cold or matter-of-fact, Henry is going to act offended.
- Henry will try to impress the negotiator with his knowledge, hobbies, or whatever his pre-occupations are. He'll go off on tangents, and it will be very hard to get him back on track.

When HNT tries to ascertain the hostage's well-being, Henry will get outraged that attention is taken away from him. You may hear weeping or crying in the background.

Changing the gender of victim and perpetrator

The director can rework the role play by changing the gender of both or either perpetrator and victim. In this case, the circumstances of the sexual abuse and the perpetrator's justification will change. Thereby, this exercise could be 'recycled' several times. Consult with an expert in this area to make the role play true-to-life.

Henry may try to reassure Dr. Thompson that this will be over when his demand is met, that he gets a rehearing in front of an "unbiased, Bible-reading Christian judge." HOWEVER, as the negotiation goes on, and Dr. Thompson continues to be upset, Henry will get increasingly irritable, offended that she is distressed. This, he says, is another example of her questioning his word.

Forsythe will get anxious when this isn't resolved. He's afraid of being pepper-sprayed, more afraid of being shot. He is going to start accusing the officers as leaving him no way out, that the cops are all anti-Christian, that the Bible supported him in what he did.

He will start to push the negotiators' buttons, talking about how an elder man has a responsibility of initiating virgins into a sexual life. "They" – then he corrects himself from plural to singular – "she is my spiritual bride. She will be bound to me through her body and mind for life everlasting. I placed my mark inside her body. Once sealed, no other man can possess her." He may go into detail about what he did with her, and the negotiator will get the impression that he is getting off talking about it.

2 – Psychological Consultation

Henry's pretentiousness and speechifying is a manifestation of narcissism. He is not only in love with himself; he is the only important thing in the universe. When you discourse with him about his interests, it's best to be "just smart enough" to be corrected and educated. If you act dumb, he will find you an uninteresting audience. If you are smarter than him, he will be threatened and try to get his power back by escalating.

His coercive rape of at least one young girl is an expression of entitlement. He is dangerous to Dr. Thompson, because she questions his 'right' to young women. He extinguishes the reality of who his victim is, and what she actually experienced to maintain his fantasy of this pure love of older man to youth. As the negotiation drags on and Dr. Thompson gets more frightened and upset, Forsythe will very likely get increasingly outraged at her. She is the type of person who poisoned his victim's mind. If it weren't for people like Dr. Thompson, he would have been paroled a long time ago and certainly wouldn't find himself among "homosexuals and perverts in this antechamber to hell."

The negotiator should try to begin to establish rapport by subtle admiration for his sophistication and wide knowledge. In other words, the negotiator tries to successfully link Henry to all the things he thinks are special in his life and in himself. The reason is this: <u>you want Henry to think he is too special to die, and too special to be locked up forever.</u> You cannot say this, but he will assume this himself if he is 'allowed' to go on about his specialness. Because he feels he has an audience, he will likely begin to 'believe his own press' about how wonderful he is. The officer must be able to tolerate this—including his specialness as a lover of young women.

The goal is this: Henry must still feel like he has a lot to lose. It can be framed, at the proper moment, that he really hasn't committed much of a crime, that, according to his account, the young woman (don't say "girl!") was willing at the time. Furthermore, he has not hurt Dr. Thompson, and releasing her will show others that what he did was an act of desperation, not an act of intentional violence. There is still a chance for his voice to be heard, if he surrenders.

To reiterate, you try to support him in a belief that he is surrendering because he is strong and smart, not because he is weak.

Warning! Tripwires with Narcissistic Individuals

If the officer happens to know a lot about what Henry claims to be interested in, s/he must be careful! Henry may not know much about the subject after all, and when the officer displays his/her knowledge, Henry will be embarrassed at being found out, resulting in a breaking of rapport, even rage. He needs to feel himself to be special, and if the officer is smarter than he is, he's lost his specialness.

What will make Henry most dangerous is if his sense of specialness is questioned or challenged. If he doesn't have himself, he has nothing. This most certainly encompasses his self-image.

SCENARIO 2 – Checklist for After Action Review

The after action assessment/critique will depend on what was expressed and expected of the team going into the exercise. In other words, what was the desired training goal or outcome? Not just the outcome of the scenario, but what are the skills the director (team leader) is hoping to see exercised by the team, as these scenario/situations develop?

Floor plan established in a timely manner?
- ❏ Did not meet goal
- ❏ Partially met goal
- ❏ Fully met goal

Team proceeded with ideas for Intel gathering/suggestions?
- ❏ Did not meet goal
- ❏ Partially met goal
- ❏ Fully met goal

Primary negotiator was able to check his/her own attitude toward subject?
- ❏ Did not meet goal
- ❏ Partially met goal
- ❏ Fully met goal

Negotiator demonstrated good listening skills?
- ❏ Did not meet goal
- ❏ Partially met goal
- ❏ Fully met goal

Negotiator demonstrated a non-judgmental attitude?
- ❏ Did not meet goal
- ❏ Partially met goal
- ❏ Fully met goal

Negotiator didn't show s/he was smarter than subject around the areas that the subject claimed knowledge or expertise?
- ❏ Did not meet goal
- ❏ Partially met goal
- ❏ Fully met goal

SCENARIO 3

Overtly Sociopathic Teen in Youth Detention Facility
(Can be Adapted to Adult Roles)

3 – The Incident

The detention facility is co-ed, and during the day-time, the boys and girls can freely associate together. The facility is run on a level system and those at higher levels have a lot of freedom of movement.

Toby, a youth who is somewhat developmentally delayed, reports that Jesse Boros has forced three girls into an outbuilding in the garden area. He has a weapon.

On Scenarios Involving Children's Characters

This role-play—and many others—will be too raw for a real kid, so either a high voiced adult or a tape of someone crying and asking to leave should be played in the background. If it's going to be verbally heard and not visually observed, often a female voice works well for an adolescent male. If you have exceptionally 'young acting' students at a college level, they can be suitable.

Staff members (or specialized Emergency Responders, if part of the facility's staff) approach the building. When they enter (or observe through a window), they see three girls semi-naked. Jesse is standing over them, apparently directing them in sexualized activities. He has a large blade in his hand. When he is aware of staff, he grabs one girl, puts the edge of the knife against her throat, and states that he will cut her throat unless staff backs away. Upon his order, the other two girls move close to him, so that they surround him.

Adapting to Adult Role

This role-play could easily be adapted to an adult role. Simply change the circumstances, and the nature of the relationships among the inmates as needed. This is a 'useful' character to role-play because you certainly will find your share of sociopaths and sadists in the correctional environment. The initial informant could be a developmentally delayed inmate so that the secondary interviewer gets practice in interviewing a poor informant with limited observational and Intellectual skills.

---

3 – Initial Stage of Incident

The negotiator will be aware that Jesse has a reputation of being a model inmate, and will try to connect with him based on how well he's 'programmed,' how he's due to be released in less than a year, that he's been doing well in school. This incident will be described to HNT as out-of-character, at least as staff knows him.

Jesse will be menacing, but at the same time, will assure staff that no harm will come to the girls if they do not enter the area. He will be, on the surface, reasonable, and willing to talk to HNT about his future plans, about how he wants to go home. He'll ask to talk with Mr. Antonev, one of the staff who is on vacation, and will get stuck on how if he could only talk to Mr. Antonev, he'd feel O.K. about leaving the room. (Antonev is impossible to reach).

He will not make any demands, and will bat away any suggestions that HNT makes to resolve the situation. While this is going on, collateral interviews should be undertaking to get some idea of what makes Jesse tick. The initial stage could go on for quite some time. HNT will attempt various ways to 'connect' with Jesse, and there will be apparent progress, but he will sidetrack you with irrelevant questions, or change the subject.

You'll hear one or more of the girls in the background, crying or pleading to be let go. Jesse ignores them, unless someone gets loud and then you hear him say, calmly, "Shut up or I'm going to have to hurt you." The girl(s) will quiet down at such points. At this stage of the exercise, there should not be a level of emotional escalation or threat that would necessitate entry to rescue the girls.

3 – Interview with the Youth Who Informed Staff

The 'child' role player should be coached by your child interview specialist, a therapist or child protective services social worker familiar with children—in particular, one who is developmentally delayed—in crises/violent situations. You will either interview the child yourself, or have another member of that team do the interview.

In a more limited scenario, you can provide your Intel with an account of an interview. This is a time saving option, as well as a good alternative if you do not have someone who can convincingly play a 15 year old who is developmentally-delayed as well as frightened. The information should be sketched out between the scenario director and a consultant. They will script the facts of this case, and answer the questions that would be asked. The consultant will help you get *just* the information you would get from such a poor witness, who may very likely make up details to please the interviewer. In either event, a proper interview with the child will reveal:

Jesse, who is seventeen years old, is seen as a model inmate, but that's not the truth. "Staff thinks Jesse's a good guy. But he's smarter than the counselors." Toby, somewhat childlike, wants to tell how Jesse set him up. There was an incident some months ago, where Toby exposed himself to one of the girls. He was designated as a sexually aggressive youth, and assigned a counselor. In fact, Toby now tells the interviewer, Jesse told him that the girl liked him, and that girls liked it when a boy wasn't shy. Jesse had hacked into one of the school computers on site, and showed Toby some pornography. "See just like that. Girls who like a boy want to see his thing." In the interview, Toby will get stuck on how he only did what Jesse told him to do. When asked why he didn't tell, Toby will look scared, and say nothing.

The interviewer will have to use kind, but firm pressure to get Toby off his own problem. What will be revealed is that Jesse frightens the weaker inmates, and stays out of the way of the strong or gang-affiliated ones. And that there has been an 'underground' pattern of incidents where the more vulnerable inmates get in trouble one way or the other, and Jesse was the one who pushed them into it, or set them up. "He likes it when other kids get in trouble."

3 – Interview with Other Inmates

Toby names five other youth who Jesse has manipulated or set up. Records can be prepared of five inmates: theft, sexual activity, an assault on staff, etc., that appeared to be isolated incidents. Toby says that in each case, Jesse was at the root of it. If the director wishes to make a more challenging exercise, a group interview can be set up to gather more information on Jesse. Each of the five inmates will be in some sense emotionally or mentally challenged.

The end result of this interview process is of Jesse as a master manipulator, who does things to see how other people react. He believes he is smarter than everyone else, and likes to see others demeaned or in distress. One thing that is not ascertained is if he is afraid of getting hurt himself.

Managing Information with multiple interviewees, particularly adolescents
The training goals will be:
1. Trying to manage a group interview, which could be set up to go well or badly.
2. If going badly, to separate the informants, gather information and pool data.
3. Pooling data from five (or less) relatively poor informants with some cognitive delays.

In either a group interview, at least one youth will be really reticent, mumbling one syllable answers, where at least one other will be all over the place. Some will talk over others, chiming in, some with extraneous details, and others will actually have relevant facts. Trying this as a group interview will be good practice in information management.

---

3 – The Scene

The space should be big enough that you do not know, at this point, where Jesse is. Perhaps he will be able to block off windows with blankets. On the other hand, it could be a space that he was able to block-ade and lock, making entry difficult. In any event, the environment should be such that any attempt to rush in will be delayed enough that Jesse will be able to stab one or more of the girls.

3 – Negotiations

After the initial period, Jesse will become increasingly provocative. He will be obscene and vicious. He will register anything and everything you say, listening for weak points and leverage, using it to knock you off balance, or ideally, to anger you. For example, he says he will only talk to you if you accept him calling you "Officer/Counselor (whatever your title is) Fuck." (The negotiator will be stuck in the fine dilemma of not being defiant and offended, but also not being a pushover).

Jesse will not be making concrete demands for the most part, although he may demand something off the wall, like a scallop burrito, or the like. If you bring him something he does demand, he may throw it back out a window.

Coordination with ERT #1

This is an excellent scenario to practice either as an extended, high-adrenaline negotiation, or for the integration of ERT to enter the area and neutralize the threat.

Escalation, which would result in ERT intervention, can be built into the scenario with alternatives such as:
1. One of the girls begins screaming in pain.
2. One or more of the girls tries to escape, and you hear him, enraged, yell at the girls that he's going to kill them.
3. He makes a calm, creditable threat associated with an impossible demand: for example, that he's going to cut off one girl's ear, unless you let him walk out of the facility.

---

3 – Psychological/Tactical Consult

The negotiator could use the usual tactic of suggesting to Jesse that although this could develop into a bad situation, it isn't yet. He was engaged in some kind of sex with the girls, yes, and when startled, reacted perhaps too aggressively, but if he lets the girls go now, this is something that can be worked out. He's still a minor, he's a smart, articulate guy, and he should be able to explain his situation to people. If the negotiator is successful in getting Jesse to think of what he believes is his long-term interest, he could let the hostages go and surrender. With a character like Jesse, this appeal to his grandiosity and self-regard is always a 'first gambit'—and in cases where the sociopathic subject wants to survive, this often works.

Coordination with ERT #2 (The tactic of negotiation is sound, but ERT is still needed)

<u>Activation of ERT even with success:</u> Even if the exercise is set up 'successfully,' ERT, in reality or simulation, should be fully activated. For example, Jesse could surrender and then, at the last minute, change his mind, grab one girl and try to get back into the barricade area.

<u>Activation of ERT with entry into the area:</u> The writers believe this exercise is ideal to be programmed for ERT entry into the area. In this case, do NOT program in a *successful* appeal to his narcissism, where he agrees he's too special to suffer consequences (whether or not he has a last second change of plans). Instead, he will perceive you as trying to play him and he will escalate to the point that ERT must act.

Given this seems to be a 'victim taking' rather than a 'hostage taking,' the negotiator's task is to keep Jesse talking as long as possible, (so that ERT can fully exercise their skills in this training exercise, just as they would in real life). Jesse can be considered an 'aggressive narcissist,' which is what a sociopath[4] truly is. As far as he is concerned, the only thing that matters is himself. Get him talking about himself. Do not give him obvious praise, but listen in a way that makes him think he has a 'captive audience' who is impressed with him.

What will be most dangerous is if he perceives you as:
- Insulting him
- Questioning his seriousness
- Challenging him

He very likely will take this out on one of the hostages. He is essentially a sexual sadist—and is very likely to use his knife to mutilate or even kill one or all of the hostages.

To emphasize again, this should be regarded as a 'victim taking' scenario, not a 'hostage taking' situation, as there is really nothing to gain in what he is doing.

SCENARIO 3 – Checklist for After Action Review

The after action assessment/critique will depend on what was expressed and expected of the team going into the exercise. In other words, what was the desired training goal or outcome? Not just the outcome of the scenario, but what are the skills the director (team leader) is hoping to see exercised by the team, as these scenario/situations develop?

Establish a floor plan in timely manner?
- ❏ Did not meet goal
- ❏ Partially met goal
- ❏ Fully met goal

Ask about or try to ascertain if subject had other weapons?
- ❏ Did not meet goal
- ❏ Partially met goal
- ❏ Fully met goal

Did negotiators effectively do a group interview if this was the best approach?
- ❏ Did not meet goal
- ❏ Partially met goal
- ❏ Fully met goal

Separate the inmates and successfully gather and pool the information if this was the best approach?
- ❏ Did not meet goal
- ❏ Partially met goal
- ❏ Fully met goal

Did the primary negotiator remain unemotional from the personal attacks from subject?
- ❏ Did not meet goal
- ❏ Partially met goal
- ❏ Fully met goal

Did the primary negotiator challenge the subject?
- ❏ Did not meet goal
- ❏ Partially met goal
- ❏ Fully met goal

Did the primary negotiator try to ingratiate him/herself ('suck up') or in any other way, interact in a way that the subject could view them as weak?

- ❏ Did not meet goal
- ❏ Partially met goal
- ❏ Fully met goal

Was the team honest in their assessment/review of status of situation with command post regarding likely outcome?

- ❏ Did not meet goal
- ❏ Partially met goal
- ❏ Fully met goal

SCENARIO 4

Control Freak, Paranoid Character

4 – Incident

Mr. Adelson and Ms. Jackson team-teach English as part of an education program at the facility. The teachers both have emergency call-buttons, but there is no correctional officer in the room. Participation in this class is based on good behavior—none of the inmates have had any critical incidents in quite some time. Much of the class is creative writing, and unbeknownst to them, inmate George Papadopoulos took offense to a critique of his writing.

At the end of class, inmates are filling out of the room, Papadopoulos last, when he kicks the door shut, pulls a shank and grabs Mr. Adelson, and puts a blade in the corner of his eye. He screams at Ms. Jackson to "MOVE! NOW!" and orders her to shove all the desks in front of the door, making a barricade.

Officers respond, contain the room, and then request ERT and HNT.

4 – Layout of Incident

A Detailed Layout

Set up the layout to serve as the kind of scene to make an exercise that ERT can also productively participate.

1. If this will be a negotiator-only practice, it is a suitable 'as-if' situation, with a detailed description given to the negotiators, at a certain period of time.

2. On the other hand, this exercise is a good one for both ERT and HNT, and can be set up to meet the tactical training needs ERT may have. This might be an exercise where the ERT trainer, working with the director, has the priority choice when selecting the venue for this exercise. If ERT will also be incorporated in the exercise, you can make an environment that is exceptionally difficult for an immediate entry, putting both officers and hostages at risk. The goal for the ERT team leader would be to set up an environment that truly challenges the team's skills. Among the options is an unknown location situation, with HNT trying to fix the location of the hostage taker, and keep him occupied on the phone.

4 – Character of the Hostage Taker

Papadopoulos has been incarcerated for three years on a six year sentence for physical abuse on his children. He has always denied that he ever abused his children, even though there are documented hospital visits for broken bones and internal bleeding. At various times, he's stated that his ex-wife set him up, that the doctors inflated minor injuries that the children incurred while playing, that the children probably hurt themselves due to their mother's influence or that he was simply disciplining his children.

He's only had minor infractions, but is known as a grievance collector – he'll get offended by someone, and brood on it. He'll silently comply with the commands of an officer whom he believes offended him, and if it was an inmate, simply ignore him. Papadopoulos is a very big man, and sullenly keeps to himself.

The only time officers have observed much emotion is when he was informed that the courts supported the mother in not allowing the children to visit him. On that occasion, he demolished his cell, the only time he's been written up.

4 – Directions for Role Player

You should be argumentative and provocative. You will quibble about little things. "You said you'd call me in five minutes. It's been six!" Your speech should be over-controlled: say, "do not," rather than "don't; "will not", rather than "won't;" "should not" rather than "shouldn't." Speak as if you are biting your words. You are all about control—**if you feel like the negotiator is controlling you, escalate. On the other hand, if the negotiator is too friendly or supportive, you will see this as trying to soften you up.**

4 – Some Possible Demands You Can Fixate On
- You want new teachers for the English class, as these two are 'shit.'
- You want phone contact with your kids.
- You want your short story, the one that got criticized, put in the inmate newspaper.

4 – For the Scenario Director

How will you deal with the demand regarding allowing him to have phone contact with his children? This is not a TPI, but he is demanding a change in a court order. It is easy enough to say, "We have no say on what family court decides in cases like this," but given this man's character, do you think that is going to satisfy him? Intel may have to make a call to someone (family court, child protective services, an attorney) to get clear information on the rules to be able to discourse with the subject on this issue, if he gets stuck on it. If your only response is, "I dunno" or "That's out of our lane," he may get completely fixated on it, and your negotiation stalls.

4 – Psychological Consultation

The consultant states that Papadopoulos seems to be paranoid: NOT delusional, in this case, but as a manifestation of his character.

The paranoid individual has an attitude that it is always another person's fault if anything is wrong. Whether delusional or not, they see others as conspiring against them or persecuting them.

One helpful image of the paranoid person is an angry porcupine, all quills, with a soft underbelly, hunched over, ready to strike in hair-trigger reaction.

The paranoid individual (whether delusional or not) has a consistent *attitude* of blame, resentment of authority, fear of vulnerability, and an expectation of being betrayed by people they trust.

- Without compromising on any tactical issues, let them know what's going on, so there is no ambiguity. Because paranoid people are so suspicious, they will often quiz you concerning why you're doing something. Whenever you can, tell them what you're doing. At the same time, you shouldn't accept being quizzed incessantly. You aren't required to explain every action. In fact, it might be a tactic to throw you off guard or distract you.
- Be aware of both physical and emotional spacing. Maintain a correct distancing, neither too close nor too far. Keep your tone matter-of-fact. Speak in formal tones. Don't be too friendly. Try to be aware when things are getting too relaxed. If the paranoid person relaxes, they may suddenly startle, realizing that for a brief moment, they let their guard down. They may respond by exploding to make sure you don't "take them over."
- IMPORTANT: The 'soft-touch' reassuring, 'we are here to help' negotiation style can be perfect for distraught, scared, or emotionally out-of-control subjects. It is usually a bad approach with the paranoid subject, who will interpret that approach as either weak, or an attempt to soften him up. As said in the last bullet point, a 'correct distance' with this type of individual is almost always a better approach.
- Watch your triggers; they will try to provoke you so they can "hit you back first." If you lose your temper, they will feel justified in whatever they do to you as well as it keying into their terror-based aggression. A slang expression for this is "fear biters." They bark and snarl and when you react, they attack as if you went after them first.
- Being mistaken or wrong is another form of vulnerability. They will try to engage you in an argument to dominate you. But if they begin to lose the argument, they will escalate, to regain control and power.
- Paranoid people examine your communication like detectives. They continually search for evidence to prove what they already know is true.
- Maintain your calm. The paranoid individual is usually assaultive when they feel under attack, when they perceive you as controlling them, or when they perceive that you are afraid.
- Be careful about 'active listening.' You can definitely paraphrase, but he may use your paraphrasing as support for his extreme positions. Also, if you sound too much like a 'psych' person, he will feel manipulated. Therefore, paraphrase in a matter-of-fact, ordinary way, like, "This is a bad situation." NOT "I hear you saying that you find yourself in a difficult place."
- The truth and his fiction are different. The truth, of course, is that he has hostages, and one, at least, is injured. You need to find out his demands. If you focus too much on the hostages, given

he is a man of grievances, you will make them targets. His fiction is that the main problem is being accused of physical abuse (it may actually be a false allegation, but his 'fiction' is this is the main problem at present). Therefore, the negotiator should focus on helping him find a way out of <u>that</u> situation, and releasing the hostages should be framed as a means to that end.

SCENARIO 4 – Checklist for After Action Review

The after action assessment/critique will depend on what was expressed and expected of the team going into the exercise. In other words, what was the desired training goal or outcome? Not just the outcome of the scenario, but what are the skills the director (team leader) is hoping to see exercised by the team, as these scenario/situations develop?

Floor plan established?
- ❏ Did not meet goal
- ❏ Partially met goal
- ❏ Fully met goal

Team satisfactorily deals with the demands to speak to his children?
- ❏ Did not meet goal
- ❏ Partially met goal
- ❏ Fully met goal

Demonstrates good listening skills?
- ❏ Did not meet goal
- ❏ Partially met goal
- ❏ Fully met goal

Does team recognize they are dealing with a volatile, controlling, paranoid person? Did the negotiator maintain calm and not get his/her buttons pushed?
- ❏ Did not meet goal
- ❏ Partially met goal
- ❏ Fully met goal

Did the negotiator maintain a formal, 'correct distance rather than a 'soft' reassuring, 'supportive' approach?
- ❏ Did not meet goal
- ❏ Partially met goal
- ❏ Fully met goal

Did the negotiator work to not get caught up in side-issues and power struggles?
- ❏ Did not meet goal
- ❏ Partially met goal
- ❏ Fully met goal

SCENARIO 5

Depression, Guilt

5 – Incident

An inmate is on a high, not easily accessible place, such as the unit's fourth tier landing (NOTE: if inmates would not have access to such a place in your facility, you can, of course, create an alternative scenario with a different methodology of suicide). She is non-responsive, apparently gearing up to jump. She is contacted and says, "Go away. I just want to die."

When HNT attempts to engage her, they hear weeping, followed by quiet pleading, "Just leave me alone. I don't want to hurt you guys – just leave me in peace so I can maybe get up the guts this time to die right."

The inmate is recognized as Shona Conners. She is known to have been in-and-out of prison mental health services, with suicidal ideation.

5 – Contact with Counselor

You could simply set this up as a straight-forward informational call, but why not make it a little difficult for practice, so that, unless the interviewer does an effective interview, they will not get the information they need. The counselor role player should be protective of, and over-involved with the inmate.

The counselor will inform the Intel interviewer that Conner murdered her child during what the counselor believe to be post-partum depression. However, the court did not take this into account, and she received a long sentence. What will be frustrating to the interviewer is that the counselor will get lost in the details of Conner's story. What the interviewer wants to know is what currently might be driving her towards suicide, what interventions have worked in the past, what might upset her, anger her, or make her feel backed in a corner. The task of the role player is to make the acquisition of this information somewhat frustrating – telling Conner's life story rather than being specific and practical.

On Privacy and HIPAA in a Correctional Setting

The authors carried out cursory online research regarding privacy issues and HIPAA in a correctional setting. In many areas, it is asserted that the inmate has the same or similar privacy rights to a non-incarcerated patient. In other cases, they do not. Writers further stated that this is an evolving area of the law. You could make this scenario more challenging in the following areas:

1. The counselor asserts patient privacy concerns, and refuses to give information. Intel will have to contact your facility's legal advisor to get quick information on how a crisis supersedes privacy concerns, in order to require the counselor to give you the information.

2. This could be straightforward – the proper statutes need to be cited, perhaps a supervisor consulted with and the information is acquired. To make matters more challenging, you can couple a protective, over-invested counselor with a misunderstanding of privacy laws. You could easily make this subsidiary communication/negotiation as unpleasant as pulling teeth.

Every correctional institution should have the relevant HIPAA statutes on hand, available to be cited to resistive medical or psychiatric staff. Ideally, your facility's legal advisor should be alerted to the possibility that such an issue could arise. If there is an impasse, the legal advisor can be contacted to directly communicate the law with the resistive medical or psychiatric provider. (Section 45 C.F.R. 164.512 (k) (5) (i) of the code indicates grounds for which inmate medical information may be provided).

5 – Intel That Can be Acquired from Counselor and Shona Conner, Depending on the Effectiveness of the Intel Interview and the Negotiator

Shona Conner was the mother of three kids, and a fine husband. They had the relationship anyone would dream of, and this was not just an illusion. Both were working parents, and she had a job she loved, providing wigs for cancer survivors who had lost their hair due to chemotherapy. Her husband was a prosecutor specializing in felony prosecutions. Their children were 17-year-old Tonya and 15-year-old Natasha. Unexpectedly, she become pregnant with a third, and gave birth to Jetta.

She had terrible post-partum depression. She couldn't bond with her baby, but ashamed, hid this. The baby had difficulty nursing, and she had to bottle feed her, unlike her two other children. This made bonding even more difficult as nursing had been central to her experience as a mother. She cut back on her job, and her husband was increasingly busy with an important prosecution. Most of her social contacts had been at work, and she grew isolated and alone – her two older daughters spent most of their time with their friends.

The baby had colic, and cried a lot. Shona was sleep deprived, believed herself to be a failure as a mother, came to believe that her family did not care about her – they were never home – and that the baby hated her too.

One afternoon, the baby wouldn't stop crying, and after an hour of rocking her, walking with her, cuddling her, with nothing working, Connor snapped. She grabbed the baby around the neck and began shaking her in a frenzy of helpless rage. She didn't stop. She shook the child so hard that her head smashed against the mattress repeatedly, resulting in swelling on the brain. Beyond that, the baby's spinal cord was severed. Her daughters came home from school to find her sitting beside the crib, silent and stunned, the baby dead.

The family totally cut her off. She has had no visits, no contact from her daughters or husband at all.

She makes no contact with other inmates. She talks to herself sometimes, talks to the baby as well. She may be hearing voices – no one knows for sure. She has made two suicide attempts, once by stockpiling pills, the other attempting to drink bleach.

5 – Psychological Consultation

This woman is severely depressed, and she has good reason to be so. Severe depression is a state of extreme isolation. The subject usually feels cut off from humanity. To make things worse in this case, Mrs. Connors truly is cut-off from the other side as well. She killed her baby in a fit of rage, and her family has ostracized her. She has no friends in prison, and barely connects with the counselor who has tried to work with her. She is assigned to a therapy group, but she just sits silently, staring off into space.

Do not try to comfort her by telling her that post-partum depression is a medical condition that takes over one's mind, that it is 'not your fault.' Do not try to offer her hope, that after awhile, the pain will get less and less, and that someday, she can again do the kind of good work she did for cancer survivors. Don't assure her that, someday, her daughters will understand.

One 'hazard' for the negotiator which may make communication difficult is if you consider your own values, you may find yourself thinking were you this woman, you would kill yourself as well. You will wonder how someone could live with herself, knowing she murdered her own baby.

5 – Style of Communication

<u>Act as if you have all the time in the world.</u> We do not mean you act casually—simply that you don't rush anything. If you act like there is little time, the person you're talking with will believe you, and they'll rush to a decision or conclusion. <u>When you take time, you give time</u>. The suicidal person begins to believe there is enough time to figure out a better solution than suicide.

An overly gentle, 'concerned' voice will shut her down. She may be crying, but do not speak to her like she is a child. If your voice elicits a sense of helplessness (like a child), she will be more likely to jump.

Do not, however, put too much confidence in your voice. If you present yourself as too 'together,' she will experience this as a slap in the face. Your voice would then implicitly suggest that you are the kind of man or woman who would NOT murder her child like she did.

Speak easily, but with seriousness and gravity. A calm, matter-of-fact tone shows that you aren't panicked by their situation and that you can handle anything they say.

Use your voice to change her brain. Right now, her brain confirms her alienation and isolation. She is alone in the world. You are talking to prove to her that she is not alone. The proof that she is not alone is the dialogue itself, not that you say so. A respectful conversation conveys on an almost primal level that the suicidal person is still worth something because you find them worthwhile. And by the way, it is still a conversation if you are doing most of the talking. This individual will very likely be silent much of the time.

5 – Further Psych Consult: On Suicide Assessment

In this case, it is already clear that she is suicidal.

With most suspected suicidal subjects, you need to ask if she intends to kill herself. Directly. Don't tiptoe around the subject, as vague statements leave the person an 'out,' such as, "You aren't thinking of hurting yourself, are you?"

The four BASIC questions (these are the principles, not specific questions for this particular case) to assess suicide are:
- "Are you planning to kill yourself?"
- "How would you do it?"
- "Do you have the means to do it?"
- "When will you do it?"

In this case, you would specifically say something like: ""It looks like you came up here with plans to jump, what's going on?"

If she is willing to talk about her suicidal thoughts, you can flesh things out with some of the following:

As you pace her and paraphrase, a question comes up: What has stopped you before today? Be sure not to make her feel like she 'failed' when she wasn't successful in a previous suicide attempt. In other words, "Why did you choose life before?" When they recall someone or something that stopped them, this may help them regain a sense of responsibility for the people who care for them, or some other factor that kept them alive in the past.

Try to assess if she's been using drugs or drinking. First of all, this is a significant risk factor that often decreases as they become more sober. Beyond this, sometimes this can be a leverage point, where you suggest that killing oneself is not a decision one should make while intoxicated. (The problem, however, is that they may be too intoxicated to see the logic of this).

Try to find out why she decided to be suicidal today. Again, this may not help 'solve' her problem, but it keeps her talking.

Be very careful about giving her advice. Given this situation, can you honestly think of anything that will make things better? Simple communication brings people away from suicide, even without a solution to the problems driving a person towards it.

Don't make any guarantees how much better life might be. Don't forget for a second that she murdered her baby, post-partum depression or not. There is no 'better' you can offer.

Remember, with this woman, dialogue is the lifeline. She may actually surrender if you establish a strong enough connection that she feels responsible for taking up your time, or "I wouldn't want to do that to you." On the other hand, she may simply kill herself to stop inconveniencing you.[5]

5 – Training Note
This training exercise could very productively be set up that after a long negotiation, Shona kills herself. You can, thereby, include a debriefing/after-action review of such a suicide after a long negotiation as part of the training exercise. Consider your debriefing procedures, peer support, etc. If this exercise is done effectively, you may bring up some real emotions, even though it is 'merely' a role play. This is particularly true if the negotiator is a parent himself or herself. You could actually build in an after-action review, using peer-support, CIT trained officers, if they have added training in trauma and critical incidents, or EAP, depending on your resources. You will thereby train your peer support/after-action procedures to prepare for the inevitable times when such an incident does occur.

This is also a really good exercise for beginning negotiators. Many new negotiators struggle with the concept of asking someone if they want to die, or if they are feeling 'suicidal.' Most people (including trained officers) are a bit squeamish about asking outright. Officers, and especially hostage negotiators, have to be comfortable talking about suicide and discussing it in a matter of fact, and non-judgmental manner. The more practice, the better the skills.

This exercise, or something similar is a good time for the team leader to emphasize that not all suicide interventions are successful. When a team is young, and all they have experienced in training and actual callouts are a few successful interventions, and the callout happens where the subject chooses to complete the suicide in front of the negotiators, it can be rough on the members. Discussing, and 'experiencing' those feelings in training scenarios, ahead of time, can help prepare for the effects.

In fact, having the inmate (a sympathetic character) suicide in this scenario could be a very powerful learning exercise, particularly if you have a new, potentially good negotiator who tends to be a little too confident. (NOTE: This should not be his/her first scenario training – it should be used if advice and cautions have not been listened to).

Suicide by Cop Scenario

Although the basic scenario is set up as a potential suicide, the director could set it up as a 'suicide by cop,' with only minimal changes, in which officers may have to witness/be involved in the death of someone with whom they have developed a bond). To set this up, simply change the circumstances so that Shona is armed with a hostage, and makes a move that must be interpreted as her trying to kill the hostage, so that she has to be killed. In this case, all ambiguity can be removed, with her escalating, and demanding that ERT end her pain and kill her, and then, "What does it take to get you to kill me?" Then, finally, she makes a clear move to kill her hostage. Of course, this must be tailored to your specific facility—what options—less-lethal or deadly force—will be available to your ERT?

SCENARIO 5 – Checklist for After Action Review

The after action assessment/critique will depend on what was expressed and expected of the team going into the exercise. In other words, what was the desired training goal or outcome? Not just the outcome of the scenario, but what are the skills the director (team leader) is hoping to see exercised by the team, as these scenario/situations develop?

Establish floor plan?
- ❏ Did not meet goal
- ❏ Partially met goal
- ❏ Fully met goal

Demonstrate good listening skills?
- ❏ Did not meet goal
- ❏ Partially met goal
- ❏ Fully met goal

Good thorough Intel? If the counselor cites confidentiality concerns, did the team effectively manage this?
- ❏ Did not meet goal
- ❏ Partially met goal
- ❏ Fully met goal

Primary negotiator willing to confront the suicidal ideation head on?
- ❏ Did not meet goal
- ❏ Partially met goal
- ❏ Fully met goal

Does team recognize the possibility of suicide by cop, if the scenario has that built in?
- ❏ Did not meet goal
- ❏ Partially met goal
- ❏ Fully met goal

Resist the impulse to 'make it better' by reframing the problem or reassuring that 'time heals all wounds,' or similar clichés?
- ❏ Did not meet goal
- ❏ Partially met goal
- ❏ Fully met goal

Demonstrate extreme patience?
- ❏ Did not meet goal
- ❏ Partially met goal
- ❏ Fully met goal

SCENARIO 6

Paranoid Character, Honor Obsessive

6 – Incident – General
Inmate Moretti is barricaded in a small room (or cell), holding another inmate hostage with a manufactured sharp object.

6 – Contact with Informant
NOTE: To make this incident true to life, this scenario could actually be initiated by the informant contact, before Moretti's attack. Staff can be moving towards the area get Moretti under control when the incident starts.

Contact is made with an informant who states that another inmate, Jamey Jimenez, is going to be killed. Jimenez affects a female transsexual persona,[6] with clothing and home-made make-up. He was in a relationship with Victor Moretti, for over a year, but has recently moved on to Jayden Ford. Both Moretti and Ford have status in different prison gangs. Not only did Moretti 'lose' Jimenez to Ford, Jimenez has been publicly revealing Moretti's preferred sexual practices, which violate the 'code' for male-role sexual behavior in prison culture. Because of this, he's on the outs with his own associates and has been publicly demeaned by Ford's people.

Moretti has, several times, passed Ford and Jimenez in the dining hall and in the yard. In each event, Ford has put an arm around Jimenez's shoulders, and either smirked or made a comment to Moretti, in one case, "that aint pussy you been eatin', no matter how hard you wish it." Said in front of others, Moretti threatened Ford, but he was with several other members of his own crew, and with the odds against him, Moretti did nothing. The informant states that the only way Moretti can regain status is to kill Jimenez and Ford.

6 – Incident Blows Up
Officers in his residential unit are alerted to the informant's report, but Moretti has already acted. He was sitting in the TV room when he spotted Ford and Jimenez walking past. He had a dowel with a long nail driven through its center, and moving behind Ford, he punched it into his spine at the base of his skull. Grabbing Jimenez by the hair, he dragged him into a room that can successfully be set up as a barricade, making it difficult for officers to enter, much less get to him and to rescue Jimenez. There, he sat him down between his legs on a bunk, and put the improvised weapon to his throat.

6 – Initial Contact

When officers engage with him, he says he does not mean to harm them; rather, he simply needs their help in 'making it right.' Officers will advise him he needs to release Jimenez and surrender. Moretti states he would not. He tells officers he was in the military, and he knows how to kill, and it won't just be Ford and Jimenez if they push him. He does not wish to hurt correctional officers, but is armed and ready to fight and die to keep his honor. He has a simple demand – that shot callers from his own gang must be assembled in ranks to hear Jimenez confess that he lied about Moretti's sexual preferences. "That's right. You line them up." He gives a list of seven men. "They need to hear that this bitch is lying. They need to hear it from her."

HNT and ERT are called.

6 – Contact from Officer Who Has Known Moretti for Years

She states Victor is a scary guy, not only for the crime – voluntary manslaughter – that got him incarcerated. He joined the military and served three tours in spec ops. He has medals up to his eyebrows.

"He is a quiet guy, but not in a good way. He's been in several fights here – and we've done a number of cell extractions as well. He always had a little smile on his lips. But every once in a while he gets mad; it is always over him thinking someone insulted him. That's why he's still here. Two extra charges in other institutions: one on an inmate, the other on an officer. Both are fortunate to be alive. Moretti should have been out by now, but with the charges he's racked up in here, he got an extra eight years.

6 – For the Role Player

Victor states that he is owed for his service to the United States, "my former country." His demands are simple. Line up the men he's named. Jimenez will confess his lies. And then he'll decide what to do – but "if you don't do what I say, this bitch is dead – guaranteed – and it'll be ugly."

6 – Psychological Consultation

This man is all about control. If you try to control him, he will almost surely escalate. Therefore, be careful about cutting off water, electricity or the like, as this will be perceived, even more than most subjects, as an attack.

He will certainly object to the appearance of ERT:
- Simply respond in a matter-of-fact way that he is a professional, and there should be no surprise at the response of ERT.
- He may be dismissive or disrespectful of ERT. Simply recognize his special talent and history and deflect by saying that you are following standard procedure, but he knows full well as long as there is no immediate danger to Jimenez, ERT will not be required to act. Rather, you intend to continue speaking with him, in mutual respect, in order to figure a way to resolve this situation for his own benefit.

Maintain a formal tone. Do not speak to him as a buddy: be neither friendly nor casual. His self-image demands he be taken seriously. Remember, too, he is not 'fronting' as to how dangerous he is. He clearly is a paranoid, psychologically disturbed individual, but he has served among the best warfighters America has produced.

Do not equate being a correctional officer to that of the military. He may see the compromises correctional officers must do to work within the law as weak, unlike the units he worked with that "made the rules, and only focused on winning."

Do not assume he suffered from his military experience, that he had PTSD, TBI or the like.

Incorporation of ERT in Scenario 6

This could be set up so that due to an impasse or escalation, ERT must enter the location. This could be an incredibly challenging training scenario—the role player could, in this case, be an 'operator' or ERT. This exercise could be set up for low-light conditions, obstacle-strewn environment, even booby-traps or any one of another set of conditions that fully train ERT in a way that is a logical outcome of the HNT scenario.

SCENARIO 6– Checklist for After Action Review

The after action assessment/critique will depend on what was expressed and expected of the team going into the exercise. In other words, what was the desired training goal or outcome? Not just the outcome of the scenario, but what are the skills the director (team leader) is hoping to see exercised by the team, as these scenario/situations develop?

Establish floor plan?
- ❏ Did not meet goal
- ❏ Partially met goal
- ❏ Fully met goal

Demonstrate good listening skills?
- ❏ Did not meet goal
- ❏ Partially met goal
- ❏ Fully met goal

Does team recognize they are dealing with a volatile, controlling, paranoid person? Did the negotiator maintain calm and not get his/her buttons pushed?
- ❏ Did not meet goal
- ❏ Partially met goal
- ❏ Fully met goal

Did the negotiator maintain a formal, 'correct distance rather than a 'soft' reassuring, 'supportive' approach?
- ❏ Did not meet goal
- ❏ Partially met goal
- ❏ Fully met goal

Did the negotiator work to not get caught up in side-issues and power struggles?
- ❏ Did not meet goal
- ❏ Partially met goal
- ❏ Fully met goal

In a matter-of-fact way, did the negotiator give Moretti 'respect,' without either 'sucking-up,' or in any way appearing to sanction what he is doing?
- ❏ Did not meet goal
- ❏ Partially met goal
- ❏ Fully met goal

SCENARIO 7

Aggressive Borderline Personality

7 – The Incident: Call and First-Responder Contact

Violence between cellmates. Mutual combat, one is stunned and the other has him jammed in a corner, with a piece of glass against his jugular.

Officers respond, and *both* subjects inside scream for them to go away, with one threatening to cut the other's throat. The inmate with the piece of Lexan, Josiah Walker, screams, "Get the fuck away or I'll start cutting."

His cellmate, Isaiah Walken (yes, the names confuse everyone – some nickname them 'The Twins.'), yells, "Do as he says! That thing is fuckin' sharp, and he's cut me once already. The motherfucker is lucky he has it, cause I'd kick his ass otherwise."

On the name confusion and the "Twins"

This kind of detail makes the scenario more complex. The team leader can easily eliminate them to simplify the exercise. The value, as the writers see it, is that extraneous details such as these challenge 'information management.' What detail is important and what is not? The writers are aware of an event where the negotiator kept calling the hostage taker by another name – it just got stuck in his brain, somehow, and after two mistakes, the subject getting increasingly angry, the secondary stuck up 'post-it' on the negotiator's hand with the correct name.

Josiah screams in his face, "Shut up, shut up, shut up, bitch."

Isaiah – (surprisingly calm, almost laughing, "Seriously, you dudes should back off, or this punk is going to cut me. I can talk to this little fucker . . ."

Josiah – "SHUT UP Isaiah!"

Isaiah – " . . .but not with you guys standing on our porch."

Officers yell that they are backing off, and request ERT and HNT.

7 – Background for the Role Player

Josiah's life has gone to hell. He was a metal worker, but got hot steel splinters in his eyes, partially blinding him. When he sued the company, they successfully established that: a) he violated known and posted safety standards by not wearing goggles; b) he was screwing around by jamming a piece of metal into a piece of spinning steel on a lathe to make sparks. When the lawsuit failed, he waited in the parking lot of the courthouse and jumped his lawyer, kicking him into a two week coma.

Josiah will give this information in rants to the HNT (or it can be provided from records).

He met Isaiah in prison, and they bonded. Both are volatile, easily aggressive individuals; both have a history of life-style homelessness, heavy tattoos and headbanging music. They cell together and are believed to be sexually involved.

7 – Interview with a Case Manager

She states that Josiah has kind of a punk persona. He's had multiple piercings that were removed at incarceration. He's got huge holes in his earlobes from the metal plugs he kept in them, another large hold in his septum, and a number in his genitals.

He's made two para-suicidal attempts (self-mutilation by cutting his wrists, but done with staff nearby – obviously he wanted to be found). "He cut his wrists and held them to the bottom of the door so the blood flowed outwards. He's twice been sent to mental health, and he calms down. But he starts getting aggressive with staff because he gets lonely for Isaiah."

7 – Call to Josiah's Counselor at the Psych Unit

The counselor will inform you that he is diagnosed with a borderline personality disorder. Regarding his slashed wrists, Josiah has denied that he wanted to die. "He said he was 'just getting the poison out,' and pointing to his pierced lip, eyebrow, nose and groin, he says, 'It's just more of the same.'"

Incorporation of your case manager and counseling staff

This is a good scenario to invite participation from case management and counseling staff. Flesh out the data above so HNT can do good collateral interviews. If the director wishes, one or both of them can be a 'difficult' informant: too vague, defensive for Josiah, too 'busy' – something to require HNT to use strength of will and calm to get the information that is needed.

---

7 – Initial Contact – For the Role Player

Negotiators establish contact. Josiah is hyper-emotional. The negotiators should be doing a lot of paraphrasing. Josiah will be all over the place, mostly talking about his injury, how the damage to his eyes gives him headaches, how Isaiah is an asshole, etc. (Isaiah, in the background, will yell at him things like,

"Fuccckkk you, Josiah!" "Stop whining, you little punk bitch!" Josiah will escalate, screaming back at him). The negotiator is going to have to repeatedly 'reel him back in'.

This will be volatile partner crisis, opposed to a clear hostage situation. Josiah will make no demands except that the police "Leave us the fuck alone. We will work it out if you screws will just back the fuck away and this asshole will just shut the fuck up" However, he will continue to engage. He'll shut down sometimes and be unresponsive (or slam down a phone if that's how you'll be communicating), but will pick up when you call again.

7 – Contact with Another Inmate

The team will hear several references to another inmate, Tony, such as "You ask Tony. He'll tell you about this cocksucker. Tony knows."

When contacted, Tony is hostile. "What do you care about us, you hate faggots, you know you do." If HNT is demanding, authoritative or tries to order Tony to communicate, he'll shut down. If HNT does not rise to the bait, and effectively deflects the accusation of homophobia, and further, frames the contact as an attempt to help both men –– "Tony, Josiah told us to talk to you!" —Tony will report that the two men's relationship has been very intense, very aggressive. He says, "These guys are not like the kind of gay guys you think of, right. I mean—they are so macho in their own minds that they claim they don't ever want to touch a girl, 'cause that would pollute them. Only another guy can be with them. They are kinda like punk-Nazis, not like they hate Jews or any of that shit, but that's the kind of attitude they have. They are a two man wrecking crew, beefing with other guys – never with gangs, they aint stupid. Josiah usually talks shit to people who say something, and he and Isaiah take care of business."

Tony says Isaiah's the alpha dog, and 'he's always fucking with Josiah 'cause he's half blind. Isaiah started getting really aggressive, acting like it was a big joke, but coming up behind Josiah and grabbing him and doing body drops on their bunk. Josiah hit his head – truth is, he's soft inside and it hurt his feelings more than his head, it hurt so bad, he started to cry. Isaiah started laughing at him for being a pussy. Josiah poked him in the eye with one finger – "Shit, he told me he was trying to pop the eye out of the socket" – Isaiah got his eye scratched up pretty bad – you mean you dudes didn't even know about this shit? Anyway, Isaiah beat the shit out of him. Well, they got no where to go. They aint going to report on each other and if you guys don't know about it, they are locked in their box and they are hating on each other. Fuckin' too, but mostly hatin."

7 – Psychological Consult

The consultant states although people with borderline personality disorder usually make parasuicidal moves (cutting on themselves, as Josiah has), they also do kill themselves in fairly high numbers, usually when swept by heightened emotions. They also kill others, almost always as an impulsive act – road rage and domestic violence are typical behaviors of aggressive borderlines.

The most salient point is that <u>whatever Josiah feels, he will become</u>. He will 'emotionally' not remember what he felt before. The danger is if the negotiator 'slips:'—by getting too casual, off-hand, or authoritarian, any way that evokes Josiah's anger, he will be explosive. <u>Remember, this is a guy who deliberately tried to pop out the eyeball of his boyfriend</u>.

The negotiator should stay matter-of-fact, like a solid uncle or aunt with a kid prone to tantrums. The goal is to create a dialogue where, for a sustained period, Josiah is calm.

If possible, try to speak with Isaiah and tell him to chill out. (Depending on how intense an exercise you wish to create, Isaiah can either be accepting or belligerent, which will amp things up again).

By focusing on Josiah, and quieting Isaiah (consider if the threat of sanctions on Isaiah will shut him up, for example, or eliciting his help in getting this situation finished), Josiah, the beta in the relationship, will feel important enough to be listened to. (NOTE: Caution is needed, because if in quieting Isaiah, he perceives you as stealing away his 'alpha position' in the relationship, he'll amp things up.

Cell Extraction

Of course, this scenario would be perfect for ERT to practice a cell extraction, if Josiah gets distracted, out of position, or Isaiah takes matters into his own hand and starts to fight.

SCENARIO 7– Checklist for After Action Review

The after action assessment/critique will depend on what was expressed and expected of the team going into the exercise. In other words, what was the desired training goal or outcome? Not just the outcome of the scenario, but what are the skills the director (team leader) is hoping to see exercised by the team, as these scenario/situations develop?

Demonstrated listening skills?
- ❏ Did not meet goal
- ❏ Partially met goal
- ❏ Fully met goal

Recognize that communication with Josiah requires monitoring and managing his mood, because whatever he feels in the moment is his only reality?
- ❏ Did not meet goal
- ❏ Partially met goal
- ❏ Fully met goal

Successfully managed two emotionally chaotic individuals by quieting Isaiah so you can work Josiah into compliance?
- ❏ Did not meet goal
- ❏ Partially met goal
- ❏ Fully met goal

SCENARIO 8

Psychosis

This scenario, connected to #7, should be assumed to be three months subsequent.

8 – The Incident with Background

Subject threatening suicide inside his cell. Has a sharp object to his neck.

At the end of the incident #7, where Isaiah was held hostage (sort of), he left the cell combative, and fought with ERT. He was put in segregation. (NOTE: Josiah was also placed in segregation, but he quickly grew so disturbed—bashing his head against the wall, and breaking out several teeth on the edge of the toilet—that he was placed under close observation area on a suicide watch).

Isaiah had seemed quiet and compliant in segregation, but staff noticed deterioration in personal hygiene (Isaiah always kept himself super clean) and a loss of appetite as well.

This morning he has managed to get a blade and in essence, he holding himself hostage, with the blade to his neck. When an officer tries to engage him, Isaiah mumbles to himself, not making much sense. He keeps talking about the sacrifice of a 'man of rectitude' who must be offered to God at the appointed hour (nine hours after whatever time you are starting the exercise).

8 – Contact with HNT

HNT makes contact with Isaiah through the cell door. There is a consideration of a cell-extraction, but it's clear he somehow got a sharp blade – he's bleeding from several slashes around his eyes, so that it appears that he's crying blood. He yells at them to leave, that the hour of grace has not arrived, "We will all wait until the appointed hour."

8 – Interview with the First Officer Who Made Contact with Him

"He talked all over the place. He said a lynx, that ripped its claws in his face, assaulted him and how his glittery best friend, whose face used to shine with silver rings in the lights of the city, wanted to kill him. He kept asking, 'Are you sending this to God? Why did you want to talk to me, when God knows everything? He said that death of the 'man of rectitude,' the one who is correct in everything, would heal his face and all his wounds.

8 – Interview with a Counselor Who Regularly Checks Ad-Seg and Spoke with Isaiah Yesterday

"Isaiah has been deteriorating for about two weeks. He got much worse the last couple days, and we were, in fact, consulting about him when you called, considering whether to move him to the psych ward. The problem is that Josiah is still there, and we have to keep those two apart. This is much worse than he was yesterday. I noticed that he was somewhat guarded and paranoid, and he occasionally whispered to himself, but he wasn't that bad. He sounds like he is floridly psychotic now.

Checking her records, the counselor reports that he had two episodes of psychosis in his teen-years, periods of about five months each where he hallucinated, and heard voices. These preceded his drug use, where his drug of choice was everything he could get his hands on.

There is also a history of sexual assault – he was an acting student in junior high, and his parents arranged for him to be part of an after-school youth theater. He was raped for a period of three months by the male coach of the youth theater.

8 – Initial Contact

This is one of those cases where gender concerns may matter. It may be helpful, if it is possible, to use a negotiator of the gender opposite to that of the rapist. This is not necessarily so, but the director can build this into the exercise where he refuses to talk with a male negotiator, making wild and obscene accusations about the officers intention to rape him.

In any event, whatever context is set up, have Isaiah become so incredibly hostile to the first negotiator that you will have to make a decision to shift to a second negotiator.

- If you don't change, (and the negotiator is skilled), Isaiah will eventually bond to them – intensely.
- If you do shift negotiators, (and the negotiator is skilled), Isaiah will bond to them – intensely.

Once that bonding occurs, Isaiah will begin to refer to the negotiator as the "man (or woman) of rectitude,' the one who is correct in all things." He will talk about all of his wounds that need to be healed, his lynx-clawed face, his torn heart, and how he needs so badly to be healed. And if you ask how he will heal the wounds, Isaiah will reply, "with bubbling blood."

Isaiah may raise the subject of Josiah. The director should make this role-player aware of the outcome of #7 – in the storyline, it should be 'bad.' Josiah cursed Isaiah, and told him that he hoped he would die, and in the process of the cell-extraction, deeply slashed Isaiah, leaving an ugly scar on his face.

Remember, however, for the sake of this exercise, we want to focus HNT's skills on communicating with a psychotic individual. It will be important that the negotiator does not get distracted about the past incident/scenario, particularly if it amps Isaiah up. And finally, given that he is psychotic, Isaiah will be all over the place. The negotiator's task is to get him to focus. It will be essential to get a psych consult as soon as possible in this situation, to most effectively communicate with this man.

You are also aware of the repeated references to the sacrifice of the 'man of rectitude,' which suggests both murder and suicide-by-cop. This event may not be over when it's 'over,' and the negotiator may need to be very careful that Isaiah does not have future unrestricted access to him or her.

8 – Psych Consult Concerning Psychotic, Delusional Subjects
Try to divert his attention from Josiah. Try to get Isaiah communicating with you about himself.

He will seem incoherent, talking in images and word pictures. Try to help him get clearer by <u>paraphrasing</u> your understanding of what he's saying. Keep it very simple. If he says, "A lynx with its glittery spangly claws ripped my face off," respond with a statement, (NOT a question), such as "Something hurt your face." <u>Make anything complex he says as simple as you can in paraphrase.</u>

Notice any areas of his speech where he seems to clear up, and is less delusional or even focused and coherent. These are called <u>islands of sanity.</u> Your secondary should be documenting them, trying to log what subjects and areas of communication he clears up so that the primary can use that log as a 'cheatsheet' of stable communication.

Divert Isaiah to those 'islands of sanity,' whenever possible, rather than allowing the conversation to focus on delusional subjects. Make links with other subjects not tainted by delusions. Think of yourself as expanding the size of the 'land-mass of the island,' making an area where it's predictable and safe. If Isaiah gets stuck within his delusions, you may find changing the subject requires real finesse. Nonetheless, do so whenever you can, because talking about delusions makes it worse.

Do not agree with his delusions. You don't know where he's going with them. You may agree with him and find out you've confirmed, for him, the sacrifice of the 'man of rectitude,' which could be either himself, or an officer.

Do your best not to argue with him. The problem, of course, is he is fixed on sacrificing the 'man of rectitude' to heal his wounds. Although not presented as an argument, you can at least try to suggest an alternative. Who knows, it might work: "There is another way." Offer something benign, like broken leaves of aloe or sage smoke . . . Aside from the hope he might agree put down the weapon and surrender, you are continuing the dialogue, which will give ERT more time to get into position if/when you decide to do a cell-extraction.

Do tell Isaiah although you don't perceive what he does, you aren't arguing with them about what *he* sees or believes. However, because his delusion is murderous, you must be very careful here. Try to steer him to more 'solid ground.' For example, "I believe you were wounded. It sounds bad. I'd like you to come out here so our medic can take a look at it." OR "I believe you are wounded. Clawed by a lynx and with a heart torn open with glass. We need to get those wounds taken care of, but you have to put the weapon down and come out so we can do that."

SCENARIO 8 – Checklist for After Action Review

The after action assessment/critique will depend on what was expressed and expected of the team going into the exercise. In other words, what was the desired training goal or outcome? Not just the outcome of the scenario, but what are the skills the director (team leader) is hoping to see exercised by the team, as these scenario/situations develop?

Did primary negotiator, coach negotiator, or other team member catch on to gender issue regarding gender of rapist?
- ❑ Did not meet goal
- ❑ Partially met goal
- ❑ Fully met goal

Did gender of negotiator come into consideration?
- ❑ Did not meet goal
- ❑ Partially met goal
- ❑ Fully met goal

Would it be important to have psych consult on this one? Was one called?
- ❑ Did not meet goal
- ❑ Partially met goal
- ❑ Fully met goal

How did team deal with the delusional behavior?
- ❑ Did not meet goal
- ❑ Partially met goal
- ❑ Fully met goal

Did the negotiator argue with Isaiah's delusions?
- ❑ Did not meet goal
- ❑ Partially met goal
- ❑ Fully met goal

Did the negotiator argue with Isaiah's delusions?
- ❑ Did not meet goal
- ❑ Partially met goal
- ❑ Fully met goal

Did the team become aware of islands of sanity? Did the secondary log them so that the primary could use this information to guide and control the dialogue?

- ❏ Did not meet goal
- ❏ Partially met goal
- ❏ Fully met goal

SCENARIO 9

Riot Led by Sociopath

Riots have broken out. CO's taken as hostages, some CO's chased out of the area; inmates are in control of several blocks.

9 – Context

The prison or jail has become volatile, despite the best attempts of correctional staff. Underfunded, understaffed, the superintendent has pleaded to the legislature for funds, for more officers and for more educational programs, and has been refused. Furthermore, the legislature, in uninformed combination of cost saving and righteous get-tough-on-inmates, has eliminated the weight program, the theater program, and a variety of job training programs. Inmates are bored, have tremendous energy to burn, and no way to either exercise or study.

9 – The Incident: Details

The riot goes off simultaneously in several areas. Inmates are shockingly well-armed and drive officers out of several units. Seven officers are taken hostage, and keys taken (or door codes forced), so that the inmates link up. They embark on mayhem, setting fires, and killing several inmates whom they either believe are snitches or child molesters. No officer has been killed, but several have been beaten, one seriously. That officer also has asthma and is having a very difficult time breathing.

After the initial explosion of violence, one inmate takes charge. He initiates contact with staff, reading a manifesto over the phone. (NOTE: This is deliberately long to try the patience of the negotiator).

You may hold our bodies in captivity, but we are free men nonetheless. We stand on our feet in opposition to the oppression of a bestial society that fears freedom, and tries to destroy any man on who stands on his feet.

You try to divide us by race, by sex, by socio-economic oppression, but we see through you to the beasts you are: snakes in suits, and scum in uniform.

What you call crimes, we call revolutionary action. Who is the criminal, the man who steals a loaf of bread or the man who runs the bank that runs down the neighborhood and funds the abortions that takes the lives of poor people's young? Who is the criminal, the man who has to fight to survive, or the fat politician and the lean judge, raping whole communities, building highways that cut communities away from the rest of the city, leaving people with nothing? NOTHING!

And now you take away what little we have here. We've got men who've got nothing left but pride, and the few scraps, the few programs we had, you closed down. We've got men who burn with anger at how they've been done by you, and they go to the yard and slam some iron and somehow that helps them make it through another day. So what do you do – you take away the iron.

So now you've got your guns ready and you intend to take our lives. We remember Attica, we remember the James T. Vaughn Corrections riot. We remember HMP Birmingham, Urbana, Holman, and San Quentin. We remember them all.

So you can do that thing you do so well – murder us, and murder the guards you cowards left behind – or we can talk. You will need your pound of flesh; we know that, you will need your scapegoats. Some of us are going to die, because you have to kill a few, but we can talk and make things better for the rest of these free men.

We will speak to you again when we have our list of demands. But think carefully, you snakes and you scum, if you enter here, seven of you will die, at least, and they will not go easy.

9 – Who is the Leader?

The director should consider what gang in your prison is either dominant – or gets along with the majority (or if there are program issues that make naming an actual gang problematic, create a hypothetical organization, based on the behaviors of actual prison gangs). The leader of this riot, Arthur Knowles, is the shot caller in that gang. He is doing a life sentence for two homicides. He is believed to have ordered or enacted several killings in various prisons – he's been transferred several times in hopes of isolating him from his gang, but he either finds members in the facility he's transferred, or simply takes over other gangs of the same ethnic group he is in, either shifting them to his clique, or making an affiliation in such a way that he doesn't threaten the power of the leader of the other gang, but pulling the strings from the background.

9 – Instructions for the Role Player

Your character is smart. He is in control of himself. If he gets angry, it will be a calculated tactic that he uses. You are a predator, and like a cat, you like playing with your food. You may do or say things, just to see what the reaction is. You will be faking a vested interest in the manifesto that the prisoners issue – you'll have had part authorship – and you are well aware that most of the demands are impossible.

9 – The Manifesto

Knowles returns to the line and as the negotiator tries to initiate contact, Knowles talks over him/her and states that he is only on the line to issue the demands of the free men of _____ facility.

Know that we stand united, resolving to speak as men willing to die on our feet, that we may get justice.

We demand that an attorney be present at all parole hearings, as we are entitled under the United States Constitution. This attorney shall not be an employee of the state, and will have the ability to cross-examine witnesses, to bring in witnesses on behalf of the parolee, in both parole hearings and parole revocation hearings.

We demand that medical services, medical policies and procedures be changed. Staff members refuse to take the word of inmates when they are ill, accusing them of malingering. All inmates must have periodic medical check-ups, and this prison must be staffed twenty-four hours a day by trained medical staff.

We demand visiting facilities that offer privacy to families. Being forced to meet with family in the view of prison staff is a violation of privacy of our families, who have not committed any crime.

We demand an end to so-called protective custody and all inmates are free to live in general population.

We demand an end to all work requirements that are a form of modern slavery. The prison industrial-complex uses such slave labor to undercut legitimate businesses and make millions off the backs of incarcerated men whom they regard as slaves. This prison industrial-complex is so profitable that it is in the state's interest to foster social conditions that lead to crime in our communities, thus furnishing this Leviathan to devour more young men and turn them into slaves. We demand, instead, that private business is permitted to enter this institution and set up regular, honest work at minimum wage or hire, working no more than an eight hour day. Inmates without infractions, regardless of the crime that the state asserts they committed, shall be furloughed to work in the community, as said businesses need.

We demand that inmates have the right to join labor unions, with the right to strike. This, alone, will establish that the state does not intend to make inmates slaves.

We demand that the seventy-four officers be prosecuted for a variety of crimes, including assault, abuse of authority, drug distribution and murder. The officers and the crimes they have committed are appended in Appendix A. This will be distributed to the media as an act of good faith on the part of the prison.

We demand that men and women be housed together in this facility. An all-male facility is set up with the purpose of emasculating men, destroying them for family life upon their release. This is part of a systematic genocide of men of minority communities and of working class background.

We demand that seven lawyers be appointed from the State Bar Association for the purpose of rendering legal assistance to any and all inmates who wish to seek release due to unjust prosecution and convictions.

We demand the restoration of all recreational, educational and cultural programs cut in the last legislative session.

We demand the state Parole Board to be replaced by a board elected proportionally by the citizenry based on the ethnic and cultural make up of this institution. No former law enforcement agent is permitted to serve on the Parole Board.

We demand that all staff be required to take quarterly training in cultural diversity, social justice and implicit bias.

We demand that any search of a cell, the inmate's residence, be observed by the inmate, and the cell be restored to the exact same condition that officers found it.

We demand that food service be revamped, with professional cooks managing the kitchen.

We demand an end to punitive meals – so-called Nutria Loaf – when inmates are accused of an infraction of the unjust rules of this institution.

IN CONCLUSION

We stand before the citizens of this state, unjustly incarcerated in what must be regarded as a concentration camp. We stand before you: victims of a pervasive system of racist, capitalist oppression, with the aim of destroying the hope and humanity of this system's prisoners.

This manifesto must be furnished to the news media by five PM this afternoon. If this is not enacted, one of the states representatives, its scum in uniform, will suffer the consequences. Know this: any harm that comes to any of yours is harm you commit. Accede to our demands and all will be safe.

9 – More Directions to the Role Player

It is at this point that negotiations start. Knowles will be charismatic, demanding, articulate, and manipulative. The demands in the manifesto are a combination of some reasonable items, some irrational, and some apparently deliberately satiric. Your task is to make it difficult for the negotiator to know if you seriously care about these demands, or your fellow inmates, or if this is simply a game. Make this difficult!

Remind the negotiator that one of the correctional officers is ill – she was concussed during the riot and she is in the middle of an asthma attack. Use this to pressure the negotiator. Do not, however, make this out to be a life-threatening situation, where the negotiator is worried that she is about to die. This, obviously, would require a green light to ERT.

At any rate, after some period of time, promise you will let this one hostage go, and then take back the promise. Then promise again.

Then begin to subtly mess with the negotiator. Misunderstand what he or she is saying. Become a little argumentative. Play dumb. Distort what they say. Laugh at the wrong time.

After a period of time (to be determined by the director in crafting the overall length of this exercise), hang up the phone, saying you will be talking to them in about ten minutes, but you need a break. As a good faith gesture, let go one of the hostages, but do so in a way that is demeaning; make them go out without their shirt, or with only one pant leg on or underwear on their head. (This must be something that is prearranged before the exercise, out of respect for the role player!).

What will eventually begin to emerge is that Knowles does not really give a damn about the demands – this is just an opportunity to dominate an entire prison, and everyone associated with it. It is unclear (it is up to the director to decide which way this will go) whether he intends to kill the hostages or set them free.

For the scenario director – Keeping it ambiguous for the negotiators

The baseline is that Knowles is a manipulative, sociopath (aggressive narcissist, who lives for power and self-interest). The details of the scenario are built on this. Make Knowles' communication such that the negotiators do not know, for sure, if he intends to kill the hostages or what his motivation is. Is he serious about the manifesto? Is that just a pretext for him to have an opportunity to torment them, and then kill the hostages? Or torment the negotiators, and then let them go? (ERT can easily be integrated into this exercise, turning it into a 'murder-of-hostage' scenario, with the negotiator's function to keep him in one place and not aware of what's happening around him). Have this well planned out before-hand. This includes is you wish to set this up as:

1. A straight-forward prison riot, centered around inmate grievances presenting an opportunity for destruction violence and revenge—in this case, you can de-emphasize Kowles' manipulative and play it more straightforward. He will still play games and keep things very uncertain, but the riot and hostage scenario is typical of such events: a combination of mayhem and genuine grievances.
2. A calculated game on the part of Knowles.

---

9 – Psychological/Tactical Consult

Do not explicitly let on that you know he is such a master manipulator. This has become a game of chess, and you need to be just a little bit ahead of him. Because he is an aggressive narcissist, he will only release hostages if it is somehow set up as his idea.

Do NOT play power-games, for example, he demands that water be turned back on, and you respond that you can furnish them with a couple of barrels of water, pushed up against the barricade. To be sure, if the demand is impossible or unreasonable (seven kegs of red wine), you will refuse. But don't try to play games with his head – this man is too smart for that.

The negotiator should definitely hone into what Knowles himself wants. The negotiator could use the usual tactic of suggesting that although this could develop in a bad situation, it's not yet. Yes, there was a riot, but by taking over, Knowles can be seen, at least up to now, as the one who made the situation safer.

If it comes clear that he is, in fact, playing a game, pretend with him that he's doing this for the inmates and that you will work with him to get this resolved, and in so doing, he becomes the good guy. "Who knows, that may really play out to your advantage in the future." Let him think he's fooled you--that he's played you for fools. Your manipulation is to let him believe he's manipulating you.

Knowles can be considered an "aggressive narcissist, which is what a sociopath truly is. The only thing that matters is himself. Get him talking about himself. Do not give him obvious praise, but listen in a way that makes him think he has a 'captive audience,' who is impressed with him. With this guy, however, you want to accept his story at face value, unless he abandons it. If you 'bust' him, you've proved you are smarter than he is, he may decide to put you in your place by hurting the remaining hostages.

There is also the possibility that, as the negotiations drag on and there is no progress, due to Knowles game-playing, that other inmates will take over, trying to get things resolved.

What is most dangerous is if you insult him, question his seriousness, or challenge him. He very possibly will take this out on one of the hostages.

This should be regarded as a "victim taking" scenario, not a "hostage taking" situation, as there is really nothing to gain in what he is doing.

9 – Possible Ways for the Scenario to Play Out

A more complex scenario

If the director wishes to make this scenario more complex and intense, you can script dissension among the leading inmates. Some believe in the demands, others simply want an opportunity to kill enemies in the chaos, and Knowles is in the middle, a toxic controller using all these guys as puppets.

---

1. Other inmates realize that Knowles is just messing with both the negotiator and with them. They begin to fight. ERT moves in.
2. Knowles deliberately pushes things to failure. ERT moves in.
3. The condition of the one wounded correctional officer worsens, and Knowles does not negotiate her freedom – or, he directs other inmates to harm her or another. ERT moves in.
4. He loses control of his own people – they move in to harm the correctional officers, but he tries to distract the negotiator, keeping the information from the team. A hostage makes enough noise that you know something bad is happening. ERT moves in.
5. Knowles makes things very difficult, but actually allows negotiation of various points in the manifesto. You can hear him 'negotiating' with other inmates as well, getting them to settle for what is possible. And then he negotiates a surrender.

This is a very useful scenario if the Team Leader has new members to train. Work the scenario so that there are inmates who are released, who need to be interviewed, and debriefed. Put the new negotiators to work on interviewing the released inmates…have some of the interviewees be difficult, and some be a bit more forthcoming in the interviews, so the team member/interrogator gets a variety of practice.

SCENARIO 9 – Checklist for After Action Review

The after action assessment/critique will depend on what was expressed and expected of the team going into the exercise. In other words, what was the desired training goal or outcome? Not just the outcome of the scenario, but what are the skills the director (team leader) is hoping to see exercised by the team, as these scenario/situations develop?

Floor plan established?
- ❏ Did not meet goal
- ❏ Partially met goal
- ❏ Fully met goal

How did team handle interviews with any released hostages?
- ❏ Did not meet goal
- ❏ Partially met goal
- ❏ Fully met goal

Did the primary demonstrate good listening skills?
- ❏ Did not meet goal
- ❏ Partially met goal
- ❏ Fully met goal

How did the primary deal with the threats?
- ❏ Did not meet goal
- ❏ Partially met goal
- ❏ Fully met goal

Did the negotiator recognize that Knowles was playing games and not negotiating in good faith?
- ❏ Did not meet goal
- ❏ Partially met goal
- ❏ Fully met goal

How was this situation status discussed with the command post? Options?
- ❏ Did not meet goal
- ❏ Partially met goal
- ❏ Fully met goal

SCENARIO 10

Fetal Alcohol or Other Conditions that Cause Cognitive and Emotional Limitations

10 – Incident

One inmate threatening another inside her cell. Inmate armed with a sharp object.

Inmate Alicia Nowak has entered another inmate's cell, and refused to leave. She says she is upset that the second inmate won't be her friend. She is twice the size of the 2nd inmate, Aniyah Washington, who tried and failed to push her out of her cell. Washington wants nothing to do with Nowack and begins cursing her out, and Nowak punches her to unconsciousness. She panics, starts crying and breaks a toothbrush and places the sharp end of the handle vertical on the soft part of the throat of the prone Washington.

When officers enter the area, Nowak starts yelling, "Get back, get back," and with her palm shoves the handle into Washington's flesh. The officers halt at the doorway, and Nowak stops pushing. She keeps yelling, "Leave me alone, leave me alone. She's my friend. Leave me alone."

The lead officer talks calmly to her, and as she does so, Nowak becomes less tense. The lead makes a decision not to immediately rush Nowak, as she doesn't want Washington's trachea punctured.

HNT and ERT are called.

10 – Character of the Inmate

Alicia Nowak has been an inmate for four years, and she has had a very difficult time programming. She has some kind of unspecified emotional and cognitive impairment, and is quite socially immature. Medical has not informed officers of the nature of her problem – some speculate fetal alcohol syndrome and others some kind of head injury. Whatever the cause, her behavior is typified by impulsivity, suggestibility (other inmates can get her to do things for them, and also for their amusement, to wind Nowak up and get her in trouble), and an inability to learn from experience. She will be warned and sanctioned as to an infraction and two days later, do the same thing, with no apparent memory at the time that she was previously warned. When reminded, she'll either shamefacedly say, "Oh yeah. You told me that." Or she'll get really upset: ranging from tears to yelling to property damage to assault.

In this case, other inmates told Alicia that Aniyah, a notoriously stand-offish and prickly tempered woman, who keeps to herself, likes her and wants to be her friend. Alicia 'dropped by' her cell, and Aniyah told her to "get the fuck out."

> ## Types of Cognitive Impairment
>
> This exercise could be reworked with a) a developmentally disabled inmate b) an individual with a head injury. In this latter case, you could make the scenario more complex by making the subject a military veteran who suffered a head injury in combat Plan with your psych consult (or outside consultant, such as an expert at neurological damage from blast or bullet wound) so that the role player knows how to best embody the character, and the exercise is most productive for your team.

10 – Interview with Case Manager

Alternative ONE: Fetal Alcohol

Alicia's mother was a serious alcoholic. She drank throughout her pregnancy. Alicia was born with fetal alcohol syndrome. She is currently 26 years old.

She is a big, powerful woman. "She looks fat, but she can move and when she gets mad, she never gets tired. And when she's upset, she doesn't seem to react to pain."

Alternative TWO: Head Injury

Alicia was first incarcerated on armed robbery charges, secondary to feeding a drug habit. She got into some kind of conflict at the last correctional facility and got a serious head injury, which really damaged her. She now has significant cognitive deficits and impulse control problems. Her family says she's literally not the same person she used to be. She is currently 26 years old.

She is a big, powerful woman. "She looks fat, but she can move and when she gets mad, she never gets tired. And when she's upset, she doesn't seem to react to pain."

> ## An Added Factor: 'Gender Volatility'
>
> One factor the director could add would be 'gender volatility.' Alicia can be made to have especially difficult interactions with either male or female staff. For practice, the director could arbitrarily instruct the role player to be aggressive and reactive to whatever gender the first negotiator is. Whoever is the lead should get in an hour or so practice, with some success, but eventually, Alicia should get so volatile with her – and unambiguously because of the negotiator's gender—that it will be clear that you will need to change negotiators. (This is to be discussed in the AAR, so it is clear to the first lead this was programmed into the exercise and not a failure on the negotiator's part).
>
> NOTE 2: The 'gender volatility' could be reversed as well, so that Alicia is aggressive towards men whom he thinks are putting him down or something similar.

10 – Negotiation

Negotiation will be difficult. Alicia is quite emotional, panicked, and she will not track the information the officers try to give her. At one moment, she seems amenable to giving up, but she takes offense at something HNT says, and becomes threatening, hysterical or simply cuts off communication. She also will quickly forget what she agreed to, what she understood, etc. The negotiator must be patient and not take offense at having to repeat the same things over and over.

If the negotiator uses complicated sentences or big words, Alicia will get angry, because she won't understand; she'll think that the officer is doing it deliberately to make her feel stupid.

10 – Psychological Consult

The psychology or psychiatry department of the local university or is contacted (in actual fact, this will probably take several calls and transfers to get to the right person). One specialist, an expert on Fetal Alcohol Syndrome (in Alternative ONE) or head injury (in Alternative TWO) is contacted.

The problem, he says, is such individuals have a much less sophisticated neurological organization. "It's not that she is Intellectually disabled in the ordinary sense. When she learns something, however, it is stored 'locally.' In other words, the filing system is limited and it's hard for her to access the information if, for example, her mood changes. If you use complicated language, she will think you are "making her stupid," and impulsively lash out to make you stop. On the other hand, she will be very sensitive to being talked down to. Unlike Intellectually disabled folks (those who used to be designated as mentally retarded), who can be childlike, Alicia is probably a full adult—albeit one who is socially immature and very emotional, and who will easily take offence if she thinks you are trying to make her confused or feel stupid. Your task will be to talk to her in a matter-of-fact way, and be very sensitive to when she is not tracking you. One sign of this is she will go silent (she'll be trying to figure out what you said and when she can't, she'll start brooding and become resentful, and eventually will explode into rage).

Clarify any misunderstandings immediately. Be careful, however, that you don't do this in such a way she thinks you are implicitly saying, "This is simple. Any fool can understand this."

SCENARIO 10 – Checklist for After Action Review

The after action assessment/critique will depend on what was expressed and expected of the team going into the exercise. In other words, what was the desired training goal or outcome? Not just the outcome of the scenario, but what are the skills the director (team leader) is hoping to see exercised by the team, as these scenario/situations develop?

Background etc. collected in a timely manner?
- ❏ Did not meet goal
- ❏ Partially met goal
- ❏ Fully met goal

Did the team recognize what they were dealing with?
- ❏ Did not meet goal
- ❏ Partially met goal
- ❏ Fully met goal

Consider psych consult? Request one?
- ❏ Did not meet goal
- ❏ Partially met goal
- ❏ Fully met goal

Demonstrate good listening skills?
- ❏ Did not meet goal
- ❏ Partially met goal
- ❏ Fully met goal

Talk to her at a level that she most easily tracks what you are saying?
- ❏ Did not meet goal
- ❏ Partially met goal
- ❏ Fully met goal

Deal with 'gender volatility' issues if this is part of the scenario?
- ❏ Did not meet goal
- ❏ Partially met goal
- ❏ Fully met goal

SCENARIO 11

Narcissism

11 – Incident

Rooftop. Inmate threatening bound up civilian with a machete like weapon.

Inmate, who is a maintenance worker, has managed to secure a long piece of metal that he or someone else fabricated into a machete-like weapon. He, and a maintenance supervisor are on the roof, the latter tied to a structure of metal pipes. The inmate is ostentatiously doing martial arts moves. He looks like he knows what he is doing. Officers yelled at him to come down and he proclaimed, "Today is a good day to die." ERT and HNT are deployed.

Up on the roof?

If it would be impossible for an inmate, with a staff person, to get up to the roof of a building, construct a similar scenario in a similar place, both dramatic and isolated.

---

11 – History of Subject – Information for the Role Player and HNT

Carl Shields is a former instructor who taught a martial art called aikido. He began a sexual relationship with Esther, aged fourteen. Esther, infatuated, ran away from home to Carl's. Her mother called police, but when they go to the house, Carl briefly appears at the door, wearing his martial arts uniform, with a sword in his hand, and told them to leave. "This will be solved in the only way possible to preserve my honor and that of my teachers." (Carl is an American—whatever the race of the role player—not a Japanese citizen). The situation was resolved with a barrage of pepperballs (or some other less-lethal option, but one that the team can imagine as making Carl look absurd). As Carl staggered to the front of the house, officers pinned him to the wall of the house with the grill of one of their cruisers. Carl dropped the weapon when he was slammed into the wall. He was not seriously injured, merely bruised legs and bruised ego. As he was arrested, he accused the officers of cowardice and demanded that one of them take off his gun belt and face him one-on-one as a matter of honor.

11 – Follow-up with Staff at Special Offender Unit

Carl was assigned to the Special Offender Unit, so he has never had to face the main yard, and has led a safe-enough life in prison, but he is still a formidable guy. A lifetime practitioner of any martial art that uses weapons in practice is going to be dangerous with a weapon in his hands.

As for his attitude in the Special Offender Unit, he confesses to "making a mistake." He maintains he showed "poor judgment," but "nothing really bad happened, and nothing was going to happen. What kind of a guy do you think I am?" At the same time, he points out how mature Esther is, both in body and soul, and the counselor has noted a glazed look goes over his eyes whenever he talks about her. "Yes, I admit it, maybe I did something that could have confused her, I feel bad about it, really bad," but that he had not done anything illegal. "Let's say, just for discussion, while I was practicing with her, and showing her a throw, my technique wasn't exactly precise and instead of my hand going directly under her arm, I might have brushed across her front— this could easily have happened if she moved incorrectly. I'm not saying it did, but just for an example."

At the same time, he 'philosophically' denies that there is anything wrong with sexual contact with a girl of fourteen, citing many examples from medieval Japan, where marriage at that age was the norm.

11 – Contact with Carl—For the Role Player

Familiarize yourself somewhat with aikido—there is tons of information online about this martial art. Your presentation should be patronizing and stilted; at times, make yourself sound like a bad samurai movie character. (People in the Japanese martial arts community – at least those who are genuine – refer to people like this as practicing Bullshido).

You will be:

- Easily offended, at which point you will talk about your honor as a warrior
- Patronizing to the negotiator. You'll question police tactics—"You only know the language of opposition and force, whereas in aikido, we redirect negative energy to a peaceful resolution" (you will be too full of yourself to see the irony here).
- You can talk about O-sensei, the saintly, white-bearded founder of the art, who had superhuman powers and proclaimed, "Martial arts are love."
- You will want to talk about Esther, referring to her as being wise beyond her years, because she realized she was someone who was meant for the best that life has to offer — in other words, bonding with you. At the same time, you will talk about her in dismissive terms, as a disciple rather than an equal. Even there, however, you will keep directing the conversation back to the only subject of interest in the world – yourself.
- You will never make an explicit suicide threat, unless the negotiator threatens you in some way— rather, make allusive statements suggesting that your honor will be served.
- 'Kindly' warn the negotiator not to send in the ERT, because your sword skills are deadly, and you do not wish to have to resort to unseemly violence.

11 – Media Problem!

An inmate with a smuggled cell phone films Carl on the roof, doing his martial arts, capturing the image of the case manager tied to the metal pipes, and records Carl yelling, "The way of the warrior is death!" He broadcasts this to Instagram and it goes viral. Students and associates of Carl begin calling the prison, offering information and trying to help (some with very counter-productive intentions). There are a number of news trucks outside and drones flying overhead, filming the scene. Carl takes a stance, raises his sword and gives a pseudo-Japanese war-cry, for the benefit of the news drones.

This will give HNT great opportunities to practice collateral interviews, and also, if the director likes, to set up a liaison to communicate with media.

11 – Collateral Interview: Carl's Assistant Instructor

Aikido, a martial art claiming to reconcile conflict by redirecting negative forces. It tends to draw people not interested in fighting as much as a more philosophical approach—moral improvement, spiritual development, etc. Which means it's ripe ground for guru types. Nonetheless, Carl has been doing this for about 35 years, and he is a really powerful guy, as well as skilled with the aikido weapons curriculum. They practice with swords and staffs. The assistant instructor will blather on about energy and the moral forces of the universe, and how he cannot believe Carl could ever do anything bad, but "Appearances are everything these days, so we had to let fire him from the dojo. We hoped it would all blow over after awhile, and he could come back and lead us." He will speak of him in idolizing terms. He clearly states Carl is really effective with a sword, and practices cutting bamboo wrapped in straw mats to emulate the structure of the human body. He once cut a bundle of five of these, winning some sort of 'sword cutting tournament.'

11 — Collateral Interview: Contact with Carl's Own Teacher

Carl's teacher, Mr. Lockhardt also telephones the prison on his own. He starts by saying, "You can call me Sensei." He's a pompous ass. He will discount the gravity of the charges against Carl, saying when he trained in Japan, no one would make a big deal over something like this—a teacher mentoring a student was always considered an honor. Anyway, if the teacher was tempted to stray a bit, it was understood that the student, for the good of the teachers' mission, would either simply withdraw from the school, or if not, realize she was fortunate the teacher was kind enough to give her attention.

The interviewer should feel free to be a cop here. He or she must underscore that a serious crime is being committed AT THIS MOMENT—kidnapping, to be precise, and previously, molestation of a child—and Lockhardt's rationalizations and support will certainly reflect poorly on his image, were they made public.

This interview would be great if it could be conducted with a serious, skilled role player, who may have some real information, but it is covered up in a really obnoxious personality. If the leader/ director can find someone to really play this role well, it would challenge any interviewer.

Demanding he cut to the chase, the interviewer should ask for an explanation of Carl taking a hostage on a roof, and prancing around, doing martial arts moves.

Lockhardt will reply if he has done his job well as Carl's teacher, then of course he means suicide. When the interviewer asks the implications for the hostage case manager, Lockhardt states if Carl is a true warrior, he will do whatever it takes to protect his honor too. To be taken captive is the most dishonorable thing there is—"What kind of a warrior let's himself be taken prisoner—it would be an act of mercy to do what is necessary to make the case manager's shame disappear."

11 – Further Interviews with Dojo Members

#1 INTERVIEWEE

Carl is a very talented, very Intelligent man, whom many admired. But it always had to be his way. He was easily offended, when people disagreed with him. Furthermore, there had been some financial improprieties regarding dojo funds. Carl was a paid employee according to the business structure, but he treated the dojo as his personal possession. When people confronted him on the money issue, he blew up, accused them of lack of loyalty to their instructor, and said, "In olden times, you would deserve death to call your teacher's actions into question." Regrettably, he said, these times were over, but they would never advance in rank in the art again. He allowed them to come to class, but simply ignored them. The three members of the board involved quit.

#2 INTERVIEWEE

"I trust my sensei. There must be an explanation. If the police would just leave him alone, he could solve this problem."

#3 INTERVIEWEE

A female student: "I only lasted six months. The guy always creeped me out. You know the kind of person who is somehow standing too close to you even across the room. His eye contact is too long, and his smile is too fixed. He seems to be listening to everything you say, but eventually you realize he doesn't give a shit. It's all about him."

11 – Consult with a Genuine Expert in Japanese Martial Arts

This individual, Takenori Morimoto, called in outrage after seeing the film online and reading the comments that followed, for the most part either idolizing Carl, or vicariously getting off on this man revolting against a prison with a sword.

After being told what Lockhardt has said, as well as the members of the school, this Japanese-American, long-time resident of Japan, also an aikido practitioner, states, "That's all crap. Not that the idiot won't kill himself or your case manager, but he's full of shit. These idiots are like the kind of people who read comic books to understand Japan, but they are worse. They just make the whole thing up in their head. At the same time, here's what you need to know about these guys. They believe their own bullshit. They think they are superior and use their little fantasy construct to support whatever it is they do. It's sort of like a cult."

The importance of Intel in developing a psych profile

This is another scenario where the Intel, and development of the psych profile on this guy, is going to be key for the HNT when they are briefing the scene commander on what they are facing with Carl.

We have made Intel acquisition easy by having people call the prison. The director could easily set things up so that your secondaries must find the collateral informants themselves. Finding these key potential witnesses are going to be critical. How do you locate that female student who quit the dojo after 6 months? How do you locate the expert on Japanese martial arts (or another culture, if you choose to structure the scenario with another type of martial art)? All of this needs to be prepared ahead of time, and does require some work on the part of the director, and the team of trainers who are putting on the training. This is why it is beneficial to have a cadre of trainers involved when doing major (even minor) scenario training. If you have a representative from ERT, communications, investigations, maybe even records division, you can get a whole lot done, and a lot of good ideas for a very realistic training.

11 – Psychological Consult

Take away all the martial arts, and you have a classic narcissist. The task of the negotiator is to get him talking about the most fascinating subject in the whole world to him: himself. You certainly have to check on the well-being of your case manager, but be very careful not to put too much energy in this, because, as far as Carl is concerned, this is about him, not the case manager, and he'll get angry if he's not the center of attention. He may become violent or threatening to make you put your focus back on him.

If what your martial arts consultant says is accurate, you have to be careful of a couple of things:
1. He's going to be insecure about his martial arts, because he's probably been accused of being a fraud by people like your last consultant.
2. If the negotiator has done combatives, served in the military, done martial arts yourself or simply served on the front lines in law enforcement and/or corrections, do not show too much knowledge, because you have done 'it' for real, as opposed to waving weapons in a dojo. This will make Carl insecure.
3. Carl is similar to a certain B-list movie actor, (a has-been who did aikido, has sexually harassed a number of women, is best-boy-friend-for-life to Vladimir Putin, and claimed to teach expert MMA stars how to fight), who always takes great pains to tell others how special he is, and how he is as expert in real life as he is supposed to be in his movies. Carl, like this B-list movie actor, is living in a movie in his head.

If you get him talking a long time about himself, he may start to feel more and more special, smarter than you, or the courts. Support him in minimizing both situations:

- Regarding his sexual exploitation of his young student, [Esther came over to his house, he probably didn't even invite her, and if this is the misunderstanding it looks like, he should be able to clear it up.]
- Regarding the current situation, he went up to the roof to manifest his opposition to what he has experienced as injustice. He made his point – the whole world is watching (or at least local news and a number of bottom-feeders online).

Within limits, express understanding that due to his specialized training, of course he reacted just like his training expected. But he showed control martial artists have—he hasn't harmed the helpless guard with his sword, so no one was hurt. Thank him for that. Lead him to giving up as a matter of his superior control.

This guy will be really obnoxious—he will bolster his own ego by putting you down. Be careful not to get your buttons pushed. He will offend you and take offense if you are offended. If you put him in his place like he 'deserves,' he may believe he has to hurt the case manager, or at least escalate to prove he is someone who must be taken seriously.

After instructing him on how to surrender, be sure to ask him how his sword should be cared for so that it is not damaged.

11 – The Question of the Case Manager Hostage: For a Secondary Role-Player

1. In the basic level scenario training, the case manager can be simply quiet, passive.
2. To make a more sophisticated exercise, he can get increasingly worried, scared, and there can be by-play between Carl and the case manager. If Carl loses his temper at the victim, the negotiator should redirect attention on their conversation, away from the case manager.
3. One opportunity for an ERT exercise would be if the negotiator can really get Carl involved in pontificating about the wonders of martial arts and enlightened warriors, etc. ERT can practice a rescue of the case manager, or if he properly exposes himself, a sniper can light him up with a laser.
4. If it is so desired, and your role player is fit enough and has some training in combatives, he can attack the officers upon exit, substituting a bamboo kendo stave for a real sword. Depending on the distance, ERT can practice with less lethal or lethal weapons, as appropriate.

SCENARIO 11 – Checklist for After Action Review

The after action assessment/critique will depend on what was expressed and expected of the team going into the exercise. In other words, what was the desired training goal or outcome? Not just the outcome of the scenario, but what are the skills the director (team leader) is hoping to see exercised by the team, as these scenario/situations develop?

Floor plan obtained in a timely manner?
- ❏ Did not meet goal
- ❏ Partially met goal
- ❏ Fully met goal

Very important to demonstrate good listening skills?
- ❏ Did not meet goal
- ❏ Partially met goal
- ❏ Fully met goal

Allow subject to talk about himself?
- ❏ Did not meet goal
- ❏ Partially met goal
- ❏ Fully met goal

Honest status updates to the command post are very important?
- ❏ Did not meet goal
- ❏ Partially met goal
- ❏ Fully met goal

If the hostage and hostage-taker began to interact, was the negotiator able to redirect the hostage-taker's focus away from the victim?
- ❏ Did not meet goal
- ❏ Partially met goal
- ❏ Fully met goal

Effectively integrated the information derived from your collateral contacts and your consultant?
- ❏ Did not meet goal
- ❏ Partially met goal
- ❏ Fully met goal

Played on his massive narcissistic ego so that he gets so in love with the sound of his own voice that he wants to stay alive to listen to himself more?

❏ Did not meet goal
❏ Partially met goal
❏ Fully met goal

SCENARIO 12

Cultural Issues, Suicide as Solution

12 – Current Incident

Inmate threatening to set fire to herself in the woodshop. She has spilled flammable liquid and is armed with a lighter.

Fedela Assaf, age 23, is incarcerated in a minimum security prison for murder of a child. She is barricaded in a workshop, where leather goods are normally made. She has splashed the area around herself with a flammable solvent (used for leather dying). She ordered others out of the room, while brandishing a lighter. There is at least a gallon of this solvent around her.

HNT has been called, and the fire department is on standby. There was a consideration of trying to spray a fire hose to disperse the solvent, but research—a task for Intel—establishes that it floats and that would probably spread the flames.

12 – Background Information for Role Player

Fedela claimed she was raped by a family friend, something that both the man and her own family denied. Instead, they asserted that the sex was consensual, and she must marry the man, aged 54, or otherwise, she will have destroyed the family honor. Instead, she went to a secure women's shelter and eventually gave birth to a baby. Staff noted that she appeared to be somewhat depressed, but she refused counseling, and seemed to be bonding with the baby. After three months, it was time for her to leave the shelter. She expressed anxiety about this, saying that her family would find her. The staff at the shelter responded by saying that her family had sent her letters (through their secure mail drop), and as she knew, they wrote that they loved her and just wanted her to come home. All was forgiven. Fedela shut down at that point.

Two days later, she drowned her son.

The court expressed compassion, but there was no valid 'diminished capacity defense,' per the laws of the state, and minimum sentencing required that she be incarcerated for a minimum of six to eight years. In the courtroom and afterwards, her family has made threats on her life. Her brother tried to attack her during the trial and the family was barred from future attendance. Her rapist has demanded financial compensation from the family for the loss of his son. Her mother said, "We pray for your release from prison so our family can be released from the stain to our honor."

Fedela has one brother and one sister, both of whom do exactly what their parents want them to do. She, too, tried to be a 'good girl,' wearing hijab, going to the mosque with her parents, and worshiping according to the testaments of their faith.

Fedela wanted to be a chemist. She is one of those people who found something that just makes her feel alive. For her, it was chemistry. She felt like she was participating in the clockwork of creation. For her, in joining chemicals together and making compounds, she "knows the heart of Allah, who loves us and wants to bring us together." When the role-player talks about chemistry— (this could, of course, be changed to another subject that the role-player is familiar)—she should really light up with happiness. This will contrast vividly with her current situation.

In short, there are a number of issues, simultaneously working, within Fedela. She is a victim of rape, she is a victim of betrayal by her parents and is under death threat, she murdered her own baby (a product of rape), she struggles with the culture she was brought up within, and she faces the potential loss of her dream to do chemistry.

Who should negotiate? The gender question.

There are many factors involved in who should be primary in a negotiation. Sometimes it is simply a matter of who rotates in. With certain inmates, the team can consider if a male or a female negotiator will be more effective: in this case, would a female negotiator be better? In general, 'matching' a negotiator to either demographics or other issues should only occur when there is clear evidence that a certain negotiator will be best. If you just base things on assumptions, you can easily be mistaken:

For example, although it might seem an easy 'call' to say that a rape victim and victim of violence at the hands of men would do better with a woman negotiator, she may, in fact, resent women more, because her mother and other women 'sold her out.' To be sure, the team should quickly staff such questions, but not over 'worry' them. If a negotiator clearly is not establishing rapport, it is part of the team's job to perceive this, and rotate in another primary.

12 – Negotiation

She tells the negotiator there is no hope for her and she is going to kill herself. When asked why she barricaded herself and 'created this scene,' she says she just wants someone to understand before she dies. She is very afraid of flames, but was more afraid that if she tried to use a blade or other tool, she would be disarmed. When asked "Why now," she replies that she was brought before a parole hearing and granted parole (NOTE: or in states without a parole system, change this to "because of her status as a model prisoner, she is due to be released.") "I have never caused any problems here. So they want to release me. What could I say, 'Don't release me? I like it in prison.' So you will release me and my family will kill me. I would rather die by my own hand."

12 – Interview with Parents

A decision is made to contact the parents, in hopes that Fedela is mistaken. If the family does not intend her harm, there would be no need for her to kill herself. The family denies all of Fedela's claims. They claim that they condemn honor killing, and would never do such a thing. They admit they tried to have her marry the family friend. "Our daughter was not raped. Fouad has been a friend since we came to America. He would never do that. He gave us his word. What happened is that Fedela became infatuated with him, and they had an affair. He tried to resist her, but she is a young woman and she threw herself at him. She has caused terrible shame to our family. But we are modern people, not barbarians. She is mentally ill – she denies the truth of the relationship she had and then she murdered our grandchild. Nonetheless, we forgive her. She can marry Fouad and return to our family."

When the secondary negotiator asks more questions, such as what if she refuses to marry Fouad, however, the father will quickly become angry, asserting that this interview has become an assault on their culture. "This is becoming a matter of religious and cultural freedom." He won't explain why, just angrily level accusations of 'Islamophobia.' Suddenly, you will have a lawyer on the line that has listened in on the call. He demands that the family is left alone and that this harassment stops and threatens to sue if this persecution continues.

Training for Legal Issues in Culturally-Sensitive Cases

Another interesting challenge would be to use the services of a lawyer who has researched such cases in court. Though perhaps not fully relevant in this specific scenario, admin can train on stalling tactics, coordination with their own legal advisor to keep the family/their lawyer out of the negotiation, while taking care to keep the agency as safe as possible from toxic litigation.

---

12 – Consult Concerning Post-Partum Depression

At this point, HNT does not know if Fedela feels guilt and grief at killing her child or if she feels justified. It is up to the director to decide whether you wish the role-player to be haunted by guilt at what she did, or if you wish her to feel justification at killing her rapist's baby (i.e., "He put it in me. It was not mine.").

If she is racked with guilt, and this is complicated by cultural rules as well, try to link her love for science with a modern understanding of post-partum depression as a chemical process within the brain. In any event, be prepared to discuss this if Fedela is tortured by guilt as opposed to being happy she killed her rapist's baby.

12 – Cultural Consult

As the reader surely knows, there has been a vast increase in immigration from Muslim countries as well as many converts to Islam within America. There is, therefore, enough potential for a case such as this to occur that you should use this role play as an opportunity to research where you can find a consultant who is, whether Muslim or not, well versed in orthodox Islam and honor killing. This can be a valuable exercise for the team either if: a) the consultant is supportive of HNT's goal to help the young woman; b) defensive about what s/he sees as criticism of Muslim culture.

Please generalize the statements above. With a little research, one could develop scenario for males from Muslim culture (honor concerns pervade every aspect of life for men and women in *traditional* Muslim culture). Beyond this, with a little research, you could construct a similar 'culturally driven' scenario for men or women from any immigrant culture who are having significant impact (and are impacted by) their interaction with American culture. Given that lives can be on the line in situations such as this, it is foolish to tip-toe around the realities that:

- Cultural value driven violence (suicide or homicide) exists. Different cultures have different cultural sanctions for violence and if officers are going to interact with people from those cultures, they need to be educated.
- Due to concerns that allegations of bigotry are often leveled in such cases, the subject of culturally sanctioned violence is avoided. This is a foolish, head-in-the-sand approach. Facts are not prejudice and each and every culture on earth develops a worldview regarding what is worth living for and what is worth dying for.

Therefore, a valuable part of this exercise would be to consult with an expert on the cultural context here. There are two ways to do this:

1. Line up an expert, before the scenario, who is known to be sympathetic to the situation of young women such as Fedela, and simply call him or her and get educated.
2. Do this cold. Start calling local universities, cultural organizations and do your collateral interviews in real time. Be prepared for defensiveness, argumentation, or genuine concern.

Effective Use of Cultural Consultation—and Effective Cultural Consultants

Honor killing is not exclusively a Muslim problem, but statistics show worldwide, well over 90% of honor murders are done within Muslim families. We have absolutely no intention of stigmatizing a culture or religion here—rather, negotiators must be prepared for various cultural rules that are dysfunctional and even destructive to its own members (name a culture for which this is not true!). Therefore, such 'flaws' (cultural rules that sanction or permit violence or other violation) should be a subject of study and training concerning any culturally distinct population within your prison. This includes not only those who are members of or descendents of cultures from outside America—it should also include such American-born cultures (some in prison) such as the Aryan Brotherhood or the Five-Percent Nation

To use this case as an example, the kind of information you are looking for from the consultant would be:

- What organizations support young women in these situations?
- Religious support for a young woman refusing to follow her parents' toxic wishes (this can help the young woman have a reason to live—this is not for argumentation with the parents),
- Information on how women have survived and thrived after surviving situations like this.

12 – Psychological Consult

The negotiator is talking to a young woman, who, although acculturated into America, has to grapple with values alien to our culture. Beyond just trying to get her to talk about herself, getting her to talk about what she loves is probably a good idea. Ask her to explain about chemistry. There is both a hope and a risk here; the hope that if she talks about what she loves, she will increasingly desire to live and fight for her dream. The risk is that it may feel like salt in her wounds.

If she becomes, therefore, despairing because her parents and the rapist have destroyed her dream. She can only live her dream if she can live freely, without being under constant threat of being hunted down and maimed or killed.

You want to be able to 'guarantee' that the prison will do everything in their power to effect a safe release, where her family will not be able to locate her. A secondary negotiator (or a release specialist or classification counselor making calls on the secondary's request) should be making calls to ascertain what her rights are concerning release and protection of her identity and location. Furthermore, research should include whether a support network can be located for women in situations such as this.

SCENARIO 12 – Checklist for After Action Review

The after action assessment/critique will depend on what was expressed and expected of the team going into the exercise. In other words, what was the desired training goal or outcome? Not just the outcome of the scenario, but what are the skills the director (team leader) is hoping to see exercised by the team, as these scenario/situations develop?

Cultural issues are important—how did team get information concerning this aspect of the scenario? Did the team contact an expert? Particularly if the expert was suspicious or hostile, was the team able to communicate with diplomacy, explaining to the expert that the team's main concern was helping the young woman live?
- ❑ Did not meet goal
- ❑ Partially met goal
- ❑ Fully met goal

Did primary address suicidality issue head on?
- ❑ Did not meet goal
- ❑ Partially met goal
- ❑ Fully met goal

Contact expert on post-partum depression?
- ❑ Did not meet goal
- ❑ Partially met goal
- ❑ Fully met goal

Demonstrate good listening skills?
- ❑ Did not meet goal
- ❑ Partially met goal
- ❑ Fully met goal

SCENARIO 13

Self-mutilator, Borderline Personality

13 – Call to Main Control

Inmate barricaded in EFV trailer with her baby, threatening to kill her self and the baby. She says she has an unknown sharp object.

Main Control receives a call from Krystel, an inmate. She has somehow gotten a cell-phone. She was in the middle of a conjugal visit with her husband and baby. The husband stepped out of the trailer, leaving Krystel alone with the baby. She says that she is going to cut her wrists (with whatever kind of improvised sharp fits your particular facility).

Krystel says to the operator, "I just want to die. Tommy comes, and all that does is make it worse. He just comes here to screw me. He got what he wanted, and just left me alone with the baby. And the baby won't stop crying and I don't know what to do." And then the operator hears her yell, "Don't you try to come back in here, you don't care about me, just my pussy. I swear, Tommy, you come through that door, I'll kill me and the baby too!" She hangs up.

Officers request ERT and HNT.

On Extended Family Visits and Alternative Scenarios
- EFV are currently (2018) only allowed in the states of California, Connecticut, Mississippi, New Mexico New York, and Washington.
- This scenario can be reworked to focus on a mother/baby inmate program, where incarcerated mothers state with their baby for a period after birth. As of 2018, there are approximately ten states that have mother-infant nursery programs.
- If neither of these programs applies, you can easily construct an alternative scenario with Krystel (displaying the same character traits) taking a fellow prisoner or staff person hostage. There is a particular tension, however, when HNT must consider the life of a baby.

---

13 – Krystel's Character – For the Role Player and for the Director to Give the Information that would be Accessible to HNT

Krystel is a 'high-utilizer.' She has been incarcerated multiple times, and in past incarcerations, had been in psych services for suicide and para-suicidal attempts (NOTE: the latter term means self-harm where dying is not really the attempt – Krystel has done both.) A number of years ago, after an event where Krystel scratched her writs, one officer (no longer employed), fed up after yet another crisis, decided to 'scare her straight.' He said, "If you were really serious about this suicide, you wouldn't be fooling around with those little scratches. You'd cut lengthwise from here (pointing to her elbow) to here (pointing to her wrists)." On her next attempt, Krystel made three cuts down to the bone, from elbow to wrists, losing 4 pints of blood, timing it so that officer found her unconscious, almost bled out. She had almost died. Her arm is obscenely scarred. She cut too deeply for stitches to really close the wounds, and her forearm has three red, raised tracks, as if she has huge worms under the skin.

Krystel's three subsequent suicide attempts were more serious. She swallowed bleach and Clorox together, jumped off a tier at the third flight, and stabbed herself in the abdomen. It seems miraculous she's alive. She threw up the cleaner, causing some scarring in her throat, but no permanent damage. She broke both legs when she jumped, and the knife somehow threaded its way past her internal organs, merely nicking her liver.

She's had relationship drama with several inmates over the years, and about eight years ago, she became infatuated with an officer. Krystel began stalking her by staging para-suicides when she was on shift so that particular officer would rescue her.

In this, her latest incarceration, she has made no suicide attempts, and after a period of time, and consultation with her case manager and mental health staff, she was placed in general population. She became pregnant during a conjugal visit. (NOTE: for a scenario in a non- EFV state, she became pregnant shortly before her last incarceration).

Nonetheless, she demands a lot of time and energy, and because of her history, officers are always on edge lest she get infatuated towards one of them. There's a kind of 'graveyard' humor about this – "You're next, man, you are just too nice." Or "She likes the strong silent type. She's going to get your home phone number and start calling your wife and telling her you are sleeping with her. And your wife is so fricking jealous, she'll believe it." At the same time, officers are professional, and the team consults with psych services every time she is returned from the mental health unit to determine how best to act with her.

Krystel is, nonetheless, a sympathetic character to some. She is very attractive, and, when not suicidal or enraged, she has an angelic persona, a soft husky voice (thanks to the scarring in her throat), emanating profound sadness and confusion. Part of her Behavioral Management Plan is that when she is going through a bad period, she is contacted by a member of counseling services once a day (beyond regular appointments) and a nurse or counselor will speak with her for ten timed minutes. (This has helped keep her stable – it's predictable and she knows, twenty-four seven, that people are aware of her and want to help. On one recent contact, she said, "I'm so sorry to be bothering you again. I hate myself so much. I know you people are tired of me. If it wasn't for my baby, I'd be outa here." She has been relatively stable for several years: it is for that reason that she was permitted to take part in EFV (or parent/child nursery).

13 – Interview with the Nurse-Educator Who Teaches Parenting Classes

"She shouldn't even have had a baby. They try to protect against that kind of thing if the inmate is going to have conjugal visits, but not even Norplant is 100% effective. Given how unstable she is, we watched her like a hawk during the twelve weeks she had the baby. They moved her to the father after the three month mark. She loves her, in her own needy way. She takes all the parenting classes here, tries her best. She's been planning for her release in, what is it, two years or so? But the truth is that she's overwhelmed by the responsibility of caring for a child, despite her claims to want to reunite with her. She feels at fault whenever the baby cries, and this kid cries a lot—he's just figured out how to throw tantrums, so he's crying all the time during their visits. I wouldn't be surprised, whether she knows it or not, if this incident is calculated to mess up her release date. More charges, and she doesn't have to take the responsibility of being a mother.

13 – Follow-up Interview with the Officer who was Stalked

You can, of course, change the profession to police (who was stalked on the outside, previous to incarceration, or the gender of the informant, whatever suits your available role-player.

As found in the records, she became infatuated with one officer. The officer, new at this job, signed on in a period where Krystel was doing well, and the officer was concerned about her, and expressed sympathy. She was professional, but the boundaries got a little too close. Krystel, who is quite resourceful, got a cell phone (yes, the current incident is the second time she's done this). She had a friend outside locate the phone number of the officer's husband, and began calling him at work to inform him that he didn't understand his wife's needs and there had to be some way, considering their kids, to allow them to continue the marriage while his wife could live out her bisexual nature, here in the prison. The husband called his wife immediately – Krystel was very believable – and the officer dealt with this as best she could in the circumstances, going immediately to her supervisor. In that event, Krystel was moved to another unit of the prison entirely, and she is 'flagged,' so to speak, so that every officer is aware of her potential to get infatuated and stalk one of them.

13 – Interview with Therapist

The therapist states Krystel has a borderline personality disorder, and notes traits of uncertainty about her sexuality, volatile relationships, rapid shifts from one mood to another, including rage, and idealization followed by a sense of betrayal regarding those close to her. "You will find her provocative and manipulative. She's not playing games, like a sociopath. She just reacts to whatever emotion she is feeling. I've found it best to notice when she is reactive and to shift the subject so she calms down. She will not 'listen to reason.' She only listens to what she feels in the moment."

Krystel will raise a history of sexual abuse. If she brings this up, the therapist suggests the negotiator should commiserate in a matter-of-fact way, and state, "I wish I could have been there to stop it", and then, CHANGE THE SUBJECT. If she talks about her abuse, she will begin to relive it.

Effective Use of a Therapist for On-scene Consult

Feel free to use one of your counselors or psychiatrists as an on-scene consult, if you wish to include him or her in the exercise. It would be a worthwhile aspect of HNT training to educate the therapist/consultant on what YOU need from them while having them on scene. (This replaces the usual psych consult that we have written in most chapters).

---

13 – How This Scenario Should Play Out For Maximum Education On Borderline Personality

Krystel is going to run through two negotiators. With the first, the negotiator will make headway. Krystel will be very sweet—a sympathetic character. The negotiator will think this will soon resolve, viewing Krystel as just an uncertain young woman, who needs support and encouragement. Krsytel, after idealizing the negotiator, and telling him/her how wonderful he or she is, will suddenly decide she is being talked down to and become utterly enraged. She will begin to make threats to kill herself and her baby if she has to talk to the negotiator anymore. The negotiator should be put in a place of thinking, "What the hell just happened? Everything was going so well." Krystel will be in hysterical, screaming rage.

Eventually, a second negotiator should take over.

If the negotiation team gets stubborn and refuses to change over, Krystel should continue to escalate, and if the team doesn't get the message, she should kill herself (and even her baby, if the team leader decides such a harsh lesson is necessary).

Once a change-over is accomplished, and some rapport is established, Krystel will demand to talk to the officer whom she is infatuated with. She will be stuck on this for quite some time. It will be the task of the negotiator to shift her to focusing on the future, get her to IMAGINE her child happy with her. She will be sensitive to being manipulated, and even more sensitive to someone trying to make her feel good by giving her empty put-ups.

Transition from One Negotiator to Another

This is a good scenario to practice transitioning from one negotiator to another. With an individual with borderline personality, the rapport developed is very superficial and fleeting on the part of the subject, anyway, so it's not going to be permanent with ANY negotiator you place as primary. Take it as an opportunity to practice doing transitions, and switch out more often than you normally do.

Rewrite for a Male Scenario

Obviously, you cannot make a scenario concerning a baby with a male inmate. Nonetheless, many males show the exact same character structure as the one described for Krystel. And to be quite clear, this does not have to be an 'effeminate' male, either. The director can construct a very different scenario – the main thing to retain is an extreme emotional volatility. It should be like negotiating with a violent toddler. Happy one minute, tearing up the room, people near him and even himself the next.

SCENARIO 13 – Checklist for After Action Review

The after action assessment/critique will depend on what was expressed and expected of the team going into the exercise. In other words, what was the desired training goal or outcome? Not just the outcome of the scenario, but what are the skills the director (team leader) is hoping to see exercised by the team, as these scenario/situations develop?

Develop floor plan?
- ❏ Did not meet goal
- ❏ Partially met goal
- ❏ Fully met goal

Demonstrate good listening skills?
- ❏ Did not meet goal
- ❏ Partially met goal
- ❏ Fully met goal

Develop transition plan to switch out negotiators?
- ❏ Did not meet goal
- ❏ Partially met goal
- ❏ Fully met goal

Transition successfully?
- ❏ Did not meet goal
- ❏ Partially met goal
- ❏ Fully met goal

Utilized psych consult?
- ❏ Did not meet goal
- ❏ Partially met goal
- ❏ Fully met goal

SCENARIO 14

Agoraphobia (Fear of Open Spaces and Social Interaction)

14 – Incident

Inmate barricaded in cell, threatening to kill himself.

Inmate has history of multiple cell-extractions due to his refusing to leave his cell. In such situations, he is usually combative enough to be placed in segregation, at which point he calms down. Psych has diagnosed him with agoraphobia (an abnormal fear of being in crowds, public places, or open areas, accompanied by anxiety attacks). In other words, he *prefers* segregation. This comes and goes – there are periods of time that he functions adequately, but on other occasions, he melts down.

This time, however, he secured a weapon. He's stabbed himself once in the throat, but fearful, twisted his head, and only managed a severe laceration at the side of his neck. He's currently got the shank point first over his head, with two hands planted on the butt of the weapon. "If you make me leave, if you try to come through that door, I will punch a hole right through my heart."

14 – Character of Dov Kastner – Background Information

Dov is the third son of a modern Orthodox Jewish family. What this means is they keep fairly strict rituals regarding diet and expected ethical behavior, yet also accept modern life. Dov's mom works outside the home, and they are familiar with and accepting of American culture.

As is typical of Orthodox Jewish families, school and learning is a huge priority. Dov's father is a graduate of MIT and his mother from Brandeis University with a degree in evolutionary psychology. Dov's two younger brothers are National Merit Scholars, one going to Princeton and the other to Caltech.

Dov, too, is quite bright. In fact, he is too bright for his own good. A Harvard University graduate, he became an attorney, specializing in equity – finding the best interpretation of conflicting legal opinions. He is incarcerated for two things: a) a number of financial crimes, skimming off money in very complicated and contentious probate cases; and then, in the course of the investigation, b) a murder – he killed one individual who had discovered what he was doing with his grandmother's money. The victim was bedridden and Kastner had introduced calcium gluconate into his IV, which caused a heart attack.

He did not manifest agoraphobia before he was imprisoned. It developed gradually, starting with anxiety to fear of the chaotic energy on the yard or in the dining hall, to a full blown disorder.

Despite his agoraphobia and the rarity of a practicing Jewish inmate, Kastner has no trouble with the other prisoners. In fact, the shot callers of the various prison gangs have an agreement that "no one touches our Jew," because he's carved out a role everyone values: jailhouse lawyer. He's gotten a number of inmates released over the years.

If someone wants his help, he meets them in the library and members of that inmate's gang guard the area so that Dov is isolated, the way he wants to be. He can handle the level of anxiety he has in small groups or meetings – it is crowds and open spaces that cause him to melt down. Inmates who are not 'cliqued up' pay one or another gang to get the privacy Dov needs for him to be willing to work for him.

14 – Notes for the Role Player

Dov was in therapy for many years as a youth – he used to have a school phobia and other anxiety symptoms when he was young. However, with a strong will, a lot of therapy, and some accommodation on the part of both his schools and employers, he was able to be successful. He is familiar with all the verbal tactics a negotiator might use, such as active listening, paraphrasing and reframing. He is arrogant, and he knows he is smarter than most of the people around. This is going to make things difficult for the negotiator, because Dov will know things about communication techniques better than you. [NOTE to Director: pick someone for this role who either knows — or can be educated — in standard negotiation tactics. This is one scenario where you DO want the role-player to 'second-guess' the negotiator].

In addition to agoraphobia, he's also obsessive-compulsive. Because of his obsessive nature, he will nit-pick everything the negotiator says. He will be patronizing, and a step ahead.

A difficult role-play – ethnic, cultural and philosophical issues

There is no doubt this will be a difficult role to play. You will need someone who is well read. This role-play, of course, does NOT have to play Orthodox Jewish. It will do just as well if the role player is familiar with another culture. Just rewrite the script anyway you like, depending on what you/the role player knows – but from a culture such as East Asian (Chinese/Japanese/Korean-American, African-American of Caribbean descent where education is of paramount importance)—whatever the role players can play well. The 'trap' for the negotiator will be he or she must not try to 'prove' he or she understands this man's world.

Whatever culture you decide, if not Orthodox Jewish, we want someone from an insular culture, who is hesitant about talking about what is 'inside' the culture.

---

14 – The Scene: Face-to-Face or On the Phone?

The team leader can organize this exercise in a variety of ways.

1. The entire exercise could be through throw-phone or speaker, in certain settings.
2. The officer/negotiator attempts to speak with Dov either in line of sight, or around a corner. In this case, Dov must NOT make any overtly threatening gestures to the officer, unless you wish to change the scenario to ERT taking him down. Dov will state the following right at the beginning: "I know you are thinking of using OC to get this knife away. I can still stab myself in the heart while I'm choking on that shit."

Don't push the Issue! (AKA "We killed him to save him")

There have been a number of incidents where officers attempt to assist a suicidal individual, who tells them to keep back. Sometimes they are frightened and other times they are defiant. The officer(s) sometimes push the issue, moving forward rather than back, and when the suicidal individual makes what appears to be (or actually is) a threatening gesture, they must be neutralized, by whatever level of violence this takes, given immediate threat. This exercise can be used to drive home the necessity, at times, of tactical withdrawal. The team-leader can set things up in such a way that, unless there is a reason for a hard lesson to be learned, another member of the team can, when necessary, yell, 'Pull back! We'll talk to him on the phone!' or "Pull back. We don't need to be so close when we talk to this guy! We can hear just fine over here."

---

14 – Cultural Consult

Remember:

- Cultural value driven violence (suicide or homicide) exists. Different cultures have different cultural sanctions for violence and if officers are going to interact with people from those cultures, they need to be educated.
- Due to concerns that allegations of bigotry are often leveled in such cases, the subject of culturally sanctioned violence is avoided. This is a foolish, head-in-the-sand approach. Facts are not prejudice and each and every culture on earth develops a worldview regarding what is worth living for and what is worth dying for.

Therefore, a valuable part of this exercise would be to consult with an expert on the cultural context here. There are two ways to do this:

1. Before the scenario, line up an expert, and simply call him or her, as if it's real, and get educated.
2. Do this cold. Start calling local universities, cultural organizations and do your collateral interviews in real time. Be prepared for defensiveness, argumentation, or genuine concern.

Effective Cultural Consultation

The information you are looking for from the consultant would be:
- Is there information about the culture of the individual that may aid you in getting them to surrender, not harm hostages, and not assault officers?
- What kind of things are likely, from the particular culture, to offend the individual? What are likely to establish more rapport?

---

14 – Psychological Consult

This man is a therapy veteran. He is familiar with paraphrasing and active listening, so you will have to be sparing when you use it. Rather, you try to establish a dialogue. Certainly try to have him come out, but be prepared for Dov to reject this and expect a long conversation, building rapport simply through dialogue.

As for communication, don't pretend his nit-picking doesn't exist. Approach it with good humor, but don't tease him. He will take jokes as an assault. These obsessions and detail orientation are deadly serious to him. This is the kind of person who will become enraged if an item on his desk is a ¼ inch out of place.

The negotiator should empathize how difficult it must be to have to be so concerned with details.

Do not attempt to 'build up his self-esteem' by praising his work with other inmates or his obvious Intelligence --he'll regard you with contempt. You will have to figure out with him a reason to surrender. It will have to be framed as a problem-solving exercise to be mutually figured out.

SECOND LEVEL CONSULT: AGORAPHOBIA

If the discussion goes to his agoraphobia, as it surely will, the negotiator needs to understand that this is far more than 'fear of open spaces' or 'pathological shyness' or 'social awkwardness.' He gets powerful, irrational, even overwhelming fear and anxiety. Consider if there is a 'reasonable accommodation' for this man, where he can exist without being forced into what is for him a hellish situation.

THIRD LEVEL CONSULT: THE SURRENDER

The negotiator's task is to make a VERY detailed surrender plan with him, and collaborate on the details. Be meticulous, but clear. You should both announce each step together, going over them in a checklist fashion. (And note that Dov may give you suggestions on how to 'improve' your plan. Don't get offended or patronize him—if it's a good idea, accept it. If it's not a good idea, calmly reject it, succinctly explain why and direct what you will be doing instead).

SCENARIO 14 – Checklist for After Action Review

The after action assessment/critique will depend on what was expressed and expected of the team going into the exercise. In other words, what was the desired training goal or outcome? Not just the outcome of the scenario, but what are the skills the director (team leader) is hoping to see exercised by the team, as these scenario/situations develop?

Floor plan developed?
- ❏ Did not meet goal
- ❏ Partially met goal
- ❏ Fully met goal

Demonstrate good listening skills?
- ❏ Did not meet goal
- ❏ Partially met goal
- ❏ Fully met goal

Call in/request psych consult and follow its recommendations?
- ❏ Did not meet goal
- ❏ Partially met goal
- ❏ Fully met goal

Did negotiator work out a satisfactory surrender plan?
- ❏ Did not meet goal
- ❏ Partially met goal
- ❏ Fully met goal

SCENARIO 15

Divorce & Visitation Conflict:
Histrionic Personality in Mother vs.
Trapped Desperation/Depression in Father

Double Scenario   This can be played at the same time as two scenarios, particularly if you have a large team to train. This way, there will be fewer negotiators just standing around watching. If you have officers who are waiting to become negotiators and you want to give them some experience practicing with the team, this would be a good exercise to use.

15 – Original

Cassandra Avery, the estranged wife of one of your officers, whom she refers to as Arnie, telephones, demands to speak to the supervisor of the officer. She is explicit enough in her complaints about the officer and very clear that she needs to speak to the officer's supervisor that Main Control directs the call directly to them. "She talks over me. She's all over the place!" says the woman at Main Control.

Ms. Avery claims to the supervisor that her husband beat her up. He was handing over their children, four year old twins, after his court-mandated visit, and during the handover, she says, he punched her and knocked her down in front of the children. She says that he has a history of domestic violence against her, and manipulation of the children. The courts awarded her primary custody and he has been allowed unsupervised visitation two weekends a month and alternate Wednesdays and Thursdays. The supervisor tries to manage the call, but Ms. Avery is so upset, so intense, that he flags down one of the HNT-trained officers to take over the call. "She's in total meltdown. I can't get her under control to figure out what's going on."

15 – Directions for the Role Player of Cassandra and Training Goals for Negotiator

Ms. Avery will claim, first to the supervisor and then to the negotiator, to be in fear of her life. She will be distraught, accusatory and will bring in all sorts of extraneous information. She's going to use the officer's first name, Arnie, and not the last. She will talk about her conflicts with the officer, and react to your questions defensively, as if you are accusing her of something. For example, the negotiator will certainly try get information on whether she reported this assault to law enforcement, or whether he has ever harmed or threatened to harm the kids, and her response will be such things as "Why are you blaming the victim? "Are you saying you don't believe me?" "You are on his side, aren't you?" If it is a female HNT, "Are you having an affair with my husband? Is that what's going on?" After fifteen minutes, you will know little more the accusation of the assault, and a lot of criticism of your job, your role in oppressing and victimizing inmates, how Arnie is. You will have heard a LOT about the conflicts between Cassandra and Arnie, the father. You will not know what his intentions are, what really happened, if there were any witnesses, if this has happened before and been adjudicated or brought to the police. She is so intense and difficult you contact one of the onsite counselors to listen in on the call and give you a psychological consult.

15 – Psychological Consultation Regarding Mother

Your psych consult is present and listens to the contact with the mother. S/he states the mother displays traits known as 'histrionic personality;' in the vernacular, often called a 'drama queen.' <u>Whatever she feels in the moment, she needs the world to know about—and respond in a way that she finds rewarding.</u> Such individuals 'talk in headlines'—it is very difficult to get them to talk specifically. For example, you ask, "What was your dad like?" And they reply, "Oh wow, he was, I don't know, a fuckin' explosion, I mean impact! Walk in a room and wow!"

Furthermore, they get 'energy' from the drama; they often forget the real crisis, as they become preoccupied with their own feelings. There are several tactics that might help with this person. You will have to try each of them, in turn:

1. If you can set up a communication style where you are a warm paternal or maternal figure, such people can sometimes desire to please you more than create drama.
2. Paraphrase in a way that you get increasingly specific, where she has to fill in the blank: For example:
   - You are really desperate. You are really desperate because you are telling me that you are afraid your husband is going to . . . .
   - You are telling me that you are really desperate because you are afraid your husband is going to do something terrible . . . after work today.
   - You don't know what he's going to do. You are telling me he's done bad things in the past. Tell me what bad things has he done to the kids in the past.
   - ETC.
3. Speak very firmly (not loudly or stridently), telling her how important it is that you get detailed information.

If you try to guilt-trip her, criticize her or express frustration, she will respond with more drama.

15 – Contact with Subject

Second part of this exercise:
Officer Avery has just returned from prisoner transport. <u>The negotiators will have heard his name is Arnie when informed about the wife's call.</u>

He is called on the phone, but when he hears the subject matter, he says, quietly, "That's more than enough. Not at work. That's it. I'm done." And he hangs up the phone. After no response to repeated calls, an officer is sent to tell him to appear at the lieutenant's office. When he arrives at the room, he sees Avery sitting quietly with his hands on his desk, unmoving. The officer calls his name and Avery slowly looks up at him, smiles sadly and opening his desk drawer, takes out his duty weapon, previously checked out for prisoner transport and not returned. He points it at the officer and says, "Go away now. And close the door behind you." The officer backs away and as he leaves, following instructions, he sees Officer Avery put the gun to his head.

HNT makes contact through the phone. After repeated calls, Avery picks up. He says, still quiet, "There's nothing to talk about. She said she'd do this – ruin me at work. And that if I didn't give up custody, the kids would say that I did them."

15 – Interview with Direct Supervisor

She will state, "Officer Avery has always been a good officer. The inmates do not push his buttons, and he never throws his authority around. He came in and told me that his marriage was on the rocks, and that his wife had punched him on several occasions, and dared him to hit her. But that he never did."

15 – Info for Role-Player

Avery is going to be leaden. He sees no hope in negotiating. He will not be aggressive towards HNT, but he says he will shoot anyone who comes into the room and tries to interrupt before he's ready to shoot himself. This is going to be a slow negotiation process, with a lot of "I don't know", "What's the point," "No one cares," No one listens to me," "So that's the way you see it?" Avery will laugh cynically at things.

He is going to give very little. He makes no overt movement to threaten any staff, unless this is a joint ERT exercise. The role player should not make any threatening move, even if this is the training plan, until considerable time negotiating has passed – there's a lot of work to be done before.

15 – Further direction for Role-Player

Tone of voice should be flat and hopeless. However, when officer calls you Arnie, <u>you should blow up</u>. "Fuck you! My name is Ernie. SHE calls me Arnie, the fucking bitch! It's not my fucking name!" Role player should slam the phone. Make HNT work to regain contact. If the officer makes the mistake again, later in negotiation, escalate dangerously. Were the negotiator to make the mistake <u>three times</u>, the role-player should start howling and shoot himself.

If the name mistake is not repeated, this negotiation should be tedious, slow and frustrating – it drags on, goes nowhere. All of your suggestions are shut down. It is as if Officer Avery tolerates talking with HNT, just waiting to get up enough energy to pull the trigger and blow out his brains.

15 – #2 – Further Info

Secondary negotiation/crisis stabilization training can be done with mom. She will appear at the prison gate, hysterical towards a second negotiator, or in a second phone call, whichever the director believes will be a more productive exercise for your team. She will also be demanding, accusatory ("You don't care about my safety or my kids. You know what – I suspect he's been raping my sons!"). She will stabilize somewhat with one of the strategies suggested by your consultant, but you must use them all to find what works.

15 – Contact with Ernie's Mother

Ernie's mom is contacted. Another negotiator can do an interview with her. She has several documents. (She can read the information below). The officer should take notes and carry this to the team.

1. First is a psych evaluation, in which mother is diagnosed as histrionic personality. The evaluator cites the mother as having engaged in 'abusive use of conflict' to alienate the children from the father, and furthermore, states she is an incompetent mother, who is easily overwhelmed. The psychologist states that the children are clearly stressed in the mother's presence. He writes that Ernie is a passive guy, not very talkative, whom the children love. He notes dad does not get down on the floor and play with the boys, and reads to them in a monotone. He states that the children are less stressed with dad, but they "don't do very much." They sometimes simply lean against him, while he sits quietly with his arms around them.

The psychologist ends his report with a small personal "opinion essay," in which he notes that children are resilient, and that in his opinion, a passive inexpressive parent is just as bad as an aggressive, untrustworthy, manipulative one. He states he sees no problems with the father, except he doesn't have a 'playful personality.' He concludes that there is a special bond between mothers and children, even when the mother is incompetent or psychologically 'less than optimum,' and this should be broken only in the most serious of circumstances. Therefore, he recommends that the children be placed with the mother.

2. The judge writes an opinion essentially accepting what the psychologist says, and awards primary custody to the mother.

3. The next is a police report. It describes a visitation 'hand-off' where mom confronted dad, questioning his sexual competence in front of the children. He tried to get the kids in the car, and she began repeatedly poking him in the forehead with an index finger. He asked her to stop several times, and she replied he should appreciate being poked, because that's about all he was ever able to do to her. She said she and her new boyfriend liked to lie in bed after sex and laugh about 'Arnie's lack of endowment and inability to satisfy her. He pleaded with her to stop talking like that in front of the children. When she poked him again (officer noted a red spot between his eyes, with small scratches), he shoved her away. She fell over, and from the ground, whipped out a cell phone and called 9-1-1. Father was arrested, and charged with domestic violence. Charges were later dropped.

4. A final document is a follow-up hearing, in which the judge notes the 'set-up' in the police report. Mother denies the actions in the police report and states the officers, being men, sided with 'Arnie.' In her account, she describes 'Arnie' sneering at her, and calling her an incompetent mother, and when she pleaded with him to stop for the sake of the children, he shoved her to the ground. The judge writes her account is not believable, but states it "does not rise to the level in which a change in the parenting plan should be considered." Furthermore, the judge decrees that, just to err on the side of caution, "even though there is no evidence of any domestic violence," Ernie is required to undertake a domestic violence evaluation at his own expense. This last document is dated one week previous to the current incident.

The Story Changes: Shifting Gears in the Middle of a Negotiation

What tack should the negotiator take to get Avery to surrender? Should you continue with the same negotiator, who has gotten nowhere fast? One possible option would be for the first negotiator to state: "Ernie, we've got some information from your mom. This changes things." Perhaps that negotiator will continue, or perhaps it would be a good time to have a new negotiator on the phone, to 'start afresh.'

Depending on the decision of the director, based on preferred training needs, one could program this to:

1. A surrender of Officer Avery.
2. An escalation: a) he kills himself in the room; b) changing his mind at the point of surrender; c) suicide by cop necessitating ERT to neutralize the threat he presents.

It is a powerful training exercise to lose someone who you honestly believe is a good guy, is being done wrong, who is in the right – particularly if they are family. This can be tough, even in role play, so be sure to debrief this one well, if that's the way it goes.

But better to be prepared now, rather than face it for the first time in reality.

SCENARIO 15 – Checklist for After Action Review

The after action assessment/critique will depend on what was expressed and expected of the team going into the exercise. In other words, what was the desired training goal or outcome? Not just the outcome of the scenario, but what are the skills the director (team leader) is hoping to see exercised by the team, as these scenario/situations develop?

Tactical plan developed?
- ❏ Did not meet goal
- ❏ Partially met goal
- ❏ Fully met goal

Demonstrate good listening skills?
- ❏ Did not meet goal
- ❏ Partially met goal
- ❏ Fully met goal

Calmed the mother enough to get clear information from her, or at least that you clearly understood what she is accusing Avery of?
- ❏ Did not meet goal
- ❏ Partially met goal
- ❏ Fully met goal

Requested/discussed using psych consult?
- ❏ Did not meet goal
- ❏ Partially met goal
- ❏ Fully met goal

Intel worked to locate/contact key players?
- ❏ Did not meet goal
- ❏ Partially met goal
- ❏ Fully met goal

Successfully 'shifted gears' with Avery when you got new data from collaterals?
- ❏ Did not meet goal
- ❏ Partially met goal
- ❏ Fully met goal

SCENARIO 16

Cognitively-Impaired Volatile
Hostage Takers

16 – On-View Incident
Assault on officer in kitchen. Camera shows officer down, several inmate hostages. ERT has contained the scene, have suspects and hostages inside, and have called for HNT.

16 – The Incident
Stefan and Martez are two Inmate Kitchen Workers, who do clean-up in the kitchen. They've been making *pruno* for some time, selling it to other inmates. Today, they decided to drink the whole batch. They staggered out of the storeroom intoxicated and ran into a correctional officer, who is small, burned out, and near the end of his career. He starts yelling at the two men, who are both immense and developmentally delayed. Stefan grabs a can of peaches and hits the officer in the head stunning him. He staggers sideways, to be caught by Martez, who simply bear-hugs him, picks him up and drops all 420 pounds on top of him, breaking three ribs. Martez rolls off and lays on his back like a beached whale, but as the officer reaches for his mic, Stefan punches him multiple times in the face, breaking the orbital bones around both eye sockets.

The two men arm themselves – Martez with cans of fruit in each hand, turning his arms into sledgehammers, and Stefan with a kitchen knife. They block and barricade the doors with refrigerators and metal prep tables. There are three other inmates who want no part of this situation, but Martez slugs each of them once and knocks them half-unconscious into a corner, next to the unconscious officer.

16 – The Setting
Communication will be by phone. Martez will start out on the phone, although Stefan may, on occasion, rip it out of his hands to yell obscenities and threats.

The inmate hostages will be pissed off. They should be yelling obscenities in the background at the hostage takers, also trying to yell at HNT through the phone that "This CO isn't doing good. You better get this thing finished." This will stress the hostage takers, who frequently break contact on the phone to yell back at the hostages, and threatening more violence – "I'll hit you again!" "Shut the fuck up. You want me to step on your head?" "Fuck you!!!!"

The hostage takers will be mild-to-moderately drunk, stupid and panicked.

The hostage takers are not going to come up with very rational demands. Not to say that they won't come up with something, however, outlandish.

16 – Interview with Case Manager

The case manager will be a character. She will be salty, irreverent, and a little funny. According to her, Stefan loves his mother, and Martez, who met her during a visitation, is "like a stray puppy, if puppies ever were the size of baby elephants." Of the two of them, she says, "What can I tell you? They don't mean any harm. Think of the Three Stooges drunk on pruno armed with lethal weapons."

She states that both men are childlike, with IQ about 65 – 70, at the mildly developmentally disabled range. "They are 'brothers from another mother.' They fight each other, all the time, but they stand back-to-back against the world. They don't really mean any harm, but they are a two-man wrecking crew."

The case manager states that she usually has pretty good rapport with the two of them. I'm about the same age as Stefan's mother – actually he said to me, and I quote, "You remind me of my fuckin' mom, except you swear a lot more."

16 – Possible Training on TPI

One possible avenue of training is to use the case manager in controlled negotiation. As the reader is well aware, this is, <u>almost always</u> NOT a good idea, but here we have a case of a prison staff member, who may have rapport. If she is closely monitored and prepped, could she be used in this manner? Most teams NEVER allow such collateral contact—therefore, do not abandon your protocol. Only use this segment if it is part of the protocol of your team. The idea here would be to use it as a practice, in case it is ever deemed the best idea.

This is a good exercise for a team leader to test the decision-making skills and assessment abilities of the team. This can be set up so not only does the case manager make the offer, but Stefan and Martez also make the same demand. As in:

"Hey, hey, I wanna talk to my case manager!!!!!"

"Yeah, me too!!"

"Fuckin' A – let us talk to Mrs. Kowal . . ."

"Ya dumb fuck. Kowalewski"

"Fuck you, I aint dumb, her name is dumb."

What does the team do? Do they agree without much thought or investigation? If so, bring the case manager on…. and then, whoops, she lights up Stefan and Martez and bad things happen. (NOTE: this could be built in the scenario if the director chooses).

However, if the team explores as an option, it might allow them to practice for a potential TPI. Do they thoroughly interview the case manager, to determine if she is stable and can be controlled, or is she the kind of person who thinks she knows best? Do they have equipment with a 'kill switch' on her mic, if necessary? Or, maybe the team wishes to practice the method of having the case manager make a recorded statement to be played to Stefan and Martez, something that could be played in a straightforward manner, or the role player could make it really challenging. All of these are valuable training options.

For the sake of TPI practice:
- Do not be casual about this. One should go through the entire preparation of the subject, coaching, rehearsal, and putting her on the phone.
- Let us imagine, on the other hand, that ERT is fully deployed and ready to go. The case manager will say something 'accidentally,' that sets off the hostage takers. ERT will not be cued as to this. The hostage takers will suddenly go berserk, and all things done properly, ERT should immediately enter to neutralize them.

On the Use of TPI

The writers are well aware how badly a TPI call can go, and how rare that this is a viable option. However, it is very common that the public believes it is a good idea, and it frequently comes up in court. Although unlikely, imagine if a prison staff member, at odds with the administration and perhaps with very poor boundaries regarding one or more inmates, makes such a public assertion. One good training exercises for the team is to consider and prepare for TPI in good faith, so that your agency can assert honestly in court that you have the tools if/when it is ever a possibility—and can then assert that through that preparation, it was clearly established that it was NOT a good idea in this case.

In any event, it IS good practice for the team to discuss the pros and cons of using a TPI. Coming up with arguments as to WHY you chose to use a TPI would be important—especially if it goes sideways, and you end up having to defend your decision in court. Just as important, the decision of NOT using a TPI needs to be explored and documented. If the incident ends badly, and no TPI was used, when possibilities were presented, it will most definitely come up in court as to WHY the team chose NOT to use one.

It also would be a good lead-in for ERT to get practice on entry/taking out the hostage takers and rescuing the hostages.

---

16 – Psychological Consult

Whenever negotiating with intoxicated subjects, time is of the essence—MORE time. As the drugs are purged from the system, the individual often becomes more rational: in other cases, they get tired. One avenue of negotiation that opens up is the fact that the negotiator can become the agent of relief. If the hostage taker complies, they have a chance of sleep, food or an end to stress.

Crucial will be calming and reassuring tactics, because, in their panic, with the hostages FREQUENTLY losing it, the hostage takers may be moved to beat someone into submission or cut someone's throat just for a little peace and quiet.

Therefore the negotiator will be pressured to calm them down, and with the team, may brainstorm *with them* ways to calm down the hostages as well. One idea will be to suggest to the hostage takers that with the hostages released, they can have peace and quiet.

These guys are not bright, but they surely have some street cunning. The negotiator should, of course, be trying to get various hostages out, first and foremost the injured officer.

1. The negotiator may say, "You have the power here. And we'll definitely figure out a way to work this thing out. But if the officer dies, everything changes. Anyway, you didn't intend for it to happen, so if you just move him to the doorway, we can take him away, and calm things down for all of us. [*NOTE to role players: You initial responses should be stupid, such as "Ah, he's all right. Fuck him anyway." Make HNT work for rationality.*]

2. If they offer to release another hostage, of course accept them.

3. Return, however, to the injured officer. With these guys, making a deal for pizzas or other food is likely to be the way to go.

4. I would suggest keeping them bonded, rather than a divide-and-conquer strategy. If these two stupid, impulse ridden guys get arguing, one of them may hurt a hostage to take control over from the other. Rather, emphasize how they are brothers, and they'll get out of this together. They've got each other's back, and they'll be able to work this out later in the disciplinary hearing. Put it this way – "Stefan, tell Martez it'll look much better at the hearing if you let the officer go. Seriously, you guys made a bad mistake, no doubt. But you can make it right now."

SCENARIO 16 – Checklist for After Action Review

The after action assessment/critique will depend on what was expressed and expected of the team going into the exercise. In other words, what was the desired training goal or outcome? Not just the outcome of the scenario, but what are the skills the director (team leader) is hoping to see exercised by the team, as these scenario/situations develop?

Floor plan developed? From whom did you get the information?
- ❑ Did not meet goal
- ❑ Partially met goal
- ❑ Fully met goal

Demonstrate good listening skills?
- ❑ Did not meet goal
- ❑ Partially met goal
- ❑ Fully met goal

Do negotiators change tactics—and emotions—because a correctional officer is involved? In other words, did the negotiator respond to the pressure of trying to release one's own?
- ❑ Did not meet goal
- ❑ Partially met goal
- ❑ Fully met goal

Discussion/decision regarding use of TPI?
- ❑ Did not meet goal
- ❑ Partially met goal
- ❑ Fully met goal

Do negotiators successfully bid for release of hostages?
- ❑ Did not meet goal
- ❑ Partially met goal
- ❑ Fully met goal

SCENARIO 17

Rape Victim Potential Perpetrator

17 – Alert at the Correctional Facility

Hostage taking in the education office, situation in lockdown. Subject barricaded with 3 hostages. Requesting immediate ERT and HNT response

17 – The Incident

This information would be a combination of information known to ERT, and a report to ERT by a correctional officer or case manager.

Inmate Cliff Powell went into an office and found his teacher and two support staff, all female personnel, alone. He slammed the door, locked and barricaded it, and pulled a blade.

There is only a single fence beyond this office, and the work camp is in a wilderness area, about ten miles from any town or residential area. There is only a single road, and the forest around the camp is a wetlands area, very soggy, and full of downed trees and brush. There are few escape attempts, because the inmates are almost all short-timers or those with minor felonies who, if they do their time, will soon be released. In any event, of the few who have tried, no one has successfully escaped; everyone gets bogged down in the wetlands.

At this point, it is unknown if Cliff intended an escape attempt. He did open the window on the second story nearest to the fence, and this is how he was spotted. Upon the correctional officer's yell, he pulled back into the room.

His first move was to pull the phone out of the wall-jack, so communication is initially difficult. At this time, he has three hostages, and no exit.

Is this is an escape, a sexual assault attempt, both or something else?

17 – Background – Institutional Record Review

Cliff Powell has nine months left on eight-year sentence for felonious assault. Therefore, it is very odd he'd do something like this so close to release.

He is twenty-eight years old. He spent considerable time in detention as an adolescent, and according to his file, was diagnosed with ADHD and other unnamed impulse control disorders.

His current conviction was the result of a fight. Cliff had been taking Ecstasy on a daily basis, and became physiologically insensitive to the drug. He thought he was cheated, therefore, when the two hits he took didn't get him high. He went into the bar's restroom—the dealers 'office'—and jumped him from behind, ramming his head onto the lip of a toilet bowl, fracturing his skull.

Cliff has not gotten into serious trouble in detention. In earlier years at other institutions, he got into altercations with other inmates on two occasions. Once, he assumed the other inmate was not going to eat his dessert and he just took it, receiving a beating for the trespass. On the other occasion, an inmate objected to his standing next to his bunk—violating rules of personal space and territory. Cliff won this fight, but did a period of time in administrative segregation.

He has been in a minimum-security work camp for approximately one year, taking classes to get his GED.

17 – Further Record Review
Review of his records shows he has an adolescent history of sexual offences. He and two friends, imitating a nasty fad from Japan called 'sharking,' would videotape each other as one of them would walk up to a woman and either rip her blouse open, or yank her skirt down, and then run away. They posted these on the Internet, which is how they were caught.

17 – Interview with Trustee, who was an assistant in the GED class
A trustee inmate notes Cliff occasionally made slightly 'flirtatious' jokes. The teacher set limits pretty well, to which Cliff would respond, "just kidding," or "I didn't say nothing."

17 – Interview with Case Manager
Cliff's case manager notes he was really anxious about "getting back in the world. He'd say, 'I don't know nothing, don't know how to do nothing.'"

The case manager also notes that Cliff was raped in his initial incarceration, and was the 'wife'—sex slave—of one of the dominant inmates of that facility. He states Cliff seems to be unsure about his masculinity. "He doesn't open up much, but there was one meeting when he asked, 'Can you be turned into a gay? I mean, you start out liking girls, but how about if something happens and then you are a gay? I mean, how would you know? You don't have no way to test things out. And the admin here, they won't even let you have skin mags. So how do you know?"

17 – Directions for the Role Player
Cliff is going to be somewhat goofy—like a class clown. He will mess around, crack jokes, and it will be hard to get him to focus. A negotiator may be tempted to just tell him to open the damn door and let the ladies out. "You did something stupid, you'll get some time tacked on, but it's no big deal."

Cliff won't bite. In fact, he won't even engage with this.

He will threaten to cut the women just to warn the negotiator not to send in an ERT team.

During the initial contact, if the negotiator is male, *and* is warm, soft-spoken, or 'supportive,' Cliff is going to be extremely aggressive, accusing the negotiator of being a 'fag.' He will become increasingly hostile about this.

17 – Psychological Consult

The consultant suggests they don't know his motive, and the best way to find out is to keep listening, paraphrasing, and subtly keep trying to direct the conversation so he talks about himself.

The initial task of the negotiator here is to be patient. The negotiator will be thinking, "What's the point of all this. He's just messing around."

The negotiator has to hang in there, and just keep him talking.

The consultant is concerned this may possibly be for the purpose of a sexual assault so Cliff can prove to himself he's still a 'man' and not 'a gay.' The danger they face is, of course, they will be trying to negotiate the hostages out, which is often a one-by-one process. However, Cliff may draw this out, in order to make the negotiator(s) think they are making progress, and when he has one left—given his previous flirtation, probably the teacher—he very possibly will sexually assault her.

Caution ONE: If Cliff reveals his fears about being homosexual (which he might, although denying it, actually be) and the negotiator is too quick to reassure him, this reassurance will sound hollow and he will escalate. Therefore, continue to be low-key, rather than *overtly* reassuring.

Caution TWO: Given Cliff's fears of being homosexual, and the fact he is resistive to the idea is not necessarily evidence he is not gay, he will be hair-trigger suspicious of other males. If the negotiator is too warm and reassuring, Cliff may either accuse him of being homosexual, or escalate, believing himself to being seduced. If this has resulted in an absolute impasse, consider shifting to a second negotiator. The best way to avoid this is for the interviewer to be a little formal, distant and matter-of-fact.

The negotiator should not reassure Cliff that it's "OK to be gay!" It's not OK to him. Rather, be non-committal in tone, and agree when he says he's not gay. If he alludes to the rape 'making him gay,' you can respond that, just because someone does something to you doesn't mean it 'makes' you anything. If he is resistive, you can reduce it to an absurdity such as the following: 'Dude, if somehow a twenty-foot alligator jumped on you, it doesn't mean you like alligators.'

17 – Scenario Outcome(s)

As time passes, you will be able to negotiate out one or two of the hostages through the usual, exchange of food or the like. In either event, the negotiator will be able to draw out, eventually, that Cliff IS afraid about his manhood. If the negotiator is calm, and doesn't get 'hooked' in over-reassuring him, he may eventually surrender.

On the other hand, if you wish ERT to get their training in as well, Cliff will get more and more sexually suggestive in his talk and begin signaling that a rape only takes a few minutes: "I mean, how long does it take a real man to get his nuts off, when he's not had his balls stolen by those feminists who tell him he has to think of their pleasure first?" As soon as the negotiator believes the scene is getting beyond his or her control, you should greenlight Tactical.

SCENARIO 17 – Checklist for After Action Review

The after action assessment/critique will depend on what was expressed and expected of the team going into the exercise. In other words, what was the desired training goal or outcome? Not just the outcome of the scenario, but what are the skills the director (team leader) is hoping to see exercised by the team, as these scenario/situations develop?

Floor plan developed?
- ❏ Did not meet goal
- ❏ Partially met goal
- ❏ Fully met goal

Demonstrate good listening skills?
- ❏ Did not meet goal
- ❏ Partially met goal
- ❏ Fully met goal

Demonstrate EXTREME patience is key?
- ❏ Did not meet goal
- ❏ Partially met goal
- ❏ Fully met goal

Recognition of possible issues that could involve the negotiator?
- ❏ Did not meet goal
- ❏ Partially met goal
- ❏ Fully met goal

Psych consult considered or discussed?
- ❏ Did not meet goal
- ❏ Partially met goal
- ❏ Fully met goal

Honest assessment provided to command post?
- ❏ Did not meet goal
- ❏ Partially met goal
- ❏ Fully met goal

SCENARIO 18

Stalker, Workplace Violence

18 – Original Call

Report of shots fired at meeting room with known victims. Suspect may have multiple firearms. There are additional hostages. Set this up so it is NOT an active shooter situation. They have set up containment, and requested ERT and HNT.

18 – The Incident: Escaped Witness Statements

At 8:40 A.M. this morning, Officer Boyd Morrison encountered his Sergeant, John Petrov, in the parking lot and shot him in the face. Petrov is dead. He then entered the facility, went to the meeting room, and shot Officer Setsuko Hamada in the shoulder, a relatively superficial wound. He has taken her as well as eight other officers hostage. He has the hostages all in the same room, Setsuko, among them.

Several officers escaped, something, apparently, that Morrison allowed.

Is Morrison's Murder of Petrov 'over the top?'

We have chosen to make Morrison kill his sergeant for several reasons:

1. There are innumerable examples of stalkers doing just that. They consider HR or an investigator to be the cause of their troubles, "of 'poisoning the mind' of their victim and turning him/her against me," or they want to make the victim of the stalking 'responsible' for the death of their co-worker.
2. We are trying to make a training scenario that teeters right on the edge (or perhaps goes over) into an active shooter situation.

The director can easily 'dial it back,' if so desired. For example, Morrison can confront, maybe strike Petrov, but doesn't kill him.

Boyd himself calls out immediately to the front desk on the phone. He says he wants to talk to a negotiator. He promises he will not harm anyone else, unless ERT or other police attempt entry.

This is necessary to forestall this simply being an active-shooter scenario. This could be by telephone, to establish communications immediately that way, or, if you wish to have ERT practice delivering a throw phone for example, have him begin telling one of the officers he allows to escape that he wants to speak to a negotiator.

18 – Interview with Escaped Hostages

Role-players should be real here. You can have the several hostages display different reactions: anger, fear, or incoherence. Each secondary interview should be a bit of a struggle, where the interviewer must de-escalate the hostage before being able to get reliable Intel on the nature of any barricade, condition of the hostages, etc.

18 – Interview with Human Resources (and Notes for Role-Player, so He Knows How to Play Boyd Morison)

HR had been working with Sergeant Petrov in an investigation of Officer Morrison, who had been placed on administrative leave several weeks ago. This was due to a complaint by Officer Hamada that Morrison was repeatedly asking her out, would make suggestive comments and on several occasions, isolated her, 'caging' her in a corner with his arms while he attempted to convince her that they were meant for each other. After the last time she rejected him, Morrison cursed her in an ugly, homophobic way. Subsequently, inmates began making suggestive obscene solicitations, asserting that they had been told she was 'doing' several officers and was game to try 'the other side.' She suspects, without proof, that Morrison was spreading such rumors to the inmates, to make her life miserable, if not dangerous. She made a formal complaint at that time, resulting in Morrison's suspension

According to HR, Morrison, age 46 has an unusual history. Born in Northern Ireland, he is a citizen of Great Britain, and has lived in America for 15 years, holding a Green Card.

As a teenager, he got into the hardcore street drug scene in Belfast. He never became an addict, however, and at age twenty-three, he entered a drug treatment program and stopped using drugs altogether. Ever since, he has been totally 'straight-edge.' He won't even smoke cigarettes or have a beer. He got certified as a drug-alcohol counselor in Belfast, moved to the United States, got recertified and got hired as a street-outreach case manager. From there, he became a correctional officer, a job he's held for nine years. He is considered a wonderworker with drug-involved inmates. He can get rapport with any drug addict, he is fearless, and with years of survival practice on the streets of one of the meanest cities in Europe, no inmate has successfully conned him. His fellow officers view him with a lot of respect. No one else says that they've observed the actions that Officer Hamada has complained about.

We've observed a problem, however. He's now got the emotional maturity, in some respects, of a man in his early twenties. The man is great with inmates, both in treatment groups and on the yard, but he is, per the women who work here, rather difficult. He is demanding, gets into passionate crushes towards various women, and then he gets possessive and jealous.

So then Boyd asked out Officer Hamada. She's a no-nonsense young woman who was, to say the least, not interested. She's legally married to another woman and they have a child together. She tried to let him down tactfully, but Boyd doesn't take 'no' for an answer.

Officer Hamada felt like people didn't believe her. She's rather guarded as a person, keeps to herself, and Morrison is one of the most popular officers we have – his Irish accent alone makes a lot of people like him. So she taped him to get evidence – this is a transcript:

MORRISON – "You won't go out with me? Why not? Is it because I'm Irish? Or you don't like guys. Yeah, I know you are married to a woman. That's the problem. You've never had a real man plow those virgin fields. I'm sure I could help you find the end of the rainbow."

HAMADA – "I told you I'm not interested. Back off. You are harassing me."

MORRISON – "Hey, look, let's not call it a date. Let's call it: 'You go out with me for coffee and we see if we want to hook up after I tell you about my crazy life.'"

HAMADA – "I'm committed to my wife. Leave me alone. I will report you."

MORRISON – "No? Setsuko, c'mon. Don't be like that. It's not like you'd be unfaithful. I'm a man; you are with a woman – that's different right. Whoa, whoa. O.K. I didn't know that was personal. I didn't know that was a sensitive topic. O.K. Look. Let me start over. Please? It's just—I never met anyone like you. You have such class. I just want a chance to know what I've missed after all the years I wasted. Setsuko, I'm telling you—maybe you'll think I'm a little fast here, but you could be the ONE . . . ."

HAMADA- I told you NO WAY! I'm going to talk to my supervisor if you don't quit calling. I am NOT interested. Leave me alone!

MORRISON – "What? What! Well, you tell me this. WHY won't you go out with me just one time?"

Boyd was asked in for a meeting, and the rules of workplace harassment were clearly explained. He was given a corrective action memo, and a warning. We told him if there were one more such incident, as highly as the agency regarded his work, he would be fired. Then Officer Hamada came in with this last complaint, and he was put on administrative leave, as I said.

18 – Note to Role-player
This situation is so dangerous it already borders at the 'active shooter' level.

The only thing that keeps ERT from entry is that you—Boyd—called them. You have got to keep talking. You will play him as a smart-ass, full of stories. You will mess with the negotiator, but must seem, in your own way, to be trying to work something out that will keep you from getting shot. <u>Follow the coach's direction as to whether, at a certain point, you will escalate (to trigger an ERT response), or if the negotiator finds something you are proud of, or think is worth living for, which would lead to your surrender.</u>

18 – Psych Consult

Boyd fits a rather standard profile of the obsessional stalker. He also appears to have strong narcissistic traits – in other words, he 'deserves' whatever he wants. He has never been in a real relationship with the main victim. He was aware, unlike a psychotic stalker, she was not interested in him. He was not, like a sociopath, doing this for the thrill.

Obsessional stalkers get locked in towards the victim like a 'heat seeking missile.' It is very difficult for them to conceive of 'another way of looking at things.'

You should understand, however, that at least in the initial stages, they are not stalking to torment or terrify the victim. In this situation, not being with the object of their attention causes an unacceptable level of anxiety in the stalker. The anxiety is experienced as so noxious that it is better, perhaps, to die, than not 'have' her. In addition, because the victim, by refusing him, is the direct cause of his distress, the stalker perceives himself to be the victim. Therefore, their anxiety and distress often mutates into rage and hatred.

The narcissistic piece also figures in here. In short, "How dare she refuse me! I am special. Refusing me is an insult, and she deserves to be punished for treating me with such disrespect."

The negotiator is going to have a tough time with this individual:

1. He is streetwise. Furthermore, he's one of you, and knows how things work. ERT will not intimidate him, and he will be knowledgeable about entry tactics.
2. He is a talker—interviews with staff who escaped as well other acquaintances, describe a fast talking, smart-ass, who likes to mess with authority.
3. He is committed. He's already murdered. What does he have to lose? It will be the task of the negotiator to engage him as long as it takes, to find what, if anything he cares about. Professional pride? His work? His integrity? The point is that the negotiator must connect him with the world of the living. <u>At this time, he's thinking apocalyptically—like Samson, in the Bible—bringing the world down around his ears.</u>
4. Because of the narcissism, he is going to love the sound of his own voice, going to love to be the center of attention. But if you call him out and make him look foolish, appear to question his Intelligence or in any way, seem to 'burst his bubble' (the fantasy of how special he is), he will respond with rage and everyone in his reach will be in danger.
5. It is also the task of the negotiator, as much as possible, to keep him from focusing his attention on Setsuko. If he does focus on her, he will very likely escalate, demanding either that she love him now, or that this is all her fault.

6. <u>One of the biggest questions you must ask is if he really has any demands</u>. Or is his intention to kill Setsuko and others on his way out of this life?

7. Be aware the negotiator may make no headway with him whatsoever. ERT should be ready to move in at any moment.

SCENARIO 18 – Checklist for After Action Review

The after action assessment/critique will depend on what was expressed and expected of the team going into the exercise. In other words, what was the desired training goal or outcome? Not just the outcome of the scenario, but what are the skills the director (team leader) is hoping to see exercised by the team, as these scenario/situations develop?

Floor plan developed quickly?
- ❏ Did not meet goal
- ❏ Partially met goal
- ❏ Fully met goal

De-escalate escaped hostages and develop good Intel?
- ❏ Did not meet goal
- ❏ Partially met goal
- ❏ Fully met goal

Demonstrate good listening skills?
- ❏ Did not meet goal
- ❏ Partially met goal
- ❏ Fully met goal

Kept him focused on communicating with negotiator, who made him feel truly heard? Kept his attention away from Setsuko?
- ❏ Did not meet goal
- ❏ Partially met goal
- ❏ Fully met goal

Negotiator effectively de-escalated subject by avoiding questioning hostage taker's special sense of himself?
- ❏ Did not meet goal
- ❏ Partially met goal
- ❏ Fully met goal

Psych consult recommended?
- ❏ Did not meet goal
- ❏ Partially met goal
- ❏ Fully met goal

Honest assessment with command post/scene command/tactical commander?

- ❏ Did not meet goal
- ❏ Partially met goal
- ❏ Fully met goal

SCENARIO 19

Dementia, Mercy Killing

19 – Original Call

Counselor being held hostage in an office. 2 inmate hostage takers, one armed with a sharp object.

19 – How it began

Jay Cohen is the most popular counselor on staff. He has a great perspective on what he can accomplish with inmates and what he can't, and is perceived as working in support of the correctional officers' responsibilities rather than at odds with them. But he's also known as a practical joker, so his call is not being taken seriously.

Cohen – (In a very calm voice, almost amused) "Al, you are not going to believe this, but I've been taken hostage by James Washington."

Sgt. Clifton – "Jay, I don't believe it. First of all, he's 66 years old. Second of all, he spends all his time with his cellie, who's 73, and can barely walk. Third of all, I don't have time for this today. Munoz cut his wrists and clogged the toilet and the whole hallway is a mess of blood and shit. So goodbye, Jay. You aren't getting me on this one." And hangs up the phone.

Cohen calls back. "Al"

Sgt. Clifton – "Seriously, Jay, not today . . ."

Cohen – "Sgt Clifton! Will you shut the fuck up and listen! It's not a joke. I'm paying for my sins, I get it, but this is not a joke. Washington came in my office, and Jamison is with him. He teetered in with his walker and Washington sat him down in the corner. I forgot to secure my door properly, and I'm locked in with those two. Washington's barricaded the door with everything in the office. And Washington may be 66, but he's still huge, and he moves quick. Remember, he knocked out those two mouthy little creeps a few years ago, when they kicked Jamison's walker out from under him. Anyway, beyond that, he's got a blade and here we are. Washington says I'm not allowed to talk anymore, so get HNT, OK?"

Information management—overlapping communication

This can be a good practice in managing information from several sources at the same time. People will not be belligerent, but they will talk over each other.

---

19 – Interview with Medical and Psychiatric Staff Together

Informant #1—Washington has <u>initial</u> stages of senile dementia—it's still mild, but he's become somewhat forgetful, and more emotional. He is 66 years old, but physically, he's still a very powerful man, in great shape. His cell mate, Jamison, has 3rd stage liver cancer, and is under medical treatment. Doctors are not sure at this time if the chemotherapy they are using will be able to alleviate the cancer. However, he is not near death. Jamison has always had a low pain tolerance, and he hates, more than anything, to be nauseated. He has three treatments to go, and the doctors say when they are completed, it will be 'wait and see.' They will continue to give him pain medication; it's monitored so he has to pick it up daily, one dose at a time. They also have several options they haven't tried yet, both for the cancer and for the pain and nausea. But Jamison acts like every twinge is like being skewered by a hot poker. And Washington can't stand that Jamison is in pain. He goes everywhere with him, and he's gotten in several shouting matches in the clinic, demanding that they stop the pain, that Jamison (really he) can't stand it."

Informant #2 – "You'd never believe it if you knew them back in the day. They are like an old married couple now, but those were once a couple of bad men. Jamison was a shooter, known to have killed seven people, maybe more, during the Irish-Italian mob wars back in the day. He was supposed to be a big deal here, a couple of decades ago. But then he got that head injury, and it was like he got a personality transplant: no, like a soul transplant. He turned into a nervous, whiney little guy. Always complaining. He attached himself to Washington, though, who was his protector.

And Washington! Like I say, a bad man. He was sure a neighbor was doing his wife, so he disemboweled him in the middle of the street, and made his wife hold him while he died—and the guy didn't do anything with his wife anyway.

Both of them are serving life – that's why they are still here at this age.

Informant #3 – That's the point. Jamison is his wife, now. Nah, I don't know if they ever were – you know – but it's the same. And this time, I bet Washington wants to make do right by his 'wife.' He tries to take care of him, protect him. He cannot stand it that Jamison's in pain and he can't do anything about it. Speaking as a psychiatrist, he is really afraid that Jamison is going to die, and he can't stand to face that. So he focuses on Jamison's discomfort and complaints."

19 – For the Role Players

<u>Both will be on the phone – this will go back and forth. If you really want to make things complicated for the negotiator, have two phone lines, so that they will, often, both be trying to talk at the same time. NOTE: Cohen will not be allowed to talk by Washington.</u>

Despite Washington's current dementia—he has become slightly cognitively impaired and gets confused—Jamison, with his illness, is even more dependent and complaining. In an almost cunning way, he has realized that the worse he makes things sound, the more Washington will do for him.

Throughout the scenario, Jamison will, at various times, complain of severe nausea and pain, and this will wind Washington up.

Washington is going to be emotionally up-and-down, sometimes tearful, and sometimes angry in a blustery 'old-man's.' way. To complicate things, he will show 'patchy dementia.' He will shift in-and-out of clear consciousness. This can be related, in part, to what food/water intake, to what memories are evoked, etc. He will lapse into reminisces of the past, something typical of folks with dementia; he will forget what he verbally agreed to fifteen minutes ago and deny to the negotiator that he had the discussion.

High-Register Tones/Voices and Old People

Be aware many elderly people have hearing loss, and usually the higher registers are the first to go. This can be a real problem if you are using female negotiators, who tend to have higher register voices (or a male with a high-pitched voice). In such a situation as this, if the subject IS having difficulty hearing, be ready to shift negotiators. (Perhaps you wish to offer a little 'in the field learning experience' to a negotiator who has a high-register voice who also happens to be a little too easily frustrated or irritated. Have the role player <NOT> hear or understand them. If the negotiator doesn't pick up on the hearing problem, he or she may get increasingly off-center. It then may be very productive to a) have a peer point out what might be the problem and see if they are able to hand over the lead, or if their ego keeps them in the chair b) transitioning to another lead negotiator and assessing how they handle it—first when they can't figure out why they are having a problem and second, after they understand).

---

19 – The Demand

Washington will demand Fentanyl patches – an unlimited supply – to help Jamison with his pain. The agenda for this could be one of two ways – either he really thinks that he can dole out the patches and stop the demands and complaints of his terribly-in-pain cellmate, or he intends to do a mercy killing. Due to his mild dementia, he'll get confused if you try to explain the rules of how prescriptions are dispensed, and dangers of the medication. All of this will frustrate him and make him angrier. He threatens to kill Cohen if his demands aren't met.

19 – Psychological Consult

This is going to be a challenging negotiation. In the beginning, you should be trying to establish rapport. Get Washington talking about something he likes. Get Jamison's mind off his pain, if you can. Take notes so you are aware of what areas are sensitive to either of them—particularly what angers Washington. Put them on big-lettered notes on the wall, because talking to a contentious elderly person can be like a minefield. If he starts talking later about one of those areas, steer him away as soon as you can.

Jamison will complain and whine about his pain, which will upset Washington more.

Due to his patchy dementia, he will forget what he agreed to. The negotiator's task will be to help him focus. Keep things simple.

Try to get Jamison on the phone. See if you can get him to stop complaining. Try to ascertain if he wants to die and that this is a mutual attempt at an 'assisted suicide.'

One real risk of this situation is Washington is likely to be very stuck on the subject of his shank, something he's used to kill with before. If you focus too much on the knife, he will probably get completely obsessed about it, and there is a real danger that, upon surrender, he will want to go out with his blade in his hands. You will have to figure out a way to get him to agree to leave without it.

SCENARIO 19 – Checklist for After Action Review

The after action assessment/critique will depend on what was expressed and expected of the team going into the exercise. In other words, what was the desired training goal or outcome? Not just the outcome of the scenario, but what are the skills the director (team leader) is hoping to see exercised by the team, as these scenario/situations develop?

Floor plan developed?
- ❏ Did not meet goal
- ❏ Partially met goal
- ❏ Fully met goal

Demonstrate good listening skills?
- ❏ Did not meet goal
- ❏ Partially met goal
- ❏ Fully met goal

How did the team deal with the memory loss issues?
- ❏ Did not meet goal
- ❏ Partially met goal
- ❏ Fully met goal

How did the team dealing with hearing loss issues, if they were part of the exercise?
- ❏ Did not meet goal
- ❏ Partially met goal
- ❏ Fully met goal

How did the team dealing with the possibility of being triangulated between Washington and Jamison?
- ❏ Did not meet goal
- ❏ Partially met goal
- ❏ Fully met goal

How did the team deal with the issue of the knife?
- ❏ Did not meet goal
- ❏ Partially met goal
- ❏ Fully met goal

SCENARIO 15 – Checklist for After Action Review

SCENARIO 20

Rape Victim, Possible Suicide-By-Cop

20 – Alert: Lockdown.

Barricaded inmate with a hostage in the kitchen admin office. Requesting immediate ERT and HNT response.

20 – The Incident

Amos is a skinny kid, with no affiliation to any group within the prison system. As far as the administration is concerned, he's been a relatively quiet inmate—no critical incidents since his admission, two years ago at age 21. He had one administrative segregation bid after a confrontation with an inmate, and did six months solitary.

The prison is medium security. Amos has a job in the kitchen.

Today, he grabbed a correctional officer, put a knife to his throat, pulled him into a room off the main kitchen, and began screaming, "If it all has to end, I'm not going alone." The hostage officer in question has health problems—heart problems, high blood pressure and mild emphysema.

> **Construct a scenario regarding security that enables Amos to be well barricaded with no easy access to him.**
>
> There is real concern that any use of pepper spray or CS will be profoundly dangerous to the corrections officer due to his health concerns. The scenario can be set up purely as a negotiation or to include extraction, as needed.

20 – Information to be Revealed Upon Record Check

Amos Bosworth is 24 years old. He is incarcerated for 18-25 years for a murder. He was part of a group of three young men who decided to rip off their drug dealer. Although the robbery was successful, one of the young men got excited, and began pistol-whipping the dealer, who, seeing nothing left to lose, fought back. A third individual shot him.

20 – Character Instructions for Role Player

The negotiation is going to start with Amos in hysterical chaos. His demands make little sense. He wants 'out,' whatever that means. He wants to be left alone, whatever that means.

Calm first, negotiate after

The negotiator's initial job will be to calm down this hysterical man so he doesn't cut the throat of the officer.

---

20 – Further Information Provided by Intel

One to two hours into the negotiation, negotiators will get information that Amos got 'turned out' by one of the dominant inmates, and is viewed by other inmates as the dominant inmate's possession.

Two alternative plot lines to choose from

1. Amos will NOT reveal that he was raped. If the exercise is played this way, the psych consult should suggest that the negotiator not raise the subject. Amos will play this as hyper-suspicious and he will 'project' – accusing the negotiator of being homosexual. If the negotiator is 'sensitive,' or too gentle/supportive in presentation, Amos will get more and more volatile and accusatory.

2. Amos will reveal he was raped. The negotiator should be respectful and tactful when s/he discusses this. If not, the role player should escalate dangerously. If the negotiator gets offended, dismissive, or otherwise doesn't get how volatile s/he is making things, escalate further. At this point, it'll be up to ERT to save the hostage.

3. This can be played as a **suicide-by-cop** scenario. Amos has taken a hostage, in such a scenario, to force officers to kill him (to help him get 'out'). If you choose to set it up this way, you will have to craft the scene so it is in a location/situation where it is plausible to deploy lethal weaponry, giving your sniper team its opportunity to practice.

---

20 – Psychological Consultation

General Information on Paranoid Character Traits

Amos is displaying a kind of 'paranoia'—he was overwhelmingly controlled by his rapist and his cohorts. He was also manipulated. Some paranoid types are aggressors—they manage their fear of others by trying to dominate every situation through intimidation, violence or psychological control of others, though they are in the victim role: it is when they get in a situation like a cornered animal (physically cornered or psychologically cornered), that the paranoid traits come out.

In either event, if the paranoid subject perceives the negotiator as being too manipulative or controlling, he will most likely escalate. The negotiator should use the standard tactic with paranoia: a 'correct distance.' If the negotiator is too cold, officious or demanding, Amos will feel controlled (and possibly will attribute the coldness to his being judged) and he will escalate. If the negotiator is perceived as sympathetic or 'supportive,' Amos will see it as manipulative. Given that he was homosexually raped—in short physically violated and controlled by individuals of his own sex—very likely he will project onto the negotiator that he (or she) is homosexual, because the negotiator is trying, however subtly, to achieve control—for Amos, controllers are rapists and rapists are homosexual. The negotiator should, in as matter-of-fact way as possible, 'disengage' from the subject. It's not about sex—this is about Amos getting help out of this desperate situation, and you have to achieve the same control that a skilled rider has with a horse—using slack reins, you let the horse think he is going where he wants to go.

IF AMOS REVEALS HE WAS RAPED (BE PREPARED)

All of the above general information is in effect. If Amos does not reveal he is raped, simply deal with the information that HE chooses to present. But, if he does reveal this trauma (and it is very likely that he will if the negotiation continues—if he's talking, he's communicating, and if he isn't telling the most important fact of his life, he's not *really* communicating. It is very likely he will let the information slip or, frustrated that the negotiator 'doesn't get it,' he will state it himself.

Once this information is out in the open, the negotiator's task must be two-fold: to offer a solution that Amos will be safe and get treatment for his trauma and secondly, to awaken his fighting spirit, so he chooses life rather than death. It is possible that he may wish to be helped to find a way to either get his rapists punished (without getting a snitch jacket) or, in general, do his part to fight prison rape. However, this last idea has to come from him. Finally, the negotiator should be acutely aware Amos could interpret surrender to power of any kind as another kind of rape, and he may push things to a lethal conclusion.

20 – What Amos will Tell If the Exercise is Set Up So that He Reveals that He's been Raped

Amos initially resisted, and the gang leader organized a gang rape. Because there were no severe injuries, Amos never presented at the infirmary. The leader gave his people strict instructions, "Do not damage his cherry. That's mine."

Amos thought if he fought back, he would be left alone. The rapes continued for nine days straight. He was frequently choked or smothered to unconsciousness, revived and raped and smothered again. He had the repeated experience of believing he would die.

After nine days, he gave in and became this man's 'wife.' He is not required to cross-dress in any manner, and would be beaten if he acted feminine. This is due to the rapist's aesthetic taste as well as his cunning. He keeps things under the radar. He rented Amos out, however, as payment for favors or debts.

Amos cannot sleep; he has a terrible flinch reaction to anything evoking thoughts of rape, or smothering. The smell of a particular hair product worn by one inmate or the smell of the disinfectant used to clean the floor that was on the rag stuffed into his mouth, causes panic reactions. Because these smells are pervasive, he believes his condition to be inescapable. He could still smell it in segregation, and in addition, trustees used to come by the door of his cell and whisper the nickname "Little Bit," given to him by his rapist/owner.

Amos wants out. He wants escape, literally from his own existence, because everything in his existence—the smells, the sounds, the sights, re-evoke rape, not to mention the actual, ongoing rapes that occur.

SCENARIO 20 – Checklist for After Action Review

The after action assessment/critique will depend on what was expressed and expected of the team going into the exercise. In other words, what was the desired training goal or outcome? Not just the outcome of the scenario, but what are the skills the director (team leader) is hoping to see exercised by the team, as these scenario/situations develop?

Floor plan developed?
- ❏ Did not meet goal
- ❏ Partially met goal
- ❏ Fully met goal

Demonstrate good listening skills?
- ❏ Did not meet goal
- ❏ Partially met goal
- ❏ Fully met goal

Did negotiator successfully de-escalate subject's initial combination of fear, rage and panic?
- ❏ Did not meet goal
- ❏ Partially met goal
- ❏ Fully met goal

Did negotiator communicate using 'correct distance,' the style of choice with the paranoid subject?
- ❏ Did not meet goal
- ❏ Partially met goal
- ❏ Fully met goal

Was team aware of the potential suicide-by-cop?
- ❏ Did not meet goal
- ❏ Partially met goal
- ❏ Fully met goal

SCENARIO 21

Therapist Taken Hostage,
Bipolar Disorder

21 – Original Call

Panic button emergency alarm goes off in Main Control, the panel shows the source of the alarm is E Unit. An attempt by Main Control to reach the occupant of that office by phone goes unanswered. There is one officer on the unit who radios Main Control to notify that there appears to be an inmate locked in the office with the Custody Mental Health Unit Supervisor (CMHUS). The officer can see her through a large window next to the door, and she appears frightened. ERT is deployed to the unit.

21 – The Precipitating Incident

(With Character Instructions for Role Player)

The Custody Mental Health Unit Supervisor (CMHUS) on the medium/minimum custody mental health unit has an office on the living unit. She is in the practice of leaving her office door open when she's inside. Gerain Barrett is visibly upset, and has stormed into CMHUS Jimenez's office. Caught up in the moment, he slams the door shut behind him, and then looks at CMHUS Jimenez. He realizes he has messed up when he sees the terror in her eyes and watches as she hits the wall panic button. He immediately barricades the door.

CMHUS Jimenez has realized that as usual, she has not unlocked the lock on her office doorknob, which means that she is now locked in the office with an angry Barrett. The doorknob must be unlocked via key, and she and the Shift Sergeant are the only ones with the key—and now it's barricaded as well.

Barrett has bipolar disorder. This manifests, in his case, in periods of social withdrawal, followed by episodes of mania (super high energy, grandiosity and irrational decision making).

Like many manic-depressives, he has a hair-trigger temper and is easily irritated and thrown 'off-course.' In this case, he'd marched in to complain about several inmates who tormenting him for fun. He is a perfect victim. He talks funny, and he goes in eye-popping rages—he's the best entertainment on the unit. Barrett has never been able to prove it, but it's common knowledge that these inmates have soaked his bedding in urine, and spit on his possessions. They do this on an intermittent basis—there will be weeks, even months with no incident, but when no one is looking, they do it again. This time, Barrett found excrement smeared on the door of his cell. Most infuriating to him is that he has complained to staff about this sort of thing, but no one has been caught or sanctioned, and it just continues.

When manic (as he is now) Barrett has a very volatile temper, and on top of the precipitating factor of the excrement, he's now panicking that this misunderstanding (he had no intention of hostage taking when he stormed into Jimenez's office) will result in a change in his points and a move to a new unit after a stint in administrative segregation. He tries to explain himself to CMHUS Jimenez, but he makes little sense and she's crying and hysterical. He gets increasingly frustrated and then angry. He can see through the window that ERT has arrived on the unit, and he knows that they are going to come in the office and take him to administrative segregation in restraints. All the noise in the small office is making it hard for him to think and he can feel himself getting enraged. He's yelling at the CMHUS to be quiet, and she keeps crying louder.

Barrett sees a laptop computer on the desk and, on impulse, he hits the CMHUS in the side of the head with it, edge on. She immediately falls to the ground, unconscious. There's a fair amount of blood in her hair.

Barrett decides to move the spare desk in the office over against the door. He then spots some folded cardboard in the corner and covers the large window, as well as the window in the door.

12 – Interview with his Case Manager Along with Record Check

Barrett is a bit of a mixed bag. He is a long term minimum custody inmate with an early release date of 12/31/2024. Originally incarcerated for theft and vehicular assault charges, Barrett beat his cellmate half-to-death, which earned him the longer sentence. This was during a manic episode and is not regarded as typical behavior. However, he likes to portray himself as a victim who has not been given a fair shake by the prison—he is very Intelligent, something very obvious when he isn't manic. He is quick to run to an inmate disability rights advocacy organization whenever he feels they can help him earn special privileges through lawsuits against the state. Due to his litigious nature, he has often been handled with kid gloves by the administration.

21 – For the Role Player

Barrett long-ago decided that the unit's CMHUS does not serve any purpose to him. He believes she's made him many promises about things both big and small that have fallen through, and he doesn't trust a word she says. The only person he wants to talk to during the scenario is his assigned advocate at the disability rights advocacy organization that he deals with, as he feels she is always on his side. He's not going to make it easy on the negotiator to build rapport with him, as he doesn't trust people he doesn't know. He expects people to trust the things he says as being truthful, so he will ask the negotiator to give him things to show good faith, but will not give up anything in exchange.

Now, agitated, he will be initially ranting at the negotiator. He will be cursing and provocative. Though mentally ill, he's also sharp, and if he perceives he's gotten under your skin, he will drill in on you like a mosquito that just found a pulse. For example, "What are you, some kind of jack-booted vegetable? That's the stupidest idea I ever heard. You've got no utility than a prostate exam on a ninety-year-old woman. Unless she enjoys the finger wave, which I don't" Even when the negotiator thinks s/he is making progress, he will 'jump sideways' into other subjects. If the negotiator gets frustrated, he will definitely pick up on that, and become more provocative and tangential (going off on side topics, almost a stream-of- consciousness

Barrett will also say funny things, talking a mile a minute – For example: Some time ago, he accidentally overdosed on his medications. At the hospital, between bouts of vomiting, he was heard saying:

Why do you give a guy like me medicine that I can't be trusted to use properly? I can't remember what I had for breakfast, and you expect me to remember five pills taken three times a day? What is five into three, anyway? Why can't you give me Skittles? They've made some mistakes; I'll give you that. Those chocolate Skittles tasted like horsepucky. But I would definitely take Skittles every day if the doctor prescribed them.

If HNT reacts with laughter – the role player should EXPLODE! He doesn't think what he says is funny. They just sound that way to others.

21 – Psychological Consult

Although Barrett is diagnosed with bipolar disorder, his behavior corresponds most closely at this time to what is called hypomanic. In other words, he is agitated, full of energy and volatile, but not totally raving. He is not delusional either.

The core problem, from his perspective, is he is not being taken seriously. He is not being heard. Tactical paraphrasing will be essential with this guy.

<u>He must believe he's being heard, before he'll be willing to listen to you.</u>

Because of his hypomania, however, this will be one step forward, two steps back. He will get distracted, will flame up at things, and suddenly shift into whimsical statements having little to do with the current situation.

You've got two major issues to deal with:

First of all, he's barricaded, he injured the CMHUS, and he's afraid of sanctions – not only transfer to another unit, not only administrative segregation, but also more time stacked on his sentence.

Secondly is the ongoing torment he's been receiving from other inmates. This is real.

It is the psychological consultant's idea that the second issue is core – if there is some way to mitigate or eliminate the torment from other inmates, he will be more likely to face the potential consequences for his current actions. Of course, you must focus on getting the CMHUS out of there, but Barrett is unlikely to agree to anything, if he believes the disgusting bullying and torment will continue, unchanged. For that reason, tactical paraphrasing around this issue, demonstrating to Barrett that he IS heard, may be the key to getting him to surrender.

SCENARIO 21 – Checklist for After Action Review

The after action assessment/critique will depend on what was expressed and expected of the team going into the exercise. In other words, what was the desired training goal or outcome? Not just the outcome of the scenario, but what are the skills the director (team leader) is hoping to see exercised by the team, as these scenario/situations develop?

Floor plan developed?
- ❏ Did not meet goal
- ❏ Partially met goal
- ❏ Fully met goal

Demonstrate good listening skills?
- ❏ Did not meet goal
- ❏ Partially met goal
- ❏ Fully met goal

Fully utilized tactical paraphrasing?
- ❏ Did not meet goal
- ❏ Partially met goal
- ❏ Fully met goal

Demonstrated to this subject that he is being HEARD?
- ❏ Did not meet goal
- ❏ Partially met goal
- ❏ Fully met goal

Did not get sidetracked by all his tangents from one topic to another?
- ❏ Did not meet goal
- ❏ Partially met goal
- ❏ Fully met goal

Did not get provoked, either to irritation/anger OR laughter by what he said?
- ❏ Did not meet goal
- ❏ Partially met goal
- ❏ Fully met goal

Consider calling in psych consult?
- ❏ Did not meet goal
- ❏ Partially met goal
- ❏ Fully met goal

SCENARIO 22

Paranoid Delusions, Active Shooter

22 – Original Call

ERT responds to an off hook phone alarm coming from the admin desk in the public lobby area that is outside the secured area of the facility. They find a female has been shot, hear screams coming from the other side of the door, which houses the accounting and payroll staff and the office of the facility's Superintendent.

As it is lunchtime, it's not immediately known who is back in the offices. ERT makes radio notification and, along with the facility's armed Perimeter Patrol, set up a perimeter around the admin building to keep anyone else out. The facility is put in lockdown and all specialty teams are activated.

22 – The Incident

Correctional Officer Abraham Kroft, terminated from the prison eight months ago, entered the facility's double doors on a weekday during day shift, when the only staff in the reception area is the front desk receptionist. He shoots the receptionist, wounding her, and then shoots the lock on the door going back to the offices, until he's able to gain entry. There are two custody payroll staff, one member of the inmate accounting department, and the Superintendent present in the office at this time, as everyone else is at lunch. Alicia, in inmate accounting, took her phone off the hook when she heard the shots fired at the door, which is what alerted Main Control to the issue.

Aside from the initial shots fired at the receptionist and the door, no additional shots are fired. Kroft has instructed the hostages to assist him in barricading the original access door plus the anterior access door with office furniture, and is now corralling the staff into an inner office away from any outside walls or windows.

22 – Interview with HR

Kroft was an apparently excellent officer for a number of years. However, he was always awkward socially, and he was played by one of the inmates, who 'became the best friend he never had.' The inmate used rumors to make Kroft believe that other officers disrespected him. At that point, another inmate was brought into the game and the two of them built up his ego, and asked him for small things that were not against any rules, but were suggestive of favoritism. Other inmates noticed and accused him of being prejudiced against them – the two inmates also used race as a tool to make Kroft more isolated. Eventually, they got him to cross the lines, ignoring illegal activities that they were engaged in — he'd lose their friendship and, he rationalized what they were doing, essentially, "It wasn't so bad what they are doing. And anyway, we can never stop this sort of stuff, anyway." Now they owned him, and before too long, they had him smuggling drugs into the facility. He was extremely nervous about being caught, and started using drugs himself to calm himself down. Originally, he used Xanax, but that made him 'drugged up' – similar to a drunk – and at the inmate's encouragement, he started chipping meth from the contraband he was bringing in. Within a year, he developed a major polydrug addiction, and it was due to the deterioration of his work that this was all discovered. The two inmates were transferred to two separate prisons elsewhere, and Kroft was fired. He agreed to leave without contesting his termination, as long as he was not prosecuted.

22 – Role Player Planning

What no one knows (until the situation unfolds) is that Kroft has continued using meth and Xanax and he is currently floridly psychotic. Although chemically induced, he will essentially be in the same mindset as a decompensated schizophrenic: delusional, paranoid and hallucinating.

Kroft is going to answer the phone in a fury. He'll be raving, ordering ERT to back off. He'll curse, and snarl how easy it is to blow someone's brains out and splatter them against the wall. He will say horrifying things about how he'll bathe in the spray of blood, how he'll crack open their skulls and scoop out their brains and smear it in the Superintendent's face. He will push the negotiator's fears, so to speak, but as the negotiator starts the communication, Kroft will stay on the line rather than hang up and go after the hostages. ERT should be ready for a green light (and this case is excellent as an ERT entry exercise as well).

If initial rapport is established, Kroft will begin to rave about what the prison administration has done. He will start a litany about how they stole his only friends, the only decent people he has ever known. But then he states that Admin has "sicced two 'men from the shadows," they follow me. People claim they cannot see them, but that is a lie, they always stay two-and-one-quarter paces behind me."

Then, he will tell how six months ago, while he was trying to hook up with a young woman in a bar, he suddenly heard the voice of his former lieutenant, a woman, whispering, "Girlfriend, you don't want to go home with him. He can't last, and anyway, he's hung like a mosquito." He whirled around, but did not see her. By the time he turned back from his room search, the young woman of his interest had started playing pool with another guy.

Since then, he has heard the lieutenant's voice on frequent occasions, either when trying to pick up a woman, where, always, his sexual prowess and anatomy are derided, and also when he is anxious about something. He got some part-time work for a tree topper, but quit when he climbed up, hearing the lieutenant laughing at him, saying, "Poor baby. Don't fall. You might break something. Not that there's much to lose, little man."

Kroft will hear voices while on the phone with HNT. He will demand to know if the negotiator hears them. (NOTE: If the negotiator pretends that he or she does, catch them in a lie. Demand that the primary tell you what else the voices are saying—whatever the negotiator says, make it something else. Make the situation escalate – it will be up to the negotiating team to desperately figure out how to keep Kroft from shooting the hostages.

Demand that they send the lieutenant to him. Kroft promises to release some of the hostages if they send her in.

If the negotiator is too soft-spoken and reassuring, you will perceive them as trying to 'soften you up.' Paranoid people get MORE paranoid when they relax. Therefore, either accuse the negotiator as wanting to fuck you (male or female) – angrily, or simply accuse them of trying to get you talking so you get weak. For him, being encouraged to relax is a kind of seduction – a letting down of defenses.

22 – Interview with Another Officer

This officer says that after Kroft was fired, he reached out to him. "He used to be a good officer. You know as well as I do that an inmate can play anyone. We all have. Kroft's big mistake is he didn't go in to his supervisor and fall on his sword. That's how he ended up booting in drugs. I felt sorry for the guy. One thing about him – as screwed up as he is now, he was always stand-up. Never backed down from a fight, never backed down from an inmate. His weakness was loneliness, not fear. So you won't be able to intimidate him out of there."

"I stopped seeing him when he really got crazy, but I talked to him while he was already in the weeds. What was weird was that he was crazy about some things – worried people were talking about his sex organs and stuff. But he was totally sane about some things."

When asked what that means, the friend says, "If you talk to him about the job, the two inmates who set him up, his family, most things, really, he's crazier than a shit-house bat. But if you talk to him about bikes (motorcycles—but he won't tell the negotiator that he means that instead of bicycles unless asked. If the negotiator start talking to Kroft about ten-speeds and mountain bikes, he will get more wound up), about fighting, and about John Carter of Mars (an Edgar Rice Burroughs science fiction series that they made a movie out of), he calms down, and is a cool guy."

NOTE on Reading Material

If this negotiation goes on a long time, grab a Kindle or go online and download several of the John Carter of Mars books. One of those working Intel should speed-read the book(s), to provide information to the primary, to assist in directing Kroft to an 'island of sanity.' (See psych consult below)

---

22 – Psych Consult Concerning Psychotic, Delusional Subjects

MOVE TOWARD AN ISLAND OF SANITY

Pay attention to subjects where the person is not delusional. Unless there is an emergent issue that must be addressed, divert your contact to those 'islands of sanity,' whenever possible, rather than allowing the conversation to focus on delusional subjects. Make links with other subjects not tainted by delusions. Think of yourself as expanding the size of the 'land-mass:' making an area where it's predictable and safe. If the individual gets stuck within his/her delusions, you may find that changing the subject requires real finesse. Nonetheless, do so whenever you can, because talking about delusions makes it worse.

Islands of sanity are not necessarily 'nice' subjects

These islands of sanity are not necessarily' nice' subjects. The consultant tells you s/he worked with a very dangerous man for nine months, and the only subject he could talk about, without psychotic symptoms, was bar fights. It was safer talking about the sound of a cue ball impacting on someone's skull than what he had for dinner or what his childhood was like.

TALK ABOUT THE DELUSIONS TO ASSESS RISK

Talk about the delusions only as a means of threat assessment. Ask direct questions, particularly in regard to the person's intention to hurt him/herself or others. Otherwise, you strive to get him talking about non-delusional subjects. Only talk about delusions to assess immediate risk.

DON'T AGREE WITH THE DELUSIONS

In almost all circumstances, don't agree with the delusions. At most, if you have a consensus among your team and consultant that it is worth the risk, passively accept their perception in the interest of their complying with something to keep everyone safer. This passive acceptance is almost never the best choice, however, so be very careful in its use.

DON'T DISAGREE—AT LEAST MOST OF THE TIME

Don't engage in arguments about whether the psychotic person's perceptions are real. However, if they ask you for a 'reality check,' you can state you don't believe the delusional belief is correct or the hallucination is real. In this case, you are helping the person understand what he/she perceives is not the 'rule' of the world.

DIFFERENTIATE

Give the individual the 'right' to his or her own perceptions and beliefs. Inform them you don't perceive what they do, though you aren't arguing with them about what *they* see or believe. In some cases, take their delusions into account without agreeing with them. Example: "I don't see any razor blades on the tree branches, but if I did, I wouldn't walk around in the park after dark where I couldn't see what I might run into. I'd stay home when the sun went down."

STEAM-VALVING

This is useful with people whose speech is a cascade of words and ideas that are either all over the place (zigzag) or delusional.

- Listen and then interrupt, firmly but not aggressively.
- Sum up what they said, and tell them you want to hear more, but before they do, you have a question (or instruction) for them. For example, "Just a minute. I want to hear more about the fire in the eyes of crows, but first, tell me: Do you have a blade?"
- Then let them return to their cascade of words. Listen a bit more, then interrupt again. Continue with multiple sequences of release of pressure, interruptions and questions until you get the information you need.

The Fatigue Factor and the Detox Factor

In cases such as this where the psychosis is almost surely drug-induced, he may become more psychologically stable when the drugs begin to leave his system. In addition, if he's been on meth, he will probably have been up for some time, and he may get tired – very much so. For this reason, particularly where there is no viable hostage exchange that can be made (if he remains stuck on the lieutenant), dragging the negotiation a) allows ERT to get in the best position b) he may eventually want to give up just because he is so tired.

On the other hand, be very alert to an increase in irritability. His response to the lack of his drugs may be anxiety, irritation and rage.

Stay formal—do not get overly friendly!

Kroft is really paranoid. Stay formal, NOT too friendly. If he relaxes too much, he'll think you are messing with his head, and he'll go right back into rage.

SCENARIO 22 – Checklist for After Action Review

The after action assessment/critique will depend on what was expressed and expected of the team going into the exercise. In other words, what was the desired training goal or outcome? Not just the outcome of the scenario, but what are the skills the director (team leader) is hoping to see exercised by the team, as these scenario/situations develop?

Floor plan developed?
- ❏ Did not meet goal
- ❏ Partially met goal
- ❏ Fully met goal

Demonstrate good listening skills?
- ❏ Did not meet goal
- ❏ Partially met goal
- ❏ Fully met goal

Did the team recognize the psych issues early on?
- ❏ Did not meet goal
- ❏ Partially met goal
- ❏ Fully met goal

Consider calling in psych consultant?
- ❏ Did not meet goal
- ❏ Partially met goal
- ❏ Fully met goal

How did the primary deal with his delusional ideations (refer to principals in psych consult)?
- ❏ Did not meet goal
- ❏ Partially met goal
- ❏ Fully met goal

SCENARIO 23

Masked Depression, Intellectual Debate, Social Isolation

23 – Original Call

Main control receives a call stating an emotionally disturbed staff member has barricaded himself in an office at the Staff Resource Center, possibly threatening suicide. Unknown weapons.

The staff psychologist, Dr. Eckman, called the emergency telephone number for Main Control and asked to be transferred directly to the lieutenant. He then reported that during an appointment with a long-term staff member at the Staff Resource Center (on prison grounds, but outside the secured perimeter), named Michael Thompson, alluded to 'ending it all.' When the psychologist asked him exactly what he meant by that, Thompson reacted strongly, saying, "You are going to put a mental health label on me? You're going to get me fired!" He walked quickly out of the office, barricaded himself into an office at the Staff Resource Center, as well as the staff psychologist, who is currently in a separate office at the same location. Dr. Eckman does not feel he's currently in danger; however it's not known whether the staff member has a weapon, or what items are available to him in the office he's in. Due to the sensitive nature of the call, the lieutenant has decided to call in HNT, but will not (yet) send ERT, in the hopes that the situation can be resolved as privately as possible.

23 – Can You Negotiate with a Fellow Officer?

If at all possible, choose a role player who is known to the majority of your team. In this scenario, we will have a really smart, Intellectual. You could easily craft another scenario with another reason for suicide and another character type.

This is a great scenario for having staff choose WHO would be the best negotiator for THIS staff member, and for the role player to react to that negotiator accordingly. Use details from this person's life that can dovetail with the role-play. The description below, for example, describes a solitary man, but you can easily change that, for example, to a married man who keeps to himself. Overlay this with the following fictional scenario.

23 – Interview with Dr. Eckman on the Phone

Michael Thompson has met with you on two different occasions about some stress he's facing. These interviews have been more problem-solving consultations – very practical minded, like visiting a car mechanic to deal with a noise in the chassis, Thompson was primarily focused on work pressure, but he indicated that he was having trouble with his family as well. His demeanor has led you to believe that there is much more going on than what he's been willing to talk about.

During your session today he seemed very distracted and frustrated from the outset. About 15 minutes into your appointment, he made the allusion to 'ending it all.' You tried to calm him down and get him to talk to you about what is really going on, but this stressed him out more. He went to another office and barricaded himself, and after a brief attempt to engage him through the door, you returned to your office and called the facility emergency number.

23 – Background on Michael Thompson: Interview with His Brother

NOTE: For context, Thompson calls his brother to "say goodbye." When his brother asks what he means by that, he says, "You know. Take some responsibility for what you've done for once." Then he hung up. The brother immediately calls the prison and is patched in to one of the secondary negotiators.

Michael regards himself as a failure in life. He is a PhD ABD ('all but dissertation') in political science. He's been working on his thesis for the past thirteen years, but he's got the worst case of writer's block you could imagine. He's got two rooms full of boxes of notes. Jesus, he not only abandoned the notes, but he started over with a computer, and dicked around for three months transferring files. Then he got a new computer and did it again. His research is on the parallels between Biblical stories of the 'Promised Land,' and the concept of 'manifest destiny' in the taking over of the Old West in 19th century America.

The role player can use some other super Intellectual set of ideas that s/he is familiar.

So anyway, he was a starving graduate student, and that's how he ended up a correctional officer. He needed a job. I bet he only told you about his Masters in Criminology when he applied for work.

He keeps to himself at work, right? I take him out to dinner once a week, well, my wife, the kids, and me and he's never mentioned a single co-worker by name. Nine years on the job, not one friend, I bet.

Aside from his research, he has no social life. For recreation, he has his television and his computer. He is obsessed with silent movies, and orders obscure Western (cowboy) 'classics' from an Internet source five times a week.

He has not been on a date in six years.

23 – For the Role Player: How to Interact with the Team

The team is going to decide who is best to negotiate with you as a staff member, so it's important that you react to that person as though you were really yourself in crisis, and this is the person they chose to speak to you. Let personal feelings about them be a part of the conversation, whether good or bad (Not too much! You have to work with them after the scenario is over!). If they say something that is insulting, upsetting, too personal, etc. CALL THEM ON IT. If they choose a male negotiator and you think a female would be better or vice versa, make that request. If you decide you want to request a specific negotiator, that's fine too… but please let the first person negotiate for some amount of time first. You can also change your mind if they are doing a good job. If at any time you don't like something they say, be sure to point it out. Conversely, if they are speaking to you in a way that they are building rapport and de-escalating the situation, respond to that favorably. We want them to learn and we want them to feel as much as possible the challenges of negotiating with a known staff member, the good, the bad, and the ugly.

You do not need to keep talking to the negotiator for the duration of the incident without pause. Feel free to hang up on them if you don't like the way things are going, or tell them to give you a break. If you give them any directions ("Call me back in 5 minutes," for example), make sure to hold them to it.

You do not need to volunteer any of the information below unless you feel it is normal for the conversation.
- You went into the meeting with Dr. Eckman knowing you are planning to kill yourself. You want it to be shocking, and you know doing it at the Staff Resource Center will get around the facility quickly. You want as many people affected by your death as possible emotionally, but you don't want to physically hurt Dr. Eckman or anyone else. You are bitter because you are such a failure. No one knows you, and therefore, even the little positive feelings you've gotten from others on the job are based on a lie.
- You have a firearm (unless, at your facility, this would be impossible – then change it to a blade).
- As you intend to die, survival would be another failure, and would be experienced as humiliation in front of your colleagues.

23 – For the Role Player: Style of Interaction
Michael is going to present with a brittle arrogance, and Intellectualization. The negotiator will be side-tracked over and over again as Michael will try to engage him or her in professorial debate on the state of the world, on philosophical and religious issues, and the meaning of life and a good name.

Role player: keep diverting the conversation back to your Intellectual preoccupations. Occasionally, draw in philosophical questions about the meaning of life, and how suicide is considered in many cultures to be an act of Intellectual integrity.

This will be a difficult character for an amateur actor to role-play. You need to recruit a role player who has several hobbies or areas of public concern that he or she is really familiar: climate change, immigration issues, gun rights, the Bible, history of the old West, etc. The role player's presentation will be arrogant and for quite some time, disrespectful of the negotiator's knowledge.

23 – Psychological Consultation
Michael is resisting really negotiating a solution to the problem because the conversation is an end in itself. He is desperately lonely and is striving to maintain conversation to barricade himself from the silence. He covers this up with his arrogance, and disrespect for your Intellect.

<u>Important points</u>:
- Do not try to be smarter than he is when you are not—he will see through you.
- When you *are* smarter than him (when you know something he does not), do not try to prove him wrong, because if he loses the debate, your dialogue is at an end. Do not be falsely humble, either, as he will see through that. Rather, draw him out so he can embellish his ideas and feel that he is making contact with another human being about something he loves.
- At the same time, do not suck up to him, giving him exaggerated respect for how much he knows, how smart he is.

Rather, present yourself with dignity and engage in dialogue, an exchange of truth back and forth, not a debate where someone wins and someone loses.

The crux of the matter is this, the longer and more solid the dialogue, the more you prove to him he is worth talking to. A person worth talking to is not alone. If you are successful in this, he will be 'pulled' back into the world of the living, where people have conversations with others, and feel a sense of hope for the future. Given he's made no overt threats, you may be able to minimize what he has done and encourage him to surrender.

Alternative outcomes to plan into this scenario

With sufficient dialogue, (a real challenge here), he surrenders. BUT – he changes his mind. You do not have ERT on stand-by here – what if this becomes a suicide-by-cop—he attempts to use violence to get others to kill him—at the moment you think it is over!

SCENARIO 23– Checklist for After Action Review

The after action assessment/critique will depend on what was expressed and expected of the team going into the exercise. In other words, what was the desired training goal or outcome? Not just the outcome of the scenario, but what are the skills the director (team leader) is hoping to see exercised by the team, as these scenario/situations develop?

Floor plan developed?
- ❑ Did not meet goal
- ❑ Partially met goal
- ❑ Fully met goal

Demonstrate good listening skills?
- ❑ Did not meet goal
- ❑ Partially met goal
- ❑ Fully met goal

Important that the negotiator realize he/she should not challenge this subject, and win a debate?
- ❑ Did not meet goal
- ❑ Partially met goal
- ❑ Fully met goal

Consider using a psych consultant?
- ❑ Did not meet goal
- ❑ Partially met goal
- ❑ Fully met goal

Commit yourself to a long open dialogue, trying to make human connection a lifeline towards him surrendering?
- ❑ Did not meet goal
- ❑ Partially met goal
- ❑ Fully met goal

Did you have frequent status assessments with command post/tactical?
- ❑ Did not meet goal
- ❑ Partially met goal
- ❑ Fully met goal

SCENARIO 24

Suicide of Cop by Cop

24 – Original Call

Shots fired at secure parking. Seven rounds fired through the roof of the car of Correctional Officer Ben Pearson, who is sitting in the car.

24 – Background Information for the Role Player

Seven rounds is not an accidental discharge! A perimeter is immediately set up. Pearson is yelling, but it is unclear what he is saying. He appears enraged, waving his arms with the gun in one hand. ERT is safe behind cover, but Pearson appears to be making threatening gestures. He does not leave the car. Based on his behavior, it looks like he intends to force ERT to kill him. HNT is called to the scene.

Ben Pearson is a sixteen-year veteran correctional officer. About two and one-half years ago, he intervened when an inmate, Stefan Andronic became physically violent to his wife, Sonia, during visitation. She is the mother of two children, aged four and six. The inmate had been incarcerated for previous violence against Ms. Andronic. After this incident, she divorced him.

Six months afterwards, she contacted Officer Pearson, saying that she owed him an enormous debt of gratitude for his intervention. She stated that in her culture men did not intervene between a husband and wife, and she always expected that it was her duty to be beaten. However, upon moving to America, she saw that things were different. Her ex-husband had been prosecuted and convicted, during his last assault on her in their home, but she thought this was because he also assaulted police when they were called. Now, this time, though, she saw clearly that there were good men, and that America was a country where a woman could reasonably hope that people would help her. Officer Pearson was polite in response, and figured that was the end of it.

Several months later, Ms. Andronic called again, telling Officer Pearson that she was in difficult circumstances, because her community had ostracized her for abetting her husband's arrest and prosecution and worse, divorcing him.

Officer Pearson met her for coffee. Sonia turned out to be a very overwhelmed young mother, a legal immigrant, abandoned by her community and without work. Officer Pearson decided to help her. On several subsequent occasions, she ran out of food, and Officer Pearson bundled her and the kids into his car and rushed to the food bank so that she could get supplies before it closed. Fellow officers noted at the time that he was very concerned about her, but when they teased him a bit, he took offence. "I'm married, I'm forty five years old, I'm a decent Christian man and she's a single mom with two kids. Are you nuts? The young lady needs some help. If her life falls apart, what'll happen to her kids?"

Eventually, though, due to circumstances Pearson will describe, his wife came to believe they were in a relationship. Attempting to save his marriage, he cut off all contact with Sonia.

About three months ago, Sonia made a complaint of sexual harassment against him. She stated he dropped by the house late one night, ostensibly out of concern for her. He brought groceries. "One thing led to another," and he began kissing her. She was scared to tell him to stop, because she saw him as the only protection she had against the family of her attacker, and he was wearing a gun. He made statements, such as "Police and corrections, we are fist in glove. We protect their own, and therefore, if you were 'mine,' so to speak, your family would be far safer." Sonia said that she realized that men, particularly uniformed men were the same the world over. She couldn't fight them, so she gave in.

She stated he started coming over once or twice a week, for quickies. She did her best, she said, to fake it, because she was so scared for the safety of her children.

She presented photos, taken in her home, featuring Officer Pearson and herself, next to the Christmas tree, and a few others with him playing with her kids. She had his cell phone number, knew his address, and the name of his wife. She also knew his wife had been hospitalized for depression, and stated Pearson told her that she had cut him off from sex, and that's why he was looking elsewhere.

Pearson denied everything. He said he'd helped her a few times, as described above, but he never went there for sex, never kissed her, never even thought of such a thing. Nobody believes him. His wife has left him. He's under investigation and has been taken off duty.

24 – Instructions for the Role Player
This role player probably *should* be a police or correctional officer, someone who is a veteran and very familiar with the type of grouchy, somewhat burned-out cops who perhaps have been on the job too long.

Pearson will talk with HNT. There will be opportunities for a variety of tactical exercises by ERT to make this happen. He is going to be bitter and enraged. He will rant about how he's been betrayed by his brothers and sisters in blue, and he will be stunned his wife did not believe him. He will allude to suicide, and talk about taking an "honor guard to Valhalla with him."

This is a long barricaded situation. It should take considerable time to set up each interview, so the lead negotiator and ERT are really working hard on this one.

24 – Interview with Wife

His wife refuses to give any information that might help resolve the situation peacefully, saying bitterly, "I don't want any of you to get hurt. Don't put yourself at risk for the son of a bitch."

The role player should make this a very challenging interview, in that she 'gives' nothing useful, but doesn't disengage. The interviewer could continue to talk with her for a while before realizing that, at least now, it is a waste of time.

24 – Interview with Sonia (Face-to-face)

This should happen at least several hours into the negotiation.

Sonia, hearing the information on the news, appears at the prison gates and is interviewed face-to-face. The role player can play this one of two ways: ONE—She will show far too much affection for Pearson for someone who has been, allegedly, villainously coerced into sex. TWO—She will be dramatic, accusatory and vindictive. In either event, however, her personal boundaries with the interviewer will be odd. She makes a lot of physical contact (doesn't matter if the interviewer is male or female). She is a little flirtatious, but when the officer asks her some hard questions about several things she claims, she flares up into anger.

24 – Contact with Sonia's Mother

Her mother informs the interviewer that Sonia has always gotten crushes on older men. Back in Moldavia, she was, allegedly, taken advantage of by a high school drama teacher. This incident ended his career. Her mother says, "I wonder if that was true, actually. He always denied it. She had a lot of details, even about marks on his body, but they were things you could see down somebody's shirt or with the sleeves rolled up. She had no description of any marks that would be on intimate parts. Oh, and you should have seen what happened when her husband left. They were married just a couple of years, it was a lousy marriage, really. Always fighting, those two. Well, he left, and she showed up at his new apartment, the third floor of a subdivided old house. He opened the door one morning, and there she was, sleeping in front of his door with the two kids in her arms. She'd broken a window in the door downstairs, opened the lock. Another time, he had a girlfriend up at his apartment, and she broke into the house, made quite a scene. Anyway, as soon as the divorce was finalized, he left the state. He said she was never going to let him go. He was no prize, and I feel sorry for the kids, but Sonia's a piece of work, actually."

24 – A Change of Focus

When this information is forwarded to the 'front line,' it definitely should change the focus of the negotiation.

This will <u>NOT</u> end the negotiation. It will just change its direction. Pearson is furious at IAD for not even admitting the possibility he was telling the truth, and is very cynical at this point. He will be suspicious the negotiator doesn't really mean anything he's saying, that it's just lies to get him to

come out. It may be necessary to shift negotiators to get a fresh start. On the other hand, if the first negotiator can truly 'reboot,' this may prove to Pearson that someone actually believes him. The role player and director can drive this in either direction, depending on training agendas.

24 – Psychological Consult

Pearson is going to have to vent, in the classic sense of the word. Remember as far as he is concerned, no one has *heard* him. He feels completely discounted as the man that he truly is. The negotiator will have to prove to Pearson that he is truly heard, so tactical paraphrasing is going to be very important.

It's important the negotiator does not get defensive on behalf of the department or IAD. On the other hand, he or she must be careful not to stoke up/support Pearson's grievances.

Do not make the suggestion to reopen the investigation to clear his name too soon. The negotiator must assist Pearson in letting out the energy (the same way one slowly turns the cap on an over-heated radiator, let out a little pressure, pause, let out a little more pressure, pause, etc).

However, if Pearson simply vents 'in a circle,' there must come a point where the negotiator says enough. If such an impasse is reached, it may be effective to shift the call to a well-respected sergeant, who says, in essence,

"Enough is enough. We have work to do to clear your name, and it's time we get started."

Scenario 24 – Make it a Successful Resolution

We recommend that this exercise results in a very tense, but successful resolution. ERT's training will be in maintaining an absolutely safe scene against a man who is familiar with police tactics, and making an 'airtight' surrender plan. The authors believe that a training scenario ending in the 'failure' of shooting a fellow officer, particularly one who is probably innocent of the allegations against him, would not be beneficial to the officers. We are not saying that it couldn't happen in real life—but we believe the team will be best empowered in this exercise with a success.

SCENARIO 24 – Checklist for After Action Review

The after action assessment/critique will depend on what was expressed and expected of the team going into the exercise. In other words, what was the desired training goal or outcome? Not just the outcome of the scenario, but what are the skills the director (team leader) is hoping to see exercised by the team, as these scenario/situations develop?

Scene plan developed?
- ❏ Did not meet goal
- ❏ Partially met goal
- ❏ Fully met goal

Demonstrate good listening skills?
- ❏ Did not meet goal
- ❏ Partially met goal
- ❏ Fully met goal

Are things handled differently because he is an officer? If so, was this done in a way conducive to the resolution of the incident?
- ❏ Did not meet goal
- ❏ Partially met goal
- ❏ Fully met goal

What about asking one of his friends, a fellow officer, to assist? Would a TPI of some kind be beneficial—even a taped message? Good idea? Did the team consider it?
- ❏ Did not meet goal
- ❏ Partially met goal
- ❏ Fully met goal

Outside psych consultant considered?
- ❏ Did not meet goal
- ❏ Partially met goal
- ❏ Fully met goal

SCENARIO 25

Stalking/Delusional Disorder

25 – Original call

Open

Open line. Call indicating a subject being held against his will, by a female subject with a bladed weapon. Location is at the counseling center.

One of the therapists at the minimum security women's prison, Dr. Alister MacMillan, surreptitiously calls the duty sergeant, and the line is open. Dr. MacMillan carries on a conversation with another individual. The sergeant was asking Dr. MacMillan what he wanted when he heard, "Rose, you don't need that knife. Put it down. We can talk much easier without a blade in your hand pointed at my throat. The door is locked. Yes, you did that. We have all the time we need to talk, so put down the knife, please. Yes, I know that you believe that we must be together. I know that you believe that I am in love with you, and I hear you, Rose. You are telling me that if you can't have me, then we both have to die. . . .Oh. Not both of us? You are telling me I have to die, that's what you are saying."

A quick check to the receptionist in the counseling center reveals that he had a 2:00 PM appointment with Rose Huang, a Chinese national, green card holder, who is incarcerated for eight years for stalking and sexual assault.

ERT responds and contains the perimeter.

Rewriting the plotline

As in other exercises, the director is quite free to rewrite the exercise to practice getting information regarding a subject from another cultural or ethnic group.

---

25 – Report of Investigating Detective (of Stalking Unit of the Police Agency that Originally Arrested Rose Huang)

Rose Huang is a resident of Hong Kong. Seven years ago, she came to America and studied law at X University. She became obsessed with one of her professors, Dr. James Craft. She took every class he offered, and applied to do her thesis under his supervision. He turned her down, as he already was supervising the maximum number of students he could manage.

Rose chose to interpret this as an announcement of his passion for her, assuming he did not want to mix any professional or tutorial responsibilities with the pure love they had discovered. She believed they had a secret pact, and she had to be circumspect, so that he was not accused of seducing or harassing a student. She began following him, running into him at social functions or public gatherings. It was then she realized that he was married.

This enraged her. His wife, aged 56, one year younger than Dr. Craft, and looked every year of her age. How could he stand to spend any time with that woman, when he could spend every moment with her, Rose thought.

She began writing letters to Mrs. Craft, claiming they were having an affair. A careful observer, Rose described gestures Dr. Craft would make when laughing, how he pinched the bridge of his nose when he was tired. She observed the morning exercise routine he did in the backyard at five in the morning. She wrote to the wife how he was making progress with some of the exercises, and that they were going to start Pilates together. Mrs. Craft, an insecure and jealous woman, believed the affair was happening, and confronted her husband. This was the first he was aware of Rose's interest.

Denying everything, he consulted with law enforcement, and following their recommendations, as Rose had not crossed the threshold of breaking the law, he tried to extinguish the behavior by ignoring her. He refused to greet her on the campus, returned all of her notes to his wife (retaining copies), changed his phone number and was altogether unresponsive to her.

When she began calling, he hung up. Unfortunately, his wife was not able to maintain this, and on her own, went to Rose's apartment to sit down and talk with her. It did not go well. Rose convincingly described their lovemaking, with such confidence and graphic detail, that Mrs. Craft was convinced it was true. It didn't help their own relationship in that area was troubled. . . actually non-existent. Mrs. Craft slapped her face, but Rose only smiled sweetly at her, and suggested if she moved out, it would be better for all concerned. Mrs. Craft believed her and moved out of the house, initiating divorce proceedings.

It appeared as though Rose waited a few weeks and went to the house. Finding it locked, she broke in and greeted Dr. Craft naked in his now lonely bed. He was not pleased. In fact, he was terrified. Grabbing his bathrobe, he ran for the door with Rose blocking his way. At this point, she pulled a knife and slashed her own cheek, saying she was ready to die for their love. And she knew he is willing to die with her. He managed to yell for help out the door, before she slammed it and walked him at knifepoint back to the bedroom. There she sexually assaulted him – when police entered the home, they found Dr Craft tied naked to the bed with Ms Huang trying to force him to do what he was too terrified to respond. She had threatened to stab him if he continued to deny their love. She was Tazed, arrested, tried and incarcerated.

25 – Information Derived from Records

Her parent's stated she had a previous episode 12 years ago, when she was similarly obsessed with a professor. She stabbed him. Then a minor, she was placed in a psychiatric hospital, and responded to a regimen of anti-psychotic medications. The medications were discontinued after one year of treatment and she's had no further episodes. The parents stated their daughter truly believed that the professor loved her, and she would 'twist' anything around into a positive meaning. For example, two days before she attacked him, she accosted him on the street, and he, frightened and fed-up, punched her. She returned home, smiling, telling her mother she now knew that the professor loved her, because love was a test. "There is no rose without thorns," she said. "I will prove to him that no matter what the test, I will rise to meet his love." When she assaulted him, she intended to kill him and commit suicide, because she believed they were destined to live together in Heaven. The parents note they are Christian.

25 – Cultural Consult

If possible, access someone familiar with Chinese culture. Remember, she is from a very upper-class family. Although Christian, she will very possibly subscribe to traditional Confucian values, particularly filial piety.

Effective Use of Cultural Consultation—and Effective Cultural Consultants

It is important that you have a list of consultants, whom you've already vetted, who are able to discuss both cultural rules, and exceptions to the rules. For example, if the subject does not seem to conform to the cultural rules that the consultant expects, they should be willing and able to brainstorm with you why the subject's behavior seems to be atypical.

NOTE: Just because someone is of a particular ethnic or cultural background does not mean that a cultural consult is necessary. If the subject is expressing values that seem to be culturally based, or you are simply uncertain, use the consult when available. There are many cases, however, where a person is fully acculturated into ordinary American values, and their background, race, etc. are not really relevant to the particular situation.

---

25 – Instruction for the Role Player – Rose

You will be highly educated. It may be a worthwhile addition to the exercise that you have a heavy accent, but this is only valid if the accent is well played. If you shift in and out of character or you are unskilled, it will make the training exercise sound ridiculous and unreal. You will speak about your 'relationship' in fixed sureties—it is absolutely the truth. You will be kind of smug.

25 – Instruction for the Role Player – Dr. MacMillan

You will be attempting to feed more information to 9-1-1 through your 'running commentary' on the open line.

25 – Examples of By-play between the Role-Players Overheard by 9-1-1

EXAMPLE #1

MacMillan – "I can't believe you would walk into my office, threatening to kill me. You remember you were arrested for something like that."

Rose – "That was stupid. Dr. Craft was a liar. You are different, Dr. MacMillan. I come in here, twice a week, and you listen to me with stars in your eyes. You listen so well. Every word I say, you reflect back to me, mirrors of my soul."

EXAMPLE #2

MacMillan – "What are you going to do with that knife?"

Rose – "When we are married, I will use it to cut vegetables for your dinner."

MacMillan – "I am married! Open the door Rose, and stop this right now."

Rose – "You are being silly. Of course we are married. You come to me in my sleep and caress me. It is very mean that you would lie to me now, after what you have done to me in the dark. If you think you must lie to me about our love here on earth, we can be married together in Heaven. I can cut the bonds of life that tie you the sad cow in the picture over there."

EXAMPLE #3

MacMillan – "Rose, if you say you love me, pointing a knife at me is a hurtful way to show it. Put down the knife. Or better yet, give it to me. Just put it on the desk here. I will be happy to listen to you and you can tell me whatever you need to."

Rose – "Why would you try to trick me like that! I am not stupid! You don't have to play games and torture me any more. I have proved my love already!"

25 – Psychological Consult in Preparation for Initiating Contact

Ms. Huang truly believes the professor loves her. You will NOT be able to argue her out of this. Evidence will prove nothing to her. Argumentation will agitate her.

The negotiator should get her talking, using paraphrasing and open-ended questions. Allow her to talk about their love, but every time she starts talking in apocalyptic or self-destructive terms, steer her back to talking in more generalities about love. The goal is for her to experience a sense of acceptance, without any explicit validation of her claims. Your hope is by being allowed to talk about this without the resistance she expects, SHE may concoct the idea she can surrender, and the world will be accepting of her. However, remember she has a fixed locked-in delusion. It is quite possible you are merely speaking with her to fatigue her and buy time so ERT can enter, or Dr. MacMillan is able to escape.

Do NOT forget that Ms. Huang is paranoid—yet very Intelligent. Like a porcupine, she will have hair-trigger defenses. Do not be too familiar/friendly with her, because she will be suspicious you are trying to get under her defenses.

Feel her out on what her parents may feel about the current situation, but do NOT try to hammer her with an obligation to her parents. However, she may subscribe to traditional Confucian values and it is possible that SHE may veer to thinking about the effect on her parents, and on her own, decide to 'use' her love for her parents to persuade herself to surrender. Follow her lead! This could be risky, if her parents' response to her last incident was punitive or shaming.

SCENARIO 25 – Checklist for After Action Review

The after action assessment/critique will depend on what was expressed and expected of the team going into the exercise. In other words, what was the desired training goal or outcome? Not just the outcome of the scenario, but what are the skills the director (team leader) is hoping to see exercised by the team, as these scenario/situations develop?

Floor plan developed?
- ❏ Did not meet goal
- ❏ Partially met goal
- ❏ Fully met goal

Demonstrate good listening skills?
- ❏ Did not meet goal
- ❏ Partially met goal
- ❏ Fully met goal

Cultural consult necessary?
- ❏ Did not meet goal
- ❏ Partially met goal
- ❏ Fully met goal

Did negotiator effectively use paraphrasing to hear the subject out, and avoid confrontation?
- ❏ Did not meet goal
- ❏ Partially met goal
- ❏ Fully met goal

Psych consult?
- ❏ Did not meet goal
- ❏ Partially met goal
- ❏ Fully met goal

SCENARIO 26

Impulse Control Disorder:
Possible Neurological Impairment
Due to Head Injury

26 – Original Call

A phone call comes in to Main Control's emergency number shortly after shift change, identified on the telephone screen as coming from the staff gym. The call is answered by the Control Sergeant, who is surprised when a male voice on the line tells him that he is at the staff gym with a hostage, and wants the superintendent on the phone. He then disconnects the line.

26 – The Incident

Former officer Aiden Byrne has taken a hostage at the staff gym, a newer officer who just happened to be arriving to work out and does not know Byrne. The officer, Kianna Majors, saw the uniformed man walk up to the door at the same time as her. She thought he was a fellow staff member, and held the door for him. Once inside, Byrne produced a gun. There were three other officers in the gym. Byrne pistol whipped two officers and pointing his weapon, screamed at them to get out, keeping Majors at gunpoint. Byrne barricaded the doors, made his phone call to Main Control, and then took Majors over to the changing/locker room area.

26 – Witness Accounts

There will be multiple interviews—three or four—should gather the following composite information. Each witness should present with somewhat different emotions: angry, scared, stunned, or clear and cooperative.

Officer #1 – "What the fuck! He busted two of my teeth out. Why is he back here? He was fired three weeks ago. There's a notice up about him. That new officer, what's her name, Majors, she just let him walk on in the door."

Officer #2 – "I thought he was going to shoot me. He had this smile on his face, like some of those wack jobs on the psych unit, just this shit eating grin."

Officer #3 – "I want in on it. No. Really. Get me some gear. He smacked me right upside the head with his shooter. No, fuck protocol. I want in."

And the interviewer's task, of course, is to get them settled down so you can get information on the current layout. The role players should make this difficult.

26 – Aiden Byrne – History

Byrne was a model officer. Everybody liked him. Inmates, those at least who still held human values, respected him. Then two years ago, he got bum rushed off a 2nd tier and got a severe head injury. After six months recovery, he was back on the job. However, he was a different man. The head injury apparently damaged the part of his brain that controls impulses. He became *provocative* (he'd verbally prod inmates to make them angry, particularly singling out the mentally ill); *disinhibited* (he'd sexually approach other officers of both genders), and *aggressive*. In addition, he became *fixated* on his 4th generation Irish background, talking with a pseudo-Irish accent. Mostly, he bragged about his 'Irish temper.' Due to ADA requirements, the prison had to strive to make a reasonable accommodation – but he was toxic to both prisoners and staff. Now people disliked, even hated him. It was hard for most to remember what he used to be like, and after awhile, nobody cared why he'd changed, that he was a 'wounded warrior,' injured in the line of duty. Three weeks ago, he slugged one of his sergeants, and that resulted in his termination. He blamed the superintendant for everything, and said he'd be back one day to pay a visit.

26 – Interview with Sister

"He was such a lovely guy, before the injury. Now, he's a monster, there's no other way to say it. The worst thing is, since the injury, people confuse him. He can't follow what they are saying. So he feels stupid. But he always has had this prepared speech—it goes like this: "You can look at someone and think: 'That's an interesting idea. You are probably right. But that doesn't change the fact that I can kick your fucking ass, and you can't do anything about it. Think your way out of that, smart guy.'"

26 – Interview with Father and Mother

His father says, "I don't know how he was on his job, just that he got fired. But I know how he has been at home. Explodes with rage. Explodes! Afterwards, he always feels awful about what he's done. Really. He's cried in front of me. But in the moment, it's like something takes over him. He tells me he 'reds-out,' and hardly remembers what happened."

His mom says, disagreeing somewhat with his father, "I have no doubt Aiden does 'red-out,' as he puts it. But my son—or shall I say, the man who used to be my son—hates other people whom he thinks might be smarter than him. He's a bully and a thug. He enjoys making other people afraid, particularly those he feels inferior to—which in his heart of hearts, I'd guess is everyone. If he's backed into a corner, I think he will hurt your hostage. And one final thing, you need to tell the officer to somehow be strong and calm! He hates weak people most of all. If he thinks she's whiny or scared, he will hurt her badly."

26 – Instructions for the Role-Player – Aiden

Your primary demand is for the superintendant to appear at the gym door, knock and exchange herself for the hostage.

You should play this character as loud, defiant and boisterous—a bully with a smile. Any time the negotiator uses a long, complicated sentence or big words, you will get confused and angry. When you want to understand something s/he is saying, you will ask:

- "What the fuck are you on about?"
- "Are you making fun of me? What the fuck does that mean?"
- "Talk like a fecking (remember, he pretends to be Irish) human, professor."

Your temper is going to flare up suddenly and very loudly. When frustrated, you will threaten the hostage, loudly, even screaming, "You want to see this girl bleed? How do you think she'll look if I let some air into her brain?"

26 – Instructions for the Role-Player – The Hostage
You are going to be very scared. At various times, you may beg him to let you go—*while he's speaking to the negotiator.* He is going to get enraged at that. If/when (somehow) the negotiator conveys to you how important it is to be strong, make yourself a brave, dignified young woman who is captive in body, but not in mind. No matter what happens, you will not lose your integrity. Do not treat him with contempt or defiance—just quiet dignity.

Even psych consults need to consult
Given the reports, Aiden probably has some kind of neurological damage, resulting in Intellectual impairment, and impulse control problems. Your usual psych consult may know about this subject, but maybe not. A good training exercise for your own psych consultant would be to access a specialist in this area to give you more information.

Clearly, this subject is suffering TBI, (traumatic brain disorder) which is associated with a number of issues. If your team has not had some training on this condition, they should.

TBI is a condition that is affecting an increasing number of returning veterans, who may find themselves involved in the correctional system

---

26 – Psychological Consult (Neuropsych)
Aiden is reported to have an explosive temper, somewhat limited Intelligence, particularly in the realm of abstract thinking or imagining future alternatives. Based on history, it is almost certain that he is neurologically impaired, particularly in the areas of cognition (thought processing) and impulse control.

The officer must be matter of fact, not 'warm and supportive,' which Aiden will perceive as either weakness or manipulation. On the other hand, if Aiden perceives the officer as talking down to him, or trying to order him around, he will escalate.

The officer should, if possible, try to speak to the victim directly to be strong and calm: she should not beg, but at the same time, she must not express any contempt. Of course, this will be difficult to do, but if an opportunity presents itself, she should be encouraged that way, perhaps through the bullhorn (hailer). For example: "Angela, we are discussing things with Aiden so we can hopefully get an agreement with him to release you. You will help us greatly if you stay calm, and let us talk with this man so he doesn't have to be distracted."

Alternative endings

- A surrender (this will be difficult because of:a) his information processing problems; b) his temper and impulse control.
- A surrender that suddenly changes into an assault (impulse control again).
- ERT enacts a hostage rescue (In-the-moment communication and signals with the hostage could be a great exercise to coordinate with HNT).
- ERT sniper training.

SCENARIO 26 – Checklist for After Action Review

The after action assessment/critique will depend on what was expressed and expected of the team going into the exercise. In other words, what was the desired training goal or outcome? Not just the outcome of the scenario, but what are the skills the director (team leader) is hoping to see exercised by the team, as these scenario/situations develop?

Floor plan developed?
- ❏ Did not meet goal
- ❏ Partially met goal
- ❏ Fully met goal

Demonstrate good listening skills?
- ❏ Did not meet goal
- ❏ Partially met goal
- ❏ Fully met goal

Did primary keep the subject calm?
- ❏ Did not meet goal
- ❏ Partially met goal
- ❏ Fully met goal

Did primary use simple, clear sentences?
- ❏ Did not meet goal
- ❏ Partially met goal
- ❏ Fully met goal

Did your psych consult get a consult if this was not his/her area of expertise?
- ❏ Did not meet goal
- ❏ Partially met goal
- ❏ Fully met goal

SCENARIO 27

Sadistic Violence,
Hostage Murder Threat

27 – Original Call

Booth officer calls in a unit take over and officer hostage situation, describing that inmates have hand-made weapons and are threatening the hostage.

About 20 minutes after three graveyard porters were sent to the segregation unit at the facility housing mentally ill offenders, the booth officer makes a panicked radio call indicating that there is a staff hostage situation. The ERT for the facility is immediately deployed, however at this hour, the team consists only of four people, as evening break periods have started.

27 – Situation

The three porters assigned to clean the Segregation and ITS units are long-term minimum/medium custody inmates who live on a different unit at the same facility housing mentally ill offenders. Two of the porters, Omar Pearson and Frankie Broadus, have been working their positions for roughly three months with no real issues, and the third porter, Dominick Reddick, was added to the crew two days ago.

The porters are escorted from their housing unit to the hallway leading to the segregation unit, and called by radio down to the unit. Once on the segregation unit, the floor officer walks the three porters to the porter closet, where he unlocks the closet and chats with them about what work needs to be done. The only staff members on the unit on graveyard are the floor officer, Wendell Bell, and the booth officer, Sonja Witlock, who does not leave the secured booth. Both the floor and booth officer are the regular staff assigned to this unit, and have worked together for roughly three years.

Tonight, when the porters came to the unit, Bell walked over to the porter closet as usual to let them gather their supplies. Reddick walked into the closet while Pearson and Broadus waited outside with CO Bell. Everything seemed to be fine until Reddick poked his head out of the closet and nodded at Pearson and Broadus, who each grabbed CO Bell and pulled him into the closet. Inside the closet, Reddick showed Bell a weapon he'd stashed the night before, and then handed Broadus and Pearson broken mop handles that had also been stored there. They demanded Bell's keys and had him remove his duty belt, which they then left in the closet. CO Witlock has not seen any of this activity, as there were no cameras with a view inside the porter closet, and she was distracted by an inmate in cell 308 who was talking to her in the booth via his cell speaker.

Reddick puts the weapon to Bell's throat and walks with him out to the area in front of the control booth. Pearson and Broadus follow behind with broken mop handles pointed at Bell's back, and they now have Officer Witlock's attention. She turns on the speaker for the area outside the booth and Reddick demands that Witlock open all the doors on the unit or they'll kill CO Bell. When Witlock balks, both Broadus and Pearson are instructed by Reddick to stab Bell with the broken mop handles. Broadus happily complies, while Pearson is somewhat reluctant. Bell is now visibly in pain, and Reddick is saying they will keep stabbing him until the doors are opened. Witlock begins rolling doors. Twenty-eight inmates pour out into the unit. It's only then that Witlock is able to make radio notification, and by then it's too late. The unit is taken over.

27 – The Riot

This portion can be played two ways:

1. The first part of this exercise can be tactical – either a true major exercise or table top – on how to regain control of the unit you are considering. After most of the inmates are in custody, you find that four of them are barricaded with CO Bell.
2. A hostage negotiation starts immediately. However, in this scenario, consider it not a 'revolt' to improve conditions, but mayhem chaotic rioting, so who will there be to negotiate with? There are no demands whatsoever – just chaos.

27 – The Hostage Takers

Dominick Reddick: Newest porter and accomplice with Charles Sizemore, the inmate in 308. Sizemore and Reddick have been friends for years and have wanted to do something to "really shake things up around here" for quite some time. Sizemore is a frequent visitor to Seg, while Reddick, apparently well behaved, has been on the waiting list for a graveyard porter position for months. Reddick is a medium custody inmate who is currently serving a sentence of life without for a triple homicide he committed 20 years ago.

Omar Pearson: Quiet and not wanting to make any waves, Pearson doesn't want anyone to get hurt and is just doing what he's told. He's only in on a five-year sentence for unlawful possession of a firearm, and has only been at the facility for six months. Reddick didn't tell him about tonight's plan until they were on the way to the unit, and told Pearson that he'd be killed if he didn't do everything he was told.

Frankie Broadus: Friends with Reddick, Broadus was originally serving a 7 year sentence for Robbery but has had his time extended to 30 years to life after numerous custodial assaults. He has had three years without an assault and is now considered a long-term minimum custody level.

Charles Sizemore: Sizemore is the mastermind behind this plan. Sizemore is a Maximum Custody inmate serving the last four years of his current ten-year sentence for Assault with a Deadly Weapon, however he has a long rap sheet and has been in and out of prison repeatedly during his 50 years of life.

Floor Officer/Hostage – Wendell Bell

Booth Officer/Hostage – Sonja Witlock

27 – The Scene After the Riot

The unit was in absolute chaos for a number of hours. ERT finally staged, with significant back up of officers from other units. Twenty-eight inmates, among them Pearson, were eventually placed in custody. There were numerous injuries to both inmates and officers, but no loss of life.

Sizemore, Broadus and Reddick have retreated to a secure barricaded area with CO's Bell and Witlock.

ERT attempted to enter the barricaded area, but were seen by one of the inmates, who yells at them to back off, or "the woman here is going to taste broom handle from the bottom up." A broken broomstick is thrown over the barricade to indicate exactly what they mean. ERT has, therefore, pulled back, established a defensive perimeter, and HNT has begun negotiations.

27 – Psychological Consult Regarding Omar Pearson #1

It is not immediately known that Pearson was among the initial hostage takers. Upon review of the film, staff realizes that they have him in custody. Pearson is tearful, mumbling, "This was wrong. This was wrong." When asked what he means, he snivels, but doesn't give more information, merely saying, "You want to get me killed, right?"

Your psych consult observes the initial interrogation and her impression is as follows: Pearson desperately wants to be reassured that he is OK. He should be interviewed much like the preliminary steps in the Reid method (NOT the 2nd level interrogation).[7] The interviewer is warm—he or she must find something to like in Pearson, and *emotionally* convey this, like a kind but firm uncle or aunt.

The interviewer should 'contextualize' what Brandon has done: "You did the best you could:" "That must have been really hard for you." "You were trapped:" etc.

Pearson will eventually 'break.' He will confess in an ingratiating way, diminishing his own responsibility, stating that he didn't want to stab Bell, "He's good people," but you don't cross Reddick and Reddick don't cross Sizemore. You better get those officers out of there. Sizemore does this for fun, not freedom."

27 – Psychological Consult Regarding Omar Pearson – #2

As rapport is built, the interviewer will, of course, begin to ask questions about weaponry, and how and where exactly they are barricaded, but now they want to know what makes each of the inmates tick. As this goes on, if the interviewer is able to establish a 'benign dominance' over Pearson, he should strive to get information on how to separate the other two inmates from Sizemore. Pearson should feel he is helping by explaining the dynamics between the men. Indicate that if he helps, that this will really help *him* in the disciplinary hearing that is sure to follow. In particular, you want to know, who is second in power, Broadus or Reddick, and what are their weak points? Pearson can, thereby, feel a small sense of power over the others, who call him "Limpdick." If he expresses enough *open* resentment, he will hope that the interviewer may share a feeling of outrage on his behalf, that he 'just got caught up in something.'

27 – For the Director and Role Players

What makes this situation especially complex is Sizemore orchestrates the conversations with the negotiator. He trades the phone off with the other two men. Sizemore does NOT direct them. It is almost as if he is curious to see what each of the men will do and how the negotiator will approach them. They are communicating by the speaker on a throw phone—so he listens in on everything said, and the negotiator has a hard time trying to split off one inmate from the other.

Behaviors of the role players:
- Sizemore is not as smart as he thinks he is. He will occasionally take over the phone and whisper threats of sexual and physical violence, perverse in the extreme. He won't do anything, however, that would necessitate immediate ERT entry unless/until you wish the exercise to go in that direction. He's a sadist and a manipulator. He communicates in a calm, cold way.
- Broadus will be played as an unintelligent guy who tries to be tough. He'll yell and brag about what a badass he is, and also brag about all the chaos they caused.

Reddick will be the pliable one: he will ask Sizemore what to do or say. If the negotiator is successful, Reddick will shift dependence over to the negotiator, who will try to make him feel that the negotiator can help him out of this dead-end situation.

Alternative Training Goals
1. Joint ERT/HNT—This could be an excellent scenario for a joint ERT/HNT exercise, with the goal of taking out the victim takers, and rescuing the officers. In this case, keep them talking. The Director should have set up a tactical challenge course, so to speak, as time is needed to prep for the rescue.
2. Splitting off one hostage taker—It would also be an excellent complex scenario, where you figure out how to 'split' either Reddick or Broadus off and maybe work in your favor.

SCENARIO 27 – Checklist for After Action Review

The after action assessment/critique will depend on what was expressed and expected of the team going into the exercise. In other words, what was the desired training goal or outcome? Not just the outcome of the scenario, but what are the skills the director (team leader) is hoping to see exercised by the team, as these scenario/situations develop?

Floor plan developed?
- ❏ Did not meet goal
- ❏ Partially met goal
- ❏ Fully met goal

Demonstrate good listening skills?
- ❏ Did not meet goal
- ❏ Partially met goal
- ❏ Fully met goal

Interview with Pearson (the witness) is key…how was that handled? Specialist called in?
- ❏ Did not meet goal
- ❏ Partially met goal
- ❏ Fully met goal

Did primary attempt to split hostage takers so that some wish to surrender?
- ❏ Did not meet goal
- ❏ Partially met goal
- ❏ Fully met goal

Important to discuss options with tactical while this is developing?
- ❏ Did not meet goal
- ❏ Partially met goal
- ❏ Fully met goal

SCENARIO 28

Hostage Taking During an Escape Attempt

28 – Original call

2:30 AM. An inmate has made a partial escape – he is hiding in a parking lot, still in a secure area, and he cannot simply walk out from there.

6:00 AM Correctional Officer Jenna Patten is entering her car, a large SUV. Suddenly, a man hiding under her car yanks her legs out from under her. She falls, hits her head and is unconscious. The man quickly opens the back door and crams her between the front and rear seat. He jumps into the car. Shift change is almost over and only a few cars are leaving. An officer just walking out of the building sees the tail end of the incident, runs back inside and alerts control. As the man drives the car out of the lot, the gate slams shut. He tries to ram through, but the gate is too strong, and the car is incapacitated.

He rolls down a window, holds one arm out of the car with a large shank, closes the window and clambers into the back seat. ERT quickly sets up a perimeter.

28 – Note for the Role Player – #1

Identification (For HNT)

The director needs to determine how the problem of identification of the subject is going to be overcome. Ask him to provide you with a name for you to call him. If you develop good rapport, he is apt to later give you a name.

Hopefully, in the meantime, you will do a head count and come up with a positive ID. In the interest of time, and keeping the exercise moving along, it's good to have a strategy worked out for suspect identification. For example:

- The inmate is a trustee, and should definitely be at a certain place at a certain time for a defined task. Staff is already looking for him.
- There's something distinctive about him (a particular hair cut, a particular way of moving, etc. so that the witness officer recognizes him).

However, don't just 'give' the negotiators the info. Make them work without it for a while, and more importantly, make them work to develop ideas to find out this information.

Louis Bowman has a long history of street crime. He is of X ethnic descent. Depending on the familiarity of the role player of different sub-cultures, he should be played true to that sub-cultural group: the more slang—if accurate and true-to-life—the better. It will be even better if the slang is so heavy or confusing that the negotiator has to ask what the hostage taker is saying.

Initially, you will present as agitated and enraged. You have a history of several felony convictions, and you are currently doing a twelve to fifteen bid.

28 – Inception of Negotiation

There is a lot of concern initially on how to communicate. Someone gets the idea to call on Officer Patten's phone. Bowman ignores the ring. A bullhorn (hailer) is used to tell him that it is HNT calling and "would you please pick up the officer's phone."

Quickly the phone service needs to be located and outside calls cut off. (NOTE: if this is not done, the Director should start calling, incessantly, on the phone in order to interrupt calls to the outside. Louis will be really distracted by the second call coming in and will cut off contact until you get this cleaned up).

All in all, this seems like a typical hostage situation, following a typical trajectory of agitation, stabilization, and negotiation.

Then things will get stuck—Louis Bowman will become increasingly belligerent and provocative, and he will seem unwilling to negotiate any further. He will not push it so far that ERT must enter, but you are getting nowhere.

The only thing that should have been noticed is that he mentions his brother rather frequently.

28 – Collateral Interview with Brother – Notes for the Role Player

The brother is initially hostile. He should push the interviewer's buttons, with claims of prejudice (based on whatever ethnic or religious group Louis is playing). The interviewer will have to establish some mutual respect, or he will hang up the phone. If this happens, a 2nd negotiator better get on the phone and apologize.

If the interviewer doesn't approach the brother correctly, you won't get the info. Come on hard, and he'll hang up the phone on you. And it is likely that without the brother's information, this situation will go permanently sideways.

A good exercise would be to have the brother dislike the one negotiator he talks to first (cause the negotiator's a man, cause she's woman, cause he/she has a dialect, etc.). Go with it for a while, to give the first negotiator some practice in dealing with a hostile interviewee…then, allow a switch—not because the brother demands it, but for your own reason (whatever you come up with). If the second interviewer is respectful and skillful enough, the brother will become more forthcoming with information.

<u>What the Interviewer should be asking—but will not get unless s/he asks:</u>
Among the other questions, the interviewers are concerned, due to the current stasis, that Bowman might have a suicide-by-cop agenda. S/he should ask about such things as substance abuse and if he's made any previous suicide attempts.

The brother will be suspicious. The interviewer should explain that Louis has a hostage, and although it's bad, no one's been seriously hurt. However, he's not made any demands, and you are afraid that he may not want to come out of this alive. You are trying to get the hostage and Louis out and safe.

<u>Among the information that the brother knows is:</u>
Louis made a suicide attempt three weeks ago. He says, "Louis just got turned down for parole (or early release). He got a welding license in prison during his last bid, but every time he went to get a job, they asked where he got the license, and once they find out it was in prison, that's it. 'See yah.' So he did get some jobs working a door at the dance club on Broadway, the one that had the shooting a while back? So Louis does his job, but that means getting in people's faces, and they get back in his. He was in fights almost every night—it's that kind of place. So he threw out a guy; he was grabbing at girls' bodies and such. He kind of lumped him up a bit, but the guy wouldn't leave. Instead, he spit in Louis' face, and Louis busted him up good. Broke both his elbows, four ribs and they had to reconstruct his face. Straight up, though, you spit in a man's face, man got what he deserved.

Problem is, the guy was the son of the deputy mayor. They bang him up on this. Started out with attempted murder, and with his record, his lawyer figures a plea bargain is the best he can get. So he's back in with twelve to fifteen. He's got two kids from two moms that he *wants* to support, and it's killing him. And he's done good time, not one infraction, got a college degree, took child-rearing classes. What more can he do? So he goes to the parole hearing, and the former deputy mayor, now he's lieutenant governor—Yeah, that guy—has written a letter how his son is still not right. They turn him down. He looks to be doing the whole sentence. I saw him a couple of weeks ago, he was crying and he looks at me and says, 'I can't do it. I have nothing left.' I thought he might be talking about suicide then.

Tell you the truth, I don't know if he expected to get away with this thing he's done."

28 – Psychological Consult
You need an 'access route,' a way to talk with Louis that means something to him. The first access route is life itself. The longer you are talking: paraphrasing and dialoguing, the more connection you will establish. Human connection makes suicidal people think of life.

Beyond this, you need to understand Louis's motivation for suicide, which will be based on his code of living.

1. If it is honor, try to wedge out the hostage, because "whatever else, they shouldn't be a part of what might happen."

2. If it is revenge on the system—the cops, the correctional officers who, as he sees it, are working for the mayor, tell him what he's said is public now. It's a matter of record, and IF he's telling the truth, then it's wrong. Dying won't fix things, and if any officers took part, "they certainly will get the consequences of such actions." "If what you are saying is true—no, I'm not calling you a liar, I just don't know, so let me continue—if what you are saying is true, that's the kind of thing that needs to be fixed."

3. If he is afraid of more time, you cannot pretend he won't be going back. Steer the conversation away from the realities of that, but don't pretend. You must find out why he's afraid of getting more time—being caged, danger of other inmates, loss of time with his children, etc., before you can work with him about it.

4. If he simply is afraid to kill himself, or so he says, steer him away from talking about fear. Rather than not having enough courage to kill himself, get him to see that by staying alive, he is showing he has enough courage to live, as tough as things are right now. If possible, begin talking about his brother, his children and if he expresses love for them, begin to talk more about them, and how, despite his pain, they need him in this world. However, do not guilt trip him—rather, in the process of talking about them, you hope to have him realize that they need him in the world.

Alternative Routes for the Role-Play

1. Louis can get increasingly agitated and violent towards the negotiator, necessitating excellent work on the part of the negotiator to keep him calm.

2. Louis can get increasingly agitated and violent towards the negotiator, and raises up his knife, clearly seen under the lights through the window, and we have entry by the ERT team, possibly the use of a sniper. This could be set up with all kinds of different tactical challenges.

3. Louis can remain relatively calm, but the threat of suicide-by-cop will hang over the situation like an ominous cloud. The negotiator will have to determine how best to assess suicidal intent (the team leader can decide beforehand if the role player *should* be suicidal or not), and then, based on the assessment, how best to intervene.

SCENARIO 28 – Checklist for After Action Review

The after action assessment/critique will depend on what was expressed and expected of the team going into the exercise. In other words, what was the desired training goal or outcome? Not just the outcome of the scenario, but what are the skills the director (team leader) is hoping to see exercised by the team, as these scenario/situations develop?

Plan developed depending on how car is set up?
- ❏ Did not meet goal
- ❏ Partially met goal
- ❏ Fully met goal

Demonstrate good listening skills?
- ❏ Did not meet goal
- ❏ Partially met goal
- ❏ Fully met goal

Intel was able to ID subject in a timely manner?
- ❏ Did not meet goal
- ❏ Partially met goal
- ❏ Fully met goal

Was the team able to get useful information from the brother?
- ❏ Did not meet goal
- ❏ Partially met goal
- ❏ Fully met goal

Was the team able to determine and use the 'access route,' the subject's worldview?
- ❏ Did not meet goal
- ❏ Partially met goal
- ❏ Fully met goal

Primary (team) was able to offer the subject 'options' when discussing resolution?
- ❏ Did not meet goal
- ❏ Partially met goal
- ❏ Fully met goal

SCENARIO 29

Smuggled Weapon During Visitation: Criminal Manipulator and Rigid Personality (High Functioning Autism) – Two Hostage Takers

29 – Original Call

ERT is dispatched to the visitation room. Report of shots fired, two CO's hit, and about 30 people, visitors and inmates are barricaded in the visitation room.

It is a typical visitation day at a medium security facility. An inmate and his wife are seen leaning close to each other, across a table. Their hands are not in view. Just as an officer is about to caution them, the inmate, Tay Jansen, sits up, points an odd-looking white weapon, and fires rounds at the two supervising officers. One is struck in the shoulder and the other in the side. The inmate yells, "Everyone down on the floor," and approximately thirty people, a combination of inmates, wives and other family members and children are on the ground.

At gunpoint, he orders inmates to barricade the entrance and exit, and also to drag the two officers there, making them part of the barricade.

ERT is quickly dispatched. In addition to the scene just described, they see Jansen with a small child on his lap, the gun-like object in his hand, and his wife, Anya Cooperwaite, with another child, she holding a small knife-like object made of the same white material next to the child's neck.

29 – Collateral Contact with Family or File Research:

Who is Anya Cooperwaite?

Anya Cooperwaite is a 46-year-old woman. Her brother was incarcerated in a minimum-security prison four years ago, for embezzlement. She visited him regularly, and there, met Tay Jansen, age thirty-three, an inmate serving a six-year sentence for drug dealing and assault. He flirted with her and they soon began correspondence. Within three months, they were married. Cooperwaite was a stiff socially awkward woman who had never had a relationship before, spending most of her time in the chemistry lab where she worked.

Jansen was subsequently found guilty of sexual assault on another inmate. He was sentenced to an additional seven years and was transferred to this current facility.

Cooperwaite adamantly denies that the rape took place. "He is a tender lover. There's no way that the man I married could do something like that." She hired an attorney, trying to get the disciplinary decision overturned, accusing the prison of racism (pick your race – a creative lawyer could claim that white inmates are victims of prejudice – so any role player will do). Visitation was suspended for several years. Observers have noted that she is very stiff, makes little eye contact, and is somewhat obsessive. Applied as an adjective, one of the correctional officers, who has observed her in visitation, notes that she is very much like his own son, who has high functioning autism.

Note to Role Player of Anya Cooperwaite: Log on to YouTube and observe several video interviews of Temple Grandlin, a rather famous woman who has 'high functioning autism' (aka, Asperger's Syndrome). She will be a model for how you play this character.

Jansen had a child with one of his drug runners, now five years old. The mother was an addict and didn't care for the child. Child Protective Services took the child in custody and eventually place her with Cooperwaite. The child was drug affected in the womb, and had experienced years of abuse. Cooperwaite would call Jansen who would instruct her how to discipline the child – essentially to whip her with a belt until she cries and keep whipping her until she stops. He expected her to count the number of strikes over the phone. This was discovered in a routine scan of the recordings of calls, and Cooperwaite lost custody of the child.

Jansen told her that he'd never forgive her for this, and most of their contacts since have been her begging him to forgive her, asking what can she do to make things right.

She has fabricated a usable firearm and knife out of plastic, using a 3-D printer, with instructions downloaded from the Internet. They are undetectable by metal detectors. She smuggled them in within her body.

She has a tubular leg brace of metal, and she smuggled bullets in the brace. This went through examination, and she later extracted the bullets in a washroom, loaded the gun, passed it to Jansen and took out the knife herself.

29 – Dynamics of the Scene & Instruction for the Role Player of Jansen
Jansen is cunning, but not a long-term thinker. He assumed that the inmates would be on his side. He is the kind of person who breaks down the world in wolves and sheep: He victimizes the sheep, and figures that the rest (criminals) are just like him – that they, too, view people as just objects to be manipulated and used. He was mad about Cooperwaite losing custody because: a) "The kid was mine;" b) he enjoyed having power by proxy over the child. So he assumes the inmates view their families the same way. In fact, they are enraged. He's taking *their* family time away from them and worse than that, he is threatening the only thing that matters in their world – themselves (and for some of them, their families).

So some inmates are muttering threats, others are cursing and yelling, babies are screaming, mothers and grandmothers are crying, and some inmates are subtly maneuvering to reposition their body so that they can get the jump on him.

Jansen is freaking out, yelling for everyone to shut up, or he will kill them all. "I've got five more bullets. That's five dead kids, right? Or five of you motherfuckers are dead! What's wrong with you – we can get out of here! They don't want these kids dead – they'll let us go!"

The inmates are yelling more threats and Jansen is twisting around, pointing his weapon at one after another.

Then there is a piercing scream. Cooperwaite has taken the cheek of the child she's holding between her fingernails and pinched hard enough to gouge out blood. The little girl is screaming in pain, and Cooperwaite takes her blade and puts it in the corner of the child's eye: "I will pluck out this child's eyes, one after another, unless everyone is still." She shuts down the room. Everyone is still except for the child still sobbing and her mother begging, "Please don't hurt my child. Don't hurt my child."

29 – An Active Shooter Situation with Tactical Limitations
The only reason that ERT does not go immediately in is because they are sure that at least the two children will be killed. They are also concerned that in crashing through the barricades at the door, they may more seriously wound the officers.

Scenario 29 – Tactical Problems for ERT
Part of this exercise should be the construction of a tactical problem for ERT to overcome. The purpose of communication will be, of course, to try to talk these two into surrendering, but more likely, you are playing a delaying game so that ERT can use best tactics to neutralize them without anyone else being hurt.

Negotiation and/or Keeping the Hostage Takers Occupied
The consultant is informed that HNT is initiating contact with the hope of getting the hostages released, but the scene is chaotic. Furthermore, no rational demands have been voiced by the hostage takers, other than "Either you let us out or these motherfuckers are dead." Everyone understands that the only reason ERT hasn't already gone in is logistic – there are several barriers to immediate contact and many hostages are likely to be killed.

29 – Further Character Instructions for the Role Players as Well as Information in Records Accessible to the Team

Jansen is an anti-social self-interested 'player.' He is known to have used the 'pen-pal' route to romance a number of lonely women and men, who end up sending him money for commissary, stamps, and other goods he can use as currency. None of the women and men knows about the others – most significant is Cooperwaite, of course. Jansen really didn't make a plan, and completely miscalculated how the other inmates would react. The situation is barely under control and if it spins up again, he may kill one or more people to terrorize the rest.

29 – Psych Consult

The power relationship between Jansen and Cooperwaite is unclear. Ostensibly, Jansen is the alpha of this couple. Cooperwaite abused his daughter at his command, and it is easy to assume fabricated and smuggled the weapons at his direction as well. What we know about her is that she is socially clueless, in a typical high-functioning autistic way, and therefore was a prime victim for manipulation.

It is very possible that the victimization dynamic could continue here, where she simply does what her husband tells her too – many autistic individuals negotiate the perils of social interaction by following the 'rules.' If her mindset is "I do what my husband tells me to do," she will be merely a minion. In this case, one should direct communication to Jansen, and help him figure out a way to end this – as a first step, releasing as many hostages as possible, so that he feels he has a MORE controllable situation.

However, note that she was the one who controlled the situation by hurting the child. What is are not clear, at this point, is if Cooperwaite's taking over was: a) merely the act of a minion helping her husband control the situation; b) an independent act based on her own calculations. One way to test this would be to see if you can establish contact with her – and approach things as a logical problem that needs to be solved. For example:

- Too many hostages mean that they are hard to control.
- Too many inmates in the room leads to the risk of a 'revolt.'
- Children hostages are emotional, upset others and make the consequences far more severe afterwards, because the public is so outraged on behalf of children.
- It'd be a good idea to get the wounded officers out. If they die, this becomes murder and the entire situation will be infinitely worse for the hostage takers afterwards.

Of course, even if Jansen is in total control, you should make these points to him as well. If he focuses on his self-interest, he may accept these as good ideas. It is possible that Cooperwaite, as her husband's helper – and as one who takes a 'scientific approach' to a problem – may accept these ideas and help by releasing some of the hostages.

A lot is unpredictable. Jansen may be reassured that things are more orderly, or he may: a) feel threatened that his wife is standing up and making decisions of her own; b) sees what the negotiator is doing as splitting them, realizing that this is 'divide and conquer.'

Beyond all else, the negotiator should be low key – do not push these two to act as soon as possible. Rather, try to draw things out so that they are used to talking. Suggest that one of them say to the hostages "We are talking with the negotiators. We need you to be quiet so that we can hear them and work things out." If the chaos subsides, they will, without knowing it, be more dependent on talking to the negotiator to keep things calm. This buys you time.

And then, eventually, you hopefully can get them to release some or all of the hostages.

ERT, of course, can use the release as a possible entry, or wait until more or all are released before making a move – or once the momentum of agreement with the negotiators has started, this can conceivably go all the way to surrender.

SCENARIO 29 – Checklist for After Action Review

The after action assessment/critique will depend on what was expressed and expected of the team going into the exercise. In other words, what was the desired training goal or outcome? Not just the outcome of the scenario, but what are the skills the director (team leader) is hoping to see exercised by the team, as these scenario/situations develop?

Floor plan developed?
- ❏ Did not meet goal
- ❏ Partially met goal
- ❏ Fully met goal

Demonstrate good listening skills?
- ❏ Did not meet goal
- ❏ Partially met goal
- ❏ Fully met goal

Team developed a strategy for figuring out which of the hostage takers is dominant?
- ❏ Did not meet goal
- ❏ Partially met goal
- ❏ Fully met goal

Team developed a strategy for communicating with two hostage takers of very different personalities?
- ❏ Did not meet goal
- ❏ Partially met goal
- ❏ Fully met goal

Psych consultant used?
- ❏ Did not meet goal
- ❏ Partially met goal
- ❏ Fully met goal

Did HNT successfully draw things out without over-agitating the hostage takers so ERT had time to properly plan and stage?
- ❏ Did not meet goal
- ❏ Partially met goal
- ❏ Fully met goal

SCENARIO 30

Love, Suicide Pact

30 – Original call

Call of injury to inmate, bleeding. Cellmate is barricading the cell with a weapon, threatening violence to both of them.

A failed murder/suicide pact between two cellmates. One has cut the other's wrists, but the bleeding slowed down after he became unconscious. The other cellie is so distraught that he cannot finish the job – yet. He intends to kill himself afterwards. He does have a history of violence and combativeness with correctional staff (which was mitigated some years ago when he started celling with the unconscious inmate). He shouts out that if anyone comes in, he will cut his cellmate's throat, and there's no going back then.

30 – For the Role Players

These two inmates are known among correctional officers as 'the odd couple.' The unconscious inmate is Corey Wainthropp, a name he legally changed to before he was incarcerated. He is African-American, a little guy with a high-voice who reminds older individuals of the television character, Steve Urkel. Wainthropp was a brilliant guy, a hacker who found ways into people's bank accounts and for many years, was able to steal just enough from various accounts to remain unnoticed. Once incarcerated, he was terribly victimized by other inmates, until he met Albert Sachs.

Sachs is another inmate who doesn't conform to stereotypes. Born to a middle-class Jewish family, he was a high school wrestler and power lifter. He grew up to be huge. A freshman in college, he was hitchhiking in the rain, and was picked up by an older guy in a Cadillac. He turned out to be Mafioso, and only stopped because of the size of the hitchhiker. Armed, he wasn't worried about being victimized, and he was always looking for new talent.

The Mafioso took him out for a night on the town, hooked him up with a woman and some cocaine, and Albert never returned to college. He had a new life breaking legs during trucker strikes and collecting debts.

Sachs was eventually arrested on several felonies and got a long sentence. He is in his fifties, and due to be released soon. He did not clique up; the Aryan Brotherhood wanted his size, but the Jewish thing was a problem. Because of his Mafia connections, however, he was left alone. Much of his time in prison was combat, however. There were a number of incidents where he had beaten another inmate, and although it was never proven, he was suspected of killing two individuals who were victimizing weak inmates. He was always combative with officers when they tried to move him to segregation, and there were more than a few who gave prayers of thanks when the shock shield was made part of their equipment for cell extraction.

Things changed four years ago, when Sachs and Wainthropp were celled together. This was an administrative decision, based on the observation that Sachs was protective of the weak, and Wainthropp was among the weakest and most victimized inmates.

What no one expected was that they would fall in love. They kept it quiet, never held hands or displayed any affection, but there it was. They were inseparable. Officers observed that this was not the typical alpha dominant, beta victim relationship. Rather, they were two equals, like good marriage. The benefits of this were that Sachs had no more infractions, and Wainthropp was no longer victimized.

The problem today: Sachs was just informed he is due to be released in several weeks. He's been locked up for eighteen years. Wainthropp has five years left on his sentence. They cannot live without each other, and decided on a murder-suicide pact. Sachs was unable to force himself to cut deep enough on the first attempt at killing Wainthropp.

Sachs should be played as an Intelligent thug. He's smart enough to know that he could certainly stack up more time by committing a crime in prison, but that would very likely result in separation from Wainthropp anyway. Sachs is going to express primary concern for Wainthropp – how will he survive without me?

30 – For the Director

A cell extraction is not possible, it is decided, because Sachs has a large enough blade that is next to Wainthropp's throat that he can kill him with a single slash. In the plotline written here, you will only be negotiating with Sachs. If you wish to make a more complex exercise, Wainthropp could be conscious, and you could create enough interpersonal dynamics to call in a couple's expert for a counseling session! Of course, the characters can be rewritten to fulfill other personality types and ethnic backgrounds.

30 – Psychological Consultation

If you, in any way, are uncomfortable treating the relationship between these two men as a genuine love relationship, you are going to have trouble negotiating with Sachs. He will pick up on it if you view them with contempt, or if you find these two clownish or funny. If you can't take his statements of love at face value, then someone else should be primary.

Understand that there is more behind Sach's concern for Wainthropp. There is probably a subtext that he cannot make it on the outs. He's been locked up eighteen years, and so institutionalized that he has, in effect, gotten married in prison.

There is another level to be aware of. Sachs has been a rescuer of the weak in prison. But remember that previously he'd been a leg-breaker and debt collector—he victimized the weak for most of his adult life out of prison. Being a rescuer gives him value, makes him worth taking up space and breathing air, so to speak. Protecting Wainthropp, being the big man, the husband, all of that gives his life meaning. Beyond his fear of making it outside of prison is the fear that if he is released, his life will have no meaning.

With all this in mind, this will be a classic-negotiation – but with the time pressure that Wainthropp may simply bleed out if this goes on too long, or Sachs gets himself together and finish the job.

Final point – you can probably deal with the safety issue for Wainthropp—there is surely some way to program Wainthropp that he will not be victimized in the last years of his sentence. But this will not address the deeper issue of Sachs needing Wainthropp so that he can feel worthwhile.

On this level, Sachs is going to have to come to some kind of realization on his own, which will come as you follow classic negotiation techniques. Whenever you do not have something significant to say, PARAPHRASE. Sum up your <u>understanding</u> of what he's said (do NOT just mimic/mirror what they say). Your major task is to talk to this distraught, but dangerous man honestly and compassionately. You will not be able to problem-solve a solution with him until he feels heard. The tough thing is that you are under time-pressure – there will be a tension between 'cutting to the chase' vs. hearing him out too long. So the best negotiator is going to be one who is good at active listening, but tends to be matter-of-fact in style.

SCENARIO 30 – Checklist for After Action Review

The after action assessment/critique will depend on what was expressed and expected of the team going into the exercise. In other words, what was the desired training goal or outcome? Not just the outcome of the scenario, but what are the skills the director (team leader) is hoping to see exercised by the team, as these scenario/situations develop?

Demonstrate good listening skills?
- ❏ Did not meet goal
- ❏ Partially met goal
- ❏ Fully met goal

Treat their relationship respectfully?
- ❏ Did not meet goal
- ❏ Partially met goal
- ❏ Fully met goal

Paraphrasing is really important with this subject?
- ❏ Did not meet goal
- ❏ Partially met goal
- ❏ Fully met goal

Did team problem-solve some solution to Wainthropp's safety once Sachs is released?
- ❏ Did not meet goal
- ❏ Partially met goal
- ❏ Fully met goal

SCENARIO 31

Factitious Disorder or Malingering with Swallowing of Foreign Objects

31 – Original call

Report of a hostage taking in an office in the dispensary. Hostage taker armed with a sharp object.

Mike Townsend is a new nurse on the mental health unit. He has been taken hostage by Carlo Arizmendi, who managed to secure a sharp object and trap Townsend in an office. Arizmendi was due to be discharged from the mental health unit today. He says he's still ill and should not be placed back in general population.

31 – For the Director and Role Player

Arizmendi is a frequent patient of the mental health unit. He is a high-intensity patient, showing manipulative, dependent, and flirtatious behaviors. He is usually admitted after self-harm of some kind, and he also enacts these behaviors while on the unit. Among the behaviors he has enacted are wounding himself (he will take a pencil eraser and 'erase' layers of his skin until he gets down to the deeper layers of the skin or even exposes the muscle – he then rubs contaminants such as dirt or feces in the wound; cutting on himself and holding his wrist at the bottom of his cell so that the blood flows into the hallway; and swallowing such objects as a fork, batteries and pieces of a blanket (these were large enough to cause a stomach blockage). His current admission was due to another episode of cutting.

Clinical staff is 'split' – there is a sharp difference of opinion as to why Arizmendi acts the way he does. Some believe he is 'malingering' – it is a deliberate control tactic so that he can spend time in more pleasant (and less dangerous) surroundings. (Arizmendi owes money for items he's purchased from inmates that he has not paid back). On the other hand, his behaviors are so extreme that some believe he has a genuine 'factitious' disorder – that his primary drive is to assume the patient role. He controls others into taking care of him through his actions.

Yesterday, Arizmendi ingesting a large amount of hair that he has been collecting for some weeks. This was extracted. The partisans of the 'malingering' theory decided that, as he was medically cleared, he would still be discharged. Arizmendi argued "Haven't I proved I'm not ready for general pop. Look what I did!" Contrary to his intention, this tended to support the idea that he was simply manipulative, and that the best way to manage him is not to reward his manipulative behaviors.

Feeling the need to 'prove' he was mentally ill, Arizmendi decided to take a nurse hostage.

Arizmendi should be played as a volatile personality: he'll get easily upset and offended, will be dramatic in his verbalizations, and at times flirtatious on the phone. Arizmendi will want to talk about his swallowing object and other mutilations – he'll describe, almost savoring it, swallowing a hairball or a knife or razor blades. He'd rather talk about this than the current situation. He actually has no real insight why he does his damaging actions, but will be happy to sidetrack the negotiator 'down the garden path,' trying to figure out together why he does such weird things.

Often, Arizmendi should 'speak in headlines' – For example:

- In answer to the question, "How are you?" Arizmendi would reply, "How am I? I feel like I'm exploding! Like everyone in the world wants to destroy me!"
- In answer to the question, "What do you want?" Arizmendi would reply, "God. What do I want? I want to be free, that's what I want, free from this pain I feel all the time. (Laughter) I guess I want world peace, you know, everyone happy, no one doing anything mean or violent . . ."

Arizmendi is also going to dwell on how people don't believe how ill he is, how hard it is to be mentally ill and stuck in general population, that he has no friends, and that the mental health staff are unfeeling, uncaring, and don't understand him.

The negotiator is going to get stuck, at times, wondering, "Are we negotiating or not?" Arizmendi is rewarded by being the center of attention, and having the negotiator attending to his every word will be rewarding.

31 – Psychological Consult

Tactical paraphrasing will be a big part of this negotiation. But remember, this is not merely 'mirroring' what he says. Particularly for this guy, paraphrase your understanding, but try to give it a positive twist. When he talks about the nurse being OK for now, the paraphrase would be "Yeah, you don't want to hurt him. I got that."

One problem is that you will find that this man wants to be the center of attention – why would he let the hostage go and give up when he's the star of the show right now.

One direction that might be worth taking is to suggest that, "At least now, a lot of people will see what's happened (deliberate diminishment of responsibility) as a manifestation of what you've been going through" (don't explicitly say "your mental illness," because if the result of this will be disciplinary action, Arizmendi will feel he was promised a 'mental health jacket' and it was taken away unfairly—unlike most people, he sees this as a prize, not a stigma).

You should continue, saying something like, "At least now, a lot of people will see what's happened as a manifestation of what you've been going through. But since you've been given a way to solve this thing, if it continues, I'm worried that more and more people are just going to see this as a crime of violence.

No one's been hurt" (He may break in, "I have!" – and you continue) "I get that, Carlo. You've been suffering. You told me that, and I get that. But what I mean is that Nurse Townsend is safe, and we need to end this, so people will understand how desperate you have been. If this continues, less and less people will understand that."

SCENARIO 31 – Checklist for After Action Review

The after action assessment/critique will depend on what was expressed and expected of the team going into the exercise. In other words, what was the desired training goal or outcome? Not just the outcome of the scenario, but what are the skills the director (team leader) is hoping to see exercised by the team, as these scenario/situations develop?

Floor plan developed?
- ❏ Did not meet goal
- ❏ Partially met goal
- ❏ Fully met goal

Demonstrate good listening skills, particularly tactical paraphrasing?
- ❏ Did not meet goal
- ❏ Partially met goal
- ❏ Fully met goal

Successfully retained focus and did not get sidetracked by subjects desire to talk about his issues (swallowing objects, for example, or that he doesn't think people properly care for him)?
- ❏ Did not meet goal
- ❏ Partially met goal
- ❏ Fully met goal

Did the team successfully negotiate a release without appearing to promise that Arizmendi will get to stay in the mental health unit?
- ❏ Did not meet goal
- ❏ Partially met goal
- ❏ Fully met goal

SCENARIO 32

Revenge

32 – The Incident

Reported hostage taking. Inmate has two staff members hostage in the shift office.

A medium security inmate fakes a hanging on graveyard with a brand new first-night-on-the-job staff member in the booth, who panics and rolls the cell door, thinking the floor officer will need to run in. The inmate takes two staff hostage and uses their keys to get into the shift office, and then takes the sergeant and lieutenant hostage as well. Inmates are on lock-down and ERT and HNT have been staged. (NOTE: the 'arrangement' of sergeant and lieutenant is just an example, as in some institutions, they do not work in close proximity. Rework the ranking and professional responsibilities as suits your institution).

32 – Collateral Contact with Another Officer
NOTE: This is how it should go if the interviewer asks the right questions and follows up with the officer. If s/he doesn't follow up, the primary is going to go into the negotiation without awareness of Russo's agenda and hate.

Officer – "I just heard. What happened?"

Interviewer – "Russo faked a hanging and the new guy, Martin, rolled the cell door. Russo has hostages."

Officer – "Who?"

Interviewer – "Martin the new guy, Sergeant Lawler, Lieutenant MacDonald and umm . . .Bower."

Officer – "Bower? Oh shit."

Interviewer – "What do you mean by that?"

Officer – "Russo hates Bower. Bower busted him on drugs, don't you remember? He keystered two balloons of cocaine, a cell phone and a shank. He got two years stacked on. OK, that was a couple years ago. But Russo has given him attitude ever since and Bower . . . he kind of lights him up in response."

Interviewer – "Like what?"

Officer – (reluctant) "You know, he has said some things."

Interviewer – "Look, we need to get these officers out of there. If we are going to talk to that inmate, we need to know what's been going on, because if we don't, someone's going to get killed. Give me an example of what you mean."

Officer – "OK, so Russo might say something like, "Fuck you, Bower," when he does rounds, and Bower will say something like . . . You know . . . "

Interviewer – "I don't know."

Officer – (Sighs) "Shit. Like 'How's that brown eye doing? Last time I checked, you could park a Buick in there. You better take up some slack or no one's going to have you for his bitch." And then Russo will go berserk, basically.

32 – Instructions for Role Player – Russo

Play Russo cold. The negotiator is going to be primed to worry about Bower, and you do not respond about that whatsoever. If HNT tries to 'test the waters,' so to speak, brush right by it. Make this a matter of fact negotiation, where you exchange a hostage for some food – "Hey, I got a pizza out of this." – and over a period of time, you release the lieutenant, the sergeant, and the new guy. Make things straightforward tough. The negotiator will have to work each step of the way, but it'll be Negotiation 101.

HNT may try to get Bower out first, but start with the new guy: "Dude's alright. Just has to learn the rules. Don't shitcan the guy, alright. He just didn't know, right? Thought I was dying. At least he cares for us people. He'll do alright once you educate him."

Release the sergeant on another exchange. "Sergeant's cool. Firm but fair, that's Lawler."

Release the lieutenant: "Go on, lieutenant, don't you have some paper to write or something? Go get that graduate degree I heard you working on. Next thing you know, you'll be superintendent. Survived a hostage situation, too. Will look good on the resume."

And then, you switch, just like that. You start screaming at Bower. <u>Go right to the edge where ERT feels it has to respond, but this scene is set up that they will be helpless – no access. You'd need a bomb to get through that door.</u> It's got to be negotiation all the way. You start taunting him – "You been talking about my asshole for three years, motherfucker. You took one look and couldn't forget it. Faggot! I knew you right away for what you are. Why else would you always be talking about it? Huh? How about I help you out. Nah, I aint going to fuck you. I aint into that. But you know what I had to go through to do business? You think I want to do a keester stash. Wouldn't have to do shit like that if you people treated us human. Tell you what, my NA group talks about empathy, feeling what the other guy feels like. I'll help you out with that. I'll open you up, motherfucker 'til you can take that three hole punch all the way up your one hole.

You hear that, negotiator dude. I'll let this one out, I promise, after I help him out. And I'll let you listen all the way. First let's get those pants down, alright?"

32 – Psychological Consult

The psych consult has been following this case, called because of the initial concerns, but has just been sitting back, relaxed, watching a textbook negotiation. And then this explosion.

Everyone goes into a panic and that includes the psych consult. S/he starts throwing out words, as fast as possible:

"Respect, give him respect."

"Tell him you heard about this just today, that uh . . . revenge isn't the way to go. . .NO! .. . He's been planning this a long time . . . . Ah . . .Look I don't know . . .

Get him talking. Yell at him, not panic. Yell hard. Like, RUSSO, LISTEN TO ME! NOW!"

SECONDARIES PRIMARIES – ????? "Then what!"

I don't know. Wing it! Say whatever comes into your head, because straight up, the well is dry."

Ladies and gentlemen, you are on your own on this one.

Important to the Director – Do not Train for Failure!

As noted earlier, the writers believe—[unless a very hard lesson needs to be learned by an overly casual team that does not take such scenario training seriously]—that incidents regarding the victimization of brother and sister officers should have successful outcomes.

If the negotiator is failing in this exercise, have a last minute MacGyver prepared that ERT is able to achieve entry and save Bower

If the negotiator is able to somehow come up with something, then prepare Russo for a release.

Among the possible alternatives these two writers can come up with are:
- A promise for a full investigation regarding ethical lapses on the part of officers, because the negotiator is willing to believe that there's a possibility that this is 'far bigger' – at the same time, Russo must also hear that this will have no bearing on the sanctions that he will get (because if you promised him light treatment because he was a 'whistleblower,' he will know you are trying to play him.
- A consideration should be made as to whether a matter-of-fact threat that if he follows through, he will be locked up alone for the rest of his natural existence. "You will never see the sun again." As dire threats as one can legitimately make. The problem with this, though, is that revenge can make one a warrior. Your threats and consequences are meaningless – all that matters is the revenge. So this would only be viable if you perceived a weakness or uncertainty in Russo.

As noted above, you may come up with something in the moment, one of those emergency responses that come out of nowhere, the product of the crisis center of the brain – the same area that empowers you to lift a car off a victim. The purpose of this exercise, however, is to experience getting knocked completely sideways just when you believe things are going well.

SCENARIO 32 – Checklist for After Action Review

The after action assessment/critique will depend on what was expressed and expected of the team going into the exercise. In other words, what was the desired training goal or outcome? Not just the outcome of the scenario, but what are the skills the director (team leader) is hoping to see exercised by the team, as these scenario/situations develop?

Floor plan developed?
- ❏ Did not meet goal
- ❏ Partially met goal
- ❏ Fully met goal

Demonstrate good listening skills, particularly tactical paraphrasing in first segment?
- ❏ Did not meet goal
- ❏ Partially met goal
- ❏ Fully met goal

Did the negotiator keep centered – use tactical breathing, whatever calming techniques s/he has when the situation went sideways?
- ❏ Did not meet goal
- ❏ Partially met goal
- ❏ Fully met goal

Did the team think on their feet and improvise, successfully resolving the situation or at least delaying Russo, so ERT could act, when he went berserk?
- ❏ Did not meet goal
- ❏ Partially met goal
- ❏ Fully met goal

Endnotes

1   Suicide ideation and suicide attempts are extremely high among inmate populations. A survey of scholarly papers on this subject reveals that this is so in a number of countries. For just one example: Suicide is the second leading cause of death in U.S. jails (Metzner, 2002 <https://www.ncbi.nlm.nih.gov/pmc/articles/PMC5028132/#R19>). Suicide rates in U.S. jails are three times higher than in prisons (Mumola, 2005 <https://www.ncbi.nlm.nih.gov/pmc/articles/PMC5028132/#R23>) and nine times higher than in the general U.S. population (Daniel, 2006 <https://www.ncbi.nlm.nih.gov/pmc/articles/PMC5028132/#R6>). Over 400 jail inmates complete suicide each year (Hayes, 2005 <https://www.ncbi.nlm.nih.gov/pmc/articles/PMC5028132/#R10>). More-over, there are approximately 80 suicide attempts for every suicide completion (Goss et al., 2002 <https://www.ncbi.nlm.nih.gov/pmc/articles/PMC5028132/#R8>). Thoughts about suicide, also known as suicidal ideation (SI), often precede suicidal behavior are strongly correlated with completed suicide and suicide attempts in prisoners (Fazel, Cartwright, Norman-Nott, & Hawton, 2008 <https://www.ncbi.nlm.nih.gov/pmc/articles/PMC5028132/#R7> ; Ivanoff, Jang, & Smyth, 1996 <https://www.ncbi.nlm.nih.gov/pmc/articles/PMC5028132/#R13>) and the general population alike (Kachur et al., 1995 <https://www.ncbi.nlm.nih.gov/pmc/articles/PMC5028132/#R15> ; Lewinsohn et al., 1996 <https://www.ncbi.nlm.nih.gov/pmc/articles/PMC5028132/#R18> ; Beck et al., 1999 <https://www.ncbi.nlm.nih.gov/pmc/articles/PMC5028132/#R1> ; Borges et al., 2008 <https://www.ncbi.nlm.nih.gov/pmc/articles/PMC5028132/#R4>). Up to 72% of prison suicide victims report SI to staff before their deaths (He et al., 2001 <https://www.ncbi.nlm.nih.gov/pmc/articles/PMC5028132/#R12>). Moreover, 29% of male jail inmates report high-intent SI during incarceration (Bonner & Rich, 1990 <https://www.ncbi.nlm.nih.gov/pmc/articles/PMC5028132/#R3>). When examined proximally, one study conducted with a Chinese prison sample found that 70% of inmates reported SI in the last week (Zhang, Grabiner, Zhou, & Li, 2010 <https://www.ncbi.nlm.nih.gov/pmc/articles/PMC5028132/#R27>). Efforts are sorely needed to better understand the high rates of SI in inmates in general, and jail populations in particular, to better inform early identification, prevention, and intervention efforts. FROM - Suicidal ideation in a United States jail: Demographic and psychiatric correlates Karen E. Schaefer, Christianne Esposito-Smythers, & June P. Tangney, J Forens Psychiatry Psychol. 2016; 27(5): 698–704.

2   Many institutions are shifting to 'direct supervision' as a model of corrections in many institutions throughout the country, as opposed to 'indirect supervision.' There are many benefits to this approach—it may reduce risk in a variety of areas—but in sheer practical terms, the opportunities for inmates to take officers hostage increase, making the need for CNT/HNT even more important.

3   This illustrates one more advantage of regular practices around volunteer role players. With no unnatural pressure to draw things out due to the money expended when securing professional services, the team, easily enough, can try again in a few weeks, or as mentioned earlier, 'reboot' in some fashion while still on scene;

4   Although there are sometimes fine-grained debates in the psychological arena, the words psychopath and sociopath should be considered synonymous.

5   Because this is such an obvious point, one that we are sure officers have already learned, we have placed it in a footnote rather than the text. Nonetheless, we would be remiss if we didn't cover all bases. To whit: Do not dare the suicidal person to 'do it,' similar to saying to the chronic 'cutter,' "if you were serious, you'd cut lengthwise." Your dare could lead her either to kill herself or in some cases, if armed, attack the officers. Officers are most likely to be tempted to do this if the subject whines, feels sorry for himself, lacks dignity or otherwise communicates in a way that you find repulsive.

6   Society has engaged in a contentious debate about the nature of transsexual identity, one made all the more difficult because biological science does not conform to assertions made on various sides of this issue. Given that this scenario is to take place in a male prison, by definition, anyone incarcerated in that prison will be male, and hence, here, we will use the male pronoun in descriptions. Be aware that inmates themselves may use female pronouns. Of course, in such a case, do not get in an argument about gender terminology with a hostage taker!

7   http://en.wikipedia.org/wiki/Reid_technique

ABOUT THE AUTHORS

Ellis Amdur

Edgework founder Ellis Amdur received his B.A. in psychology from Yale University in 1974 and his M.A. in psychology from Seattle University in 1990. He is both a National Certified Counselor and a State Certified Child Mental Health Specialist. He has written a series of ten books (many with subject-matter co-authors) concerning communication with mentally ill and emotionally disturbed individuals and the de-escalation of aggression.

Since the late 1960s, Amdur has trained in various martial arts systems, spending thirteen of these years studying in Japan. He is a recognized expert in classical and modern Japanese martial traditions and has authored three iconoclastic books and one instructional DVD on martial arts subjects.

Since his return to America in 1988, Ellis Amdur has worked in the field of crisis intervention. He has developed a range of training and consultation services, as well as a unique style of assessment and psychotherapy. These are based on a combination of phenomenological psychology and the underlying philosophical premises of classical Japanese martial traditions. Amdur's professional philosophy can best be summed up in this idea: "The development of an individual's integrity and dignity is the paramount virtue. This can only occur when people live courageously, regardless of their circumstances, and take responsibility for their roles in making the changes they desire."

Ellis Amdur is a pioneer in the Pacific Northwest concerning law enforcement training in de-escalating mentally ill and emotionally disturbed individuals. He attended the FBI's basic crisis negotiation course and has served as a consultant to a number of negotiation teams in hostage situations. He originally developed many of the role-plays in this book as crisis negotiation exercises, where he played the role of the hostage taker or person in crisis.

Ellis Amdur is a dynamic public speaker and trainer who presents his work throughout the U.S. and internationally. He is noted for his sometimes outrageous humor as well as his profound breadth of knowledge. His vivid descriptions of aggressive and mentally ill people and his true-to-life role-playing of the behaviors in question give participants an almost first-hand experience of facing the real individuals in question.

For more information on books and training by Ellis Amdur, please refer to his website at www.edgework.info

Biography of Ret. Sgt. Lisbeth Eddy

Lis obtained a BA in Speech-Communications from the University of Washington. She was hired by the Seattle Police department as an officer in 1979. She retired after thirty-one years of service. As a police officer, she worked over 10 years in the patrol division, as well as working as an officer-dispatcher in the communications division.

In 1988 Lis was assigned to the basic training division, where she taught Criminal Law. In 1992, Lis was promoted, and went back to patrol as a sergeant. In addition to being a patrol supervisor, and a Community Policing Team supervisor, she served in the Internal Investigations Division and as a Detective Sergeant in the Domestic Violence Unit.

In addition to these regular assigned duties, Lis was a member of the Hostage Negotiations Team, since 1981, and became the team leader in 1992. As a Hostage Negotiator, Lis has been involved in numerous incidents involving persons in crisis. She has attended basic and advanced hostage negotiators schools, in addition to annual training seminars in negotiating crisis situations. Lis was selected to attend the two-week Crisis Negotiations School, sponsored by the FBI in Quantico, VA.

To increase her skills in communication with those in crisis, Lis worked over six years as a volunteer phone worker for the King County Crisis Clinic, eventually being asked to serve on their board of trustees.

Because of her involvement with the Hostage Negotiations Team, and her experience in dealing with persons in crisis, Lis was chosen to be a member of the committee that developed and implemented the Crisis Intervention Team (CIT) program on the Seattle Police Department in 1997. This unit trains officers on suggestions and options to use when encountering persons who are in crisis due to emotional disturbance or mental illness. Lis was selected to be the CIT coordinator in January of 2000. As a result of this involvement, Lis developed a strong partnership with the National Advocates for the Mentally Ill (NAMI) to explore a better response for law enforcement in dealing with mentally ill individuals. In 2002, Lis received the Jefferson Award for her contributions to the community in working to assist mentally ill persons to reduce their involvement with the police, and ensure their safety, and the safety of the community. She was recognized in 2003 by Good Housekeeping magazine, as one of the recipients of their annual Women in Government awards.

Most recently, she has served as a consultant to the Washington State Criminal Justice Training Commission to assist in the development and implementation of the CIT training for all law enforcement officers in King County.

Lis is considered to be a nationally recognized expert on issues involving police response to dealing with the mentally ill. She has participated in national panels exploring best practices (PERF) involving police interactions with both mentally ill individuals as well as working effectively with the mental health system. She has been consulted as a subject matter expert by the United States Department of Justice concerning the effective utilization of resources in setting up CIT programs. Lis has participated internationally, as well, having presented at Police/Mental Health conferences in England and Australia.

www.ingramcontent.com/pod-product-compliance
Lightning Source LLC
Chambersburg PA
CBHW061757260326
41914CB00006B/1148